Successful Scientific Writing

The detailed, practical, step-by-step advice in this user-friendly guide will help students and researchers to communicate their work more effectively through the written word. Covering all aspects of the writing process, this concise, accessible resource is critically acclaimed, well-structured, comprehensive, and entertaining. Self-help exercises and abundant examples from actual typescripts draw on the authors' extensive experience working both as researchers and with them.

Whilst retaining the accessible and pragmatic style of earlier editions, this third edition has been updated and broadened to incorporate such timely topics as guidelines for successful international publication, ethical and legal issues including plagiarism and falsified data, electronic publication, and text-based talks and poster presentations.

With advice applicable to many writing contexts in the majority of scientific disciplines, this book is a powerful tool for improving individual skills and an eminently suitable text for classroom courses or seminars.

JANICE R. MATTHEWS is a writer and educator with a broad background in the biological sciences. She has edited books, technical manuals and hundreds of scientific research papers in the veterinary and biological sciences, both in university settings and for private industry.

ROBERT W. MATTHEWS is a Josiah Meigs Distinguished Teaching Professor at the University of Georgia and a member of the UGA Teaching Academy. An insect behaviour specialist, his scientific publications number over 165 research articles.

D1125272

Successful Scientific Writing

A step-by-step guide
for the biological
and medical sciences

Third edition

Janice R. Matthews and
Robert W. Matthews

CAMBRIDGE
UNIVERSITY PRESS

CAMBRIDGE UNIVERSITY PRESS
Cambridge, New York, Melbourne, Madrid, Cape Town, Singapore, São Paulo, Delhi

Cambridge University Press
The Edinburgh Building, Cambridge CB2 8RU, UK

Published in the United States of America by Cambridge University Press, New York

www.cambridge.org
Information on this title: www.cambridge.org/9780521699273

First published 1996
Second edition 2000
Third edition 2008
Third printing 2009

Printed in the United Kingdom at the University Press, Cambridge

A catalog record for this publication is available from the British Library

ISBN 978-0-521-69927-3 paperback

Contents

vi   Contents

Contents

Preface

Times change. Today the need to communicate science information effectively is perhaps more important than it has ever been, but the past decade has witnessed a significant revolution in the manner in which we gather, process, and communicate information. The twin technologies of the Internet and personal computers have changed the way nearly everyone works (and plays).

In keeping with the spirit of change, we have extensively revised, updated, and reorganized this third edition. Whether you are a first time author/speaker or a seasoned professional in the biological or medical sciences, we hope you find this step-by-step manual useful.

Because our preface message to you in the second edition still rings true for us, we are including it here as well. Enjoy.

JRM
RWM
2007

Preface to the second edition

Mend your speech a little, lest it mar your fortune.

– Shakespeare

The catch phrase "Publish or Perish" – or its more upbeat variant, "Publish and Flourish" – seems to have as much validity as ever in the minds of scientists everywhere. The scientific community has long emphasized quantity and quality of scholarly publications as a way to judge the eminence of scientists. Granting agencies appear to do the same. Scores received by renewal applications for National Institutes of Health funding for research in universities and hospitals have been shown to correlate very strongly with the number of publications resulting from NIH grants. Perhaps it is not surprising that the publication rate of scientific information doubles about every 12 years (Stix, 1994), although few of us will be likely to match the output of a Russian chemist whose scientific productivity over 10 years totaled 948 papers, or about one publication every four days!

All this writing . . . Does it really make any difference whether it is good, bad, or ugly? We believe it does, and that it matters a great deal, for words are tools of science no less than numbers are. Research is not complete until it is communicated, and publication in a refereed journal is the fundamental unit of scientific communication. The decision not only to write, but to make the effort to write well, lies at the heart of scientific literacy. To most minds, sloppy scientific writing indicates sloppy thinking, and both are disastrous to research and research reporting.

The published word has remarkable persistence. A sloppily written or prematurely published paper can haunt a scientist to the end of his or her days. Over 30 years ago, an examination of the reasons why research grant applications were turned down showed that 12% of the rejected proposals were not approved because the investigators' previously published work did not inspire confidence. Despite vast technological advances, there is no reason to expect that scientific writing is any less important today.

Still, we never set out to be writers. Few scientists do. During our graduate training, we learned about statistics, research, experimentation; we were taught to use instruments and techniques we have seldom encountered again. There was never a word of guidance on writing a scientific paper, nor did we notice that this instruction was missing . . . at first. Once our working lives began we quickly learned that while a plumber can make a comfortable living without writing about his pipes, a scientist's career is inextricably enmeshed with (some would say enslaved by) the need to write. So, like most scientists, we have stumbled along, learning writing skills by trial and error – now and then helped along by a benevolent senior faculty member or a friendly colleague.

Now, as a new millennium begins, we find we have become that senior faculty member and, hopefully, those friendly colleagues as well. This guidebook is one outcome. Its goals are to help you to write effectively and efficiently, just as we would if we could meet with you in person. Because it forms such a major part of almost every scientist's written communication, the research article in a biological, medical, or veterinary medical journal is the book's main focus. However, the tips, techniques, and guidelines presented here apply to a variety of other writing contexts, from review articles to the popular press.

The first edition of *Successful Scientific Writing* began as a brief manual requested by graduate students and new researchers affiliated with the University of Georgia's College of Veterinary Medicine, and their colleagues in human medicine and the biological sciences. This edition has been reorganized and expanded to offer increased guidance, additional examples, and more hands-on exercises.

When you picked up this book, did you fear that it would center on split infinitives, case and tense, and other matters that sound only too much like English composition class? They will be covered – but we promise this won't be grammar class revisited. We do not aspire to present you with a comprehensive reference work or stylebook, chock-full of detailed grammatical and stylistic rules and obscure exceptions to them. Where such specialized information might be desirable, we try instead to point you toward relevant resources.

Efficiency and effectiveness include far more than wordsmithing. While good writing seems synonymous with a great deal of revising, rereading, and polishing, we believe that effective scientific writing is not as difficult to accomplish as many people try to make it. We hope to show you how to develop a strong organizational framework for both the task and the document, how to access the literature more effectively, and how to tailor your approach to your individual style. We have shared a potpourri of techniques which have been useful in our own writing – covering aspects as varied as overcoming writer's block, using word processors, and constructing tables and graphs. To illustrate the guidelines and suggestions, we have provided abundant examples and exercises, many of which are based upon actual manuscripts slated for publication in scientific journals in the biological and medical sciences.

Our scientific community is rapidly becoming an international one, and English is becoming a truly global language. New sections in this edition cover using the Internet and email, and special tips when writers and readers have different first languages. Because we are most accustomed to American spelling, grammar, abbreviations, and punctuation, we have usually followed American conventions in these matters. However, we have tried to point out British equivalents or alternatives whenever possible.

Any book can only do so much, especially in as personal an area as writing. Learning to write skillfully is, always has been, and must continue to be a hands-on experience. However, it needn't be the random, slow, haphazard process that typically occurs in academic circles. Whether you use this book as an alternative to a formal course in science communication or to complement such a course, we hope that you will find that studying and applying this material increases your awareness of scientific writing style. Our goal is to help ease your approach to the writing that your chosen profession in the sciences will invariably call upon you to do.

J. R. M.
J. M. B.
R. W. M.

1

Preparing to write

Find a subject you care about and which you in your heart feel others should care about. It is this genuine caring, not your games with language, which will be the most compelling and seductive element in your style.

– Kurt Vonnegut

Most of us were drawn to science because, like Vonnegut, we found a subject we feel deeply about, not just because we wanted to write about it. However, all scientists recognize that research must be made known if it is to have lasting value. This is how science moves forward, with the shared word illuminating each step of discovery for the sake of others that follow.

"Scientific writing" can be defined narrowly as the reporting of original research in journals or more broadly to encompass other ways that scientists share research information with one another, such as review articles, posters, and slide-based presentations. (The term "science writing" is often used for writing about science topics for the general public.) Whatever form it takes, successful scientific writing must answer basic questions and address problems raised during the dialogs that identify and define a given subject. It must be clear, concise, and follow established formats. In many ways, its language forms a dialect all its own.

What is the most efficient way to write a paper or presentation that successfully covers all this? This book exists to help you tackle the task, step by step. In this chapter, we suggest that you back up from actual writing, and start where your research does – with a question. Learn the most effective ways of compiling background information. For help defining, organizing, and planning the content, use techniques borrowed from problem-solving strategies. Choose a journal so that you have a goal and format. Finally, take charge of the whole project by using the Process Approach.

SEARCH AND RESEARCH

Any time we reach past our own knowledge and experience to seek out, investigate, and use materials beyond personal resources, research is involved. It may be the study of a subject through firsthand observation and investigation, such as carrying out a laboratory experiment, conducting a survey, or sifting through statistical data. Or it may be the examination of studies that other researchers

1

have made of a subject, as presented in books, articles, or scientific debates. Most often it is an amalgamation of the two, for literature research and laboratory research form a powerful combination.

The first substantial writing that many beginning scientists produce is either a prospectus or progress report on their thesis, or dissertation research, or a short journal article written jointly with their supervisor or major professor. Increasingly, a detailed prospectus, including a literature review, is being requested before research projects can begin. Likewise, in business and industry, a well-written proposal often must precede approval for research projects, and its worth can influence promotion and pay. In fact, one would be hard pressed to find any scientific profession that would not require checking sources of information about a specific subject, integrating this information with one's own ideas, and presenting thoughts, findings, and conclusions effectively.

Conducting a comprehensive literature review

Conducting a comprehensive literature review is undeniably a big job. Here are a few general points of advice to help you coordinate your work, followed by tips specific to conducting computer-based searches.

Organization is a journey, not a destination

A literature review means you'll soon be handling an avalanche of papers – at the very least, personal notes, photocopies, journal reprints, and printed copies of electronic publications. It is essential to have some system in place to deal with all the information that will be converging upon you.

What system is most effective? There is no one-size-fits-all answer. The popular press is brimming with suggestions, often coupled with explicit or implicit promises of spectacular life results if one can only become properly organized (for examples, see Aslett, 1996; Bolker, 1998). Seek out such materials if you feel you need motivation, inspiration, or novel approaches, but maintain your perspective. The secret to effective and efficient scientific writing isn't simply in getting organized. It is in wanting to get the job done and committing oneself to do it. However, having a system from the beginning and consistently staying up with it can go a long way to keeping that commitment on track.

Mind your Ps and Qs

Whether you photocopy journal articles, request reprints, or print potentially helpful information from the Internet, you will soon amass a great many facts and ideas couched in the words of others. The old advice from typesetting days, "mind your Ps and Qs," is worth remembering in this new context.

First, watch the *P*s – print materials. It will be tempting to use these copies as a substitute for taking notes. However, because of the way that writing and thinking are related to each other, it is actually more effective if you can begin to digest these written materials as you go along. Adopt a good note-taking procedure right from the start. Take many more notes than you think you need and prune them later. Staple the notes to the print materials so they will remain together through the inevitable subsequent paper-shuffling.

Second, watch the Qs – quoted material. To avoid unintentional plagiarism, always write notes in your own words. Indicate their source. If you must quote directly, use extreme care to identify quoted material either with quotation marks or with the letter Q.

Use many different search strategies

Trace information in all directions through time and space. Each search strategy has different strengths and weaknesses, and will uncover a somewhat different set of information.

Later in this chapter, we will discuss computerized searches in some detail. However, the idea of networking pre-dates computer-based searches. For example, a time-honored search strategy called the Ancestry Approach starts by acquiring a research report and examining its references to find other relevant references. Through reiteration, researchers work their way back through the literature until either the important concepts disappear or the studies become so old they can be judged obsolete.

A more recent set of searching tools employs the Descendency Approach. Citation indexes identify a publication's offspring – those more recent books and journal articles that reference the earlier work.

Make it easy to relocate relevant material

Write the full journal source on each photocopy or computer printout, if the source is not printed somewhere on the page. For material obtained from online sources, list the author, if available; title, document, file, or website; date of the material; name of the database or other online source; date you accessed the source; and the full electronic address or Uniform Resource Locator (URL).

It is particularly easy to forget how one actually located online material. To minimize this problem, it is a good idea to set up an electronic bookmark that identifies a location you may want to revisit. Over time these bookmarks will accumulate into a customized list that makes it easy to locate and return to particular sites.

Use email as a timesaving resource

Being transmitted in machine-readable form, email text can be printed, revised, and sent back, or even incorporated directly into another computer file without being retyped. These abilities can be used to your advantage in many ways. References, abstracts, and even entire articles located in a particular database can be directed to your personal email address. There you can download them, then print or add them directly to your computerized literature retrieval system.

Conducting computer-based searches

The way in which we obtain information is changing rapidly. A decade or two ago, most literature searching was done manually. Computerized literature databases were searchable only through a mainframe, searching software was difficult to use, and online searching was expensive and limited in scope. Specially trained librarians did most of the searching, and researchers paid telecommunication charges for reaching the mainframe and were charged for each record received.

Today, in many fields, a literature search that once took six months to a year can often be done in less than ten minutes, and with far more thorough results. Thousands of specialized databases exist around the world. Database software has become increasingly user-friendly. Research libraries and even moderately sized community libraries buy site licenses to various indexes, and offer their clients free searching of CD-ROMs and mainframe-mounted indexes. The Internet offers direct access to both new and old sources of information.

The upshot of this revolution is that you need to know how to conduct a literature search yourself. Whether you consider this a blessing or a curse depends on your approach to the task and your knowledge of available resources.

Compilations are there to help – use them!

Research bibliographies, research registers, reference databases, and citation indexes are compilations constructed for the explicit purpose of providing relatively comprehensive lists of published information related to a topic. They can be some of your most valuable literature searching sources.

Each of these databases has limitations, however. Some contain only published research; others, only unpublished research. As with searching the Internet, one searches the database by specifying keywords; any mismatch between the seeker and the indexer is likely to result in missed articles. There can be a long time lag before references appear in an electronic index, because after publication the work must be identified and catalogued into the reference database. Thus, physically browsing for newly appearing information is still advisable. Furthermore, despite their claims, none of the online databases access all relevant journals on a topic. Use multiple sources.

Consult research bibliographies and research registers

Research bibliographies can be a great help and time-saver. They generally take the form of nonevaluative listings of books and articles relevant to a particular topic area, but it is even possible to find bibliographies of bibliographies. Research bibliographies are often maintained by single scientists or groups of individuals, rather than by a formal organization.

Prevalent in the medical sciences, research registers are databases of studies focusing on a common feature, such as subject matter, funding source, or design. Prospective research registers are unique in attempting to include not only completed research, but also research that is in the planning stage or is still under way. Some research registers are more comprehensive than others; whenever possible, determine how long a register has been in existence and how the research included in the register got to be there.

Locate and use reference databases and abstracting services

Reference databases (Table 1.1) are particularly fruitful sources of information. Maintained by both private and public organizations, these services focus on a specific kind of document (such as theses and dissertations) or field (such as agriculture or medicine). At present, most include only titles and abstracts, but full-text databases are becoming more prevalent and probably will be the norm in the future.

Table 1.1. *Examples of helpful literature abstracting and indexing databases available to biological and medical researchers. All are available in both traditional formats and online from various vendors*

Database	Description
Agricola	Covers all major areas of agricultural sciences.
Agricultural and Environmental Biotechnology Abstracts	Especially useful for genetic engineering and its agricultural implications.
Bioengineering Abstracts	Covers biomedical and genetic engineering and related fields.
BIOSIS (Biological Abstracts)	Widely used for literature in biology, agriculture, and biomedicine. Includes five different indexes – author, genus, biosystematic grouping from phylum through family, concept, and subject. Records prior to 1993 are formatted and indexed different from records since that time.
Biological and Agricultural Index	Particularly useful for environmental and conservation sciences, agriculture, veterinary medicine, and related areas of applied biology.
Books in Print	Covers in-print, out-of-print, and forthcoming books from North American publishers.
CAB Abstracts	Excellent coverage for agriculture, veterinary medicine, and biology.
Cambridge Scientific Abstracts	Source of several particularly useful databases.
CINAHL (Cumulative Index to Nursing and Allied Health)	Particularly strong coverage of the nursing and allied health professions literature.
Current Contents	Indexes recent articles in a variety of life sciences by reproducing the tables of contents of numerous journals. Authors' addresses enable contact to request a copy of the paper if the journal is unavailable. Includes abstracts.
Dissertation Abstracts	Provides complete abstracts of dissertations from U.S., Canadian, British, and other countries, plus select coverage of masters theses.

(cont.)

Table 1.1. (*cont.*)

Database	Description
General Science Index	Helpful place to start when working with a broad topic. Includes both papers in selected technical journals and nontechnical overviews, many of which are written by scientists who have also published technical papers on the same topic. (Locate the latter by searching by author names in more specialized databases.)
Journal Citation Reports (an annual volume of *Science Citation Index*)	Lists indexed journals grouped by subject field. Ranks journals by their relative "impact factors," including number of citations of a journal's papers in other publications during a given calendar year and other statistics.
Medical and Pharmaceutical Biotechnology Abstracts	Covers human health, molecular biology, and biotechnology.
PubMed (*MEDLINE*)	The online counterpart to *Index Medicus*, and one of a group of databases (MEDLARS = Medical Literature Analysis and Retrieval System) produced by the U.S. National Library of Medicine. Includes all the medical and health sciences; unsurpassed for preclinical and clinical medicine.
Science Citation Index	Widely used to locate other authors who have mentioned a paper relevant to one's topic.
Web of Knowledge	Incorporates various searchable databases (including *Science Citation Index*) from Thomson Scientific (formerly Institute of Scientific Information [ISI]).
Zoological Record	The most comprehensive index to zoological literature.

All major research libraries subscribe to numerous reference databases and have reference librarians to help first-time users. Many databases are available in more than one medium or format. The older media (print, microfilm, microfiche, and more recently CD-ROMs) require physically visiting the library. Using online reference databases can save considerable time and ensure a high degree of accuracy. Furthermore, online reference databases are sometimes updated more frequently than their CD-ROM or print equivalents. Some databases are accessible only through licensed sites, such as a university library.

Individual vendors and reference database publishers provide detailed and readily available instructions on database searching. Learn the shortcuts that make can make your life easier. For example, database software usually has the capacity to format reference citations in a variety of ways, representative of the formats most commonly found in the scientific literature. Some database software programs also can be integrated with many word processing programs to format references automatically within a document and insert them during typescript preparation. Become familiar with the most widely used formats in

Table 1.2. *Preliminary questions to ask about research design*

The basic question	Examples of ways in which it might be assessed
1. Do I know what I'm doing?	Have I drawn up a plan (a protocol) for what I intend to do? Do the proposed studies cover all the criticisms likely to be made? Are the statistical methods valid?
2. Do my proposed experiments meet accepted ethical standards?	If my experiments involve human beings or animals, do they meet accepted standards? Could my work adversely affect the environment or the place where I am doing field work?
3. What practical and political considerations need to be addressed?	Is publication of my work likely to break any official secrecy regulations? Could publication invalidate a later application for a patent? Are collecting or other permits required?
4. How will I record the work as it proceeds?	How will I record what I read? How will I record what I do? How will I ensure that my records are complete? How will I ensure that I can access the records again when I or others need them?

your discipline and select the most up-to-date and versatile tools available. Take the time to master them.

Consult citation indexes and Dissertation Abstracts

Citation indexes are a unique kind of reference database that identifies and groups together all newly published articles that have referenced (cited) the same earlier publication. Citation indexes limit entries to references in published research, both journals and books, but are quite exhaustive within these categories.

Academia houses a great deal of potentially valuable but largely unpublished material in the form of doctoral dissertations and masters' theses. Although many reference databases contain abstracts of dissertations, *Dissertation Abstracts* focuses exclusively on them. Both the printed and the computerized versions include records dating back to 1861. Increasingly, the full text can be purchased and printed. Alternatively, you may need to use interlibrary loan services to obtain a photocopy from the university at which the dissertation research was conducted.

Learn to use keyword search terms and apply Boolean logic

Most literature retrieval services are really matchmakers (Table 1.2). They have some provision for searching a subject by way of keywords – brief terms chosen (usually by a study's author) to describe the major topics included in the document. To find the document, one must specify the same keyword that the author has chosen (or a part of it; see "wildcard characters" later in this chapter).

Language gets much of its meaning through context, however. As a result, typing in keywords during an Internet search without specifying their context or relationships can lead to strange, frustrating, or humorous results. To improve the outcome, use a special system called Boolean logic to specify the relationships between search terms.

Boolean logic is named for George Boole, a mathematician who lived in the middle 1800s. It really is just a highbrowed way of describing three logical choices:

> I want this one AND that one
> I want this one OR that one
> I want this one but NOT that one

Search tools let you apply Boolean logic in various ways. A common variation allows you to choose from a menu of options that describe the Boolean logic, such as "all of these words," "any of these words," and "must not contain."

Suppose you wish to undertake a comparative study of types of skin cancer. By specifying `carcinoma AND melanoma`, you would retrieve all the hits (entries computer-matched to your search) in which both types of cancers appear in the same document, but none that mention only one. For a comprehensive search on both kinds of skin cancer, you would specify `carcinoma OR melanoma`. Either or both terms would appear in each document that is retrieved. Alternatively, perhaps you want more information on skin cancers, but know that because of its potential deadliness, there will be hundreds of entries on malignant melanoma. To narrow the results, you could specify `carcinoma NOT melanoma`. Any document about skin cancer that mentioned melanoma would be omitted from the list of retrievals.

With another system called Implied Boolean, you use "logical operators" – a plus sign in place of AND and a minus sign in place of NOT. The signs abut the front of the word, with no space between them. Precede this with other search terms you want to have it coupled with. For example, type `plastic facial +surgery` to get results for facial surgery and plastic surgery but not for the words plastic or facial alone. Use a minus sign in front of a word to ensure that a word does not appear in hits. For example, `poisoning -food` would yield information on poisoning without including entries on food poisoning.

Plan an effective search strategy

For efficient use of time and energy, carefully define the scope of your literature review right at the beginning. How extensive do you want it to be? Do you want to get a broad list that includes records even slightly related to your topic, or just a few most relevant ones? To what extent do you need to rely upon informal channels versus formal ones?

Then, be prepared for a bit of trial-and-error. Identify a limited number of concepts that may be useful to describe the research question at hand, and choose terms and accompanying logic that seem to define them. Precision is imperative. Searching for instances of a broad term like `ecology` would be akin to drinking from a fire hose, summoning thousands of hits. The list that is returned often will display the total number of items found, but only show them in batches.

Run a computerized search using your initial set of terms, and look over a sample of the records it retrieves. Are they mostly relevant? If not, revise your search. To increase the number of records, expand the lists of terms connected by OR. To retrieve fewer records, narrow the search by adding terms or concepts connected by AND or (very carefully) by NOT logic. Most databases will let you define a time period or subject area for your search; many Internet searches still will not. Another useful capability of some online databases is the option of using an index tree or thesaurus. The vocabulary is arranged hierarchically, allowing the searcher to scroll through the list and select topics to broaden or narrow search parameters as desired.

When you are satisfied with the records obtained from one information channel, but feel you do not have everything that you need or want, begin all over again with another. The results will probably be different.

Handle search results wisely

Exercise care and vigilance when entering reference citations into your personal database. While it can be tempting to add bibliographic references directly into your personal database from the literature cited sections of review articles and other publications, avoid doing so. Never incorporate a reference into your database until you have actually verified its accuracy and appropriateness.

Using the Internet wisely and well

As a successful writer, you will find yourself using the Internet repeatedly. This vast interconnected system of smaller public and private networks lets users communicate around the globe, finding and sharing information, offering commercial services, and opening vast information resources.

Remember two things, however. First, the Internet is an ever-changing entity. Printed material pointing to specific sites is sometimes outdated before it is even published, and finding something useful once doesn't mean you will be able to locate it again. The secret to dealing with this vast, chaotically organized resource and its instability is learning to understand how it works and how to use specialized tools designed to facilitate your scientific writing efforts.

Second, the Internet has no gatekeepers. Material can be, and is, posted by anyone who cares to do so. This form of publishing lets everyone have a voice, and it provides for a wealth of information. However, just because something appears – even on a really fantastically professional looking page – doesn't mean that the information necessarily is credible.

Evaluate Web entries carefully

As Gurak (2000) points out, one or more of the following characteristics indicate a credible site:

Exercise 1.1. Search strategy and Boolean logic

This is an exercise in thinking logically, not in finding answers on the Web. Here are ten publication titles. Use them to answer the questions below.

A. Trap-Nesting Wasps And Bees: Life Histories, Nests, And Associates
B. Behavior Of Three Florida Solitary Wasps
C. Winged Warriors: Insects In The Garden
D. A Cluster Of Bees
E. The Wasps Of The Genus *Pisonopsis* Fox
F. Beeswax, Twine, and Time: The Art of Candlemaking
G. Cowfly Tigers: An Account Of The Bembicine Wasps Of British Guyana
H. Honeybees Attacked At Their Hive Entrance By *Philanthus* Wasps
I. A Life History of Stinging Insects
J. A Comparative Study Of The Nesting Habits Of Solitary Bees And Wasps

Write the number(s) corresponding to the title(s) that would be retrieved for each of the following Boolean statements.

1. Wasps AND Bees   2. Wasps NOT Bees
3. Bees NOT Wasps   4. Wasps OR Bees

5. When using terms in a subject directory, you will usually get only relevant titles. When using terms in a search engine, you should expect a mixture of relevant and irrelevant titles. If you were searching for Wasps OR Bees using a search engine, which of the above titles would probably be retrieved but have little to do with them?

6. When you search one of the better subject directories, you search not only titles but annotations written by a staff person. Which of the above titles would be missed by a search engine using the keywords Wasps OR Bees, but might contain relevant information that would be retrieved by a good subject directory?

- It is an online version of a reputable published source, such as a newspaper, major media source, or an academic or professional journal
- It includes a list of works cited
- It is affiliated with a reputable educational or research institution
- The authors of the site are identified, with information about how to contact them

If most or all of these characteristics are present, you can be fairly confident that the site is likely to be credible.

The Internet and especially the World Wide Web are undeniably valuable tools. However, there is a common misconception that with their arrival, literature searching has become a breeze. Reality is closer to a description by Gould (1998, p. 8):

> If you keep in mind that the Internet just came out of the trees and got into the knuckle-walking stage of its evolution, you will be able to appreciate what is there, and reduce your frustration at working in this very young medium.

Subject directories and search engines

What if you don't know what information is out there, or where it is located? In general, there have been two different approaches to searching for information on the World Wide Web – subject directories and search engines. However, like everything else in the online universe, the clear-cut division between subject directories and search engines is changing. Many newer searching tools include both.

Keywords are used with both approaches, but in somewhat different ways. Subject directories are specialized websites that select other sites and organize them under broad subject headings; no two directories categorize their materials in the same way, and each directory covers only a small subset of the entire Internet. To use subject directories most effectively, choose broad, inclusive keywords because unique terms will often yield no results. Keep in mind, however, that failure to find information does not mean it does not exist. The directory simply may not have picked it up for indexing.

Search engines, on the other hand, are software programs that consist of comprehensive indexes of the Internet. One of the most popular of these, Google, is rapidly becoming a verb as well (as in, "google it"). However, there are many others. You can find a catalog of them, listed by category, at <search.cnet.com>. Their (nearly impossible) goal is to index every word of every Web page in their databases, but even the biggest search engines index only 60–80% of the Web (Gould, 1998). Search engine databases are created by computer programs – variously called robots, spiders, webcrawlers, or worms – that work constantly to collect and index Web pages.

When you provide keywords to a search engine, it will attempt to honor your request with a ranked list ("hit" list) of sites. However, because so much information is available, it is common to get overloaded with results that mix trivial or irrelevant results with the pertinent ones. Search engines attempt to help with this problem by applying ranking algorithms or formulas that determine the order in which the results are displayed. Small differences in these algorithms have a major effect on the results obtained, even when you use identical search terms. Thus, it is a good idea to use multiple search engines, rather than relying on the results from only one.

To use search engines effectively, choose very specific keywords and combine them in an appropriate syntax to take advantage of advanced search features.

The more uncommon the word or phrase, the more manageable the number of retrievals will be, and the fewer irrelevant documents that will appear.

Tapping other informal and formal communication channels

There are many ways to tap into the vast stream of scientific information that exists in the world. Some are informal and unmediated; others are formal, with explicit rules that restrict the kind or quality of information that is admitted into their system.

If literature searching were courtship, informal channels would be face-to-face dates, but formal channels would be blind dates arranged by friends. To carry the analogy further, the serious suitor eager for the best match should try every appropriate avenue (Cooper, 1998).

Consult the invisible college

A colleague down the hall passes along an article he feels would be of interest. A reviewer notes a relevant paper that the author has missed. A student reads a post on an Internet chat group that starts her thinking of a new interpretation for her research.

The term "invisible college" has been used widely to describe informal but systematic ways like these that scientists arrange in order to stay in contact with colleagues who are working on similar problems. In the past, the lines of communication occurred primarily one-on-one, but with the advent of the Internet, they now are also maintained through a newsgroup or a computerized mailing list management program (technically a "listserv" but often anglicized to "listserve"). Anyone can join most such mailing lists or newsgroups by sending a simple command to their host computer. Special topic groups can be found in printed directories, in Internet directories, or by searching the Internet.

Formal channels involve third parties with an element of judgment

Formal scientific communication has four major channels – professional conference presentations, personal journal libraries, electronic journals, and research report reference lists. Formal channels of communication all insert an element of judgment into the system. To enter information into them, researchers must follow explicit rules that restrict the kind or quality of information that is admitted into the system. The classic example of a formal communication channel is an article published in a refereed scientific journal. It must follow specific requirements, and both editors and reviewers judge its acceptability.

Although their selection criteria for presentations are sometimes less strict than that required for journal publication, the conferences periodically held by professional societies are also formal communication, because they accept only presentations structured to their topic area. For information to enter the system, the researcher must be a member of the society and be aware of the meeting, and the research generally must pass at least a weak peer review.

Currently, many journals appear in both paper and electronic forms. However, due to the storage capacity and favorable economics of computer technology, experts predict a future switch to solely electronic editions (Peek and Newby, 1996; Walker, 1998). As a whole, electronic journals straddle the world between informal and formal communication channels. Some evaluate submitted articles; others do not. In evaluating electronic articles, this is important information to have.

Your research: the big picture

A book like this one is not the place for a detailed procedural catalog of all the productive ways of doing research. Conducting a research study is undeniably a big job. Presumably you are being guided through that task by various mentors. However, some guidelines can always be useful, even if only as reminders.

Regularly assess your research design, progress, and direction

Begin by asking yourself some important questions about your plans for the research itself (Table 1.2). Seek advice on these matters. If necessary, modify your plans accordingly.

At regular intervals, pause to check the direction your work is taking. Force yourself to sit down and describe your progress in writing. The discipline of marshaling words into formal sentences will compel you to think about it more clearly.

CHOOSE A COMMUNICATION VENUE

Although peer-reviewed formal research publication is the major emphasis of this book, it is only one of many ways scientific data can be shared. The way scientists transmit their work to one another has changed more in the past two decades than at any time since the first appearance of scholarly journals back in the late seventeenth century.

Publication in a peer-reviewed scientific journal feels like such an important step that it can be tempting to rush to this phase – or to run from it in fear. How can one know when a study is actually ready to be shared through formal publication? Or whether it should be published at all? And if it isn't ready yet, what can be done with it in the meanwhile?

Is the research ready for formal publication?

Consider your research ready to be written up for publication when the results and conclusions fulfill at least one of these requirements:

- They are reasonably consistent, reproducible, and complete
- They represent significant experimental, theoretical, or observational extensions of knowledge
- They represent advances in the practical application of known principles
- They take knowledge of the subject a step further

In other words, are you fairly confident that the outcomes of your study are new, true, and meaningful? If yes, go for it! If the answer to all these questions is no, delay publication efforts. Sometimes, a topic that originally looked worthwhile turns out to be a dud or simply unsuitable in its present form. Don't throw away the data – just defer writing a paper based on them until further work has been done.

If you decided not to publish this work, don't hide it (or yourself) in a closet. Perhaps at the moment you simply need to consider a different venue for sharing this information.

Formal publication: the message determines the medium

Where scientific material appears is almost as important as what it says. Conversely, where it appears ideally should be determined by what it says. Thus, before going any further, a savvy writer asks four questions.

- What message do I want to convey?
- What format is most appropriate for my message?
- Who will be interested in my message?
- Where should this paper be published?

You may be able to answer these questions by yourself, but for an extra margin of safety, discuss them with a more experienced colleague. All of us can suffer from the normal human failings of inflating the importance of a message and overestimating the size and nature of its potential audience.

What message do I want to convey?

By this point, you should be able to answer this question in some detail. In essence, it can be rephrased as: "What is my research question, and what is (or probably will be) my answer?"

This is not the same as asking the "purpose" of the research. That phrasing can lead to some tremendously circular and meaningless statements: "The purpose of my research was to obtain data so I could publish them in order to get my degree so I could do more research and publish some more . . ."

What format is most appropriate for my message?

Most of us are justifiably interested in recognition for our work. The way in which a study is presented and published can determine the nature of that recognition, and in fact whether we receive any recognition at all.

For a scientist to receive professional credit for being the first to discover something new, it is not sufficient just to be the first to perceive or detect it – he or she must be the first to publish the information "validly," i.e., in a very specific way. This distinction is most important in (but not restricted to) the taxonomic sciences, in which the naming of new organisms hinges on a strict system of priority of valid publication.

What does "valid" publication mean?

"Valid" scientific publication has several essential components. It is (1) the first publication of research results (2) in a form whereby peers can assess the observations, evaluate the intellectual processes, or repeat the experiment and test its conclusions, (3) appearing in a primary journal or other source document (4) that is readily available within the scientific community. In addition, (5) the scientific paper contains certain specified kinds of information (6) organized in a certain stylized manner, i.e., it has a certain format. This is not to imply that other publication is "invalid" for any other use than this very special purpose of establishing priority of discovery.

Research paper types and validity

Though they may be designated by slightly different sets of names, research papers in the biological and medical sciences fall into four general categories – research articles, case histories, reviews, and case-series analyses – and shorter variants with such titles as research notes or brief communications. Each category is most appropriate for different sorts of messages.

Research articles and case histories are the usual avenue for valid publication of original results. Both types of papers are based on one's own experiences. A research article generally presents new data obtained through experimentation or observation. A case history usually covers such subjects as a unique, previously undescribed syndrome or disease, new information on an illness, an unsuspected causal relationship, or an unexpected outcome such as a possible therapeutic or adverse drug effect. The study may be retrospective (analyzing previously accumulated data) or prospective (with a design that pre-dates data collection).

Satisfying a requirement for valid publication, research articles and case histories have a specific set of defining characteristics. Both are structured with distinctive sections that parallel the sequence of a critical argument. They present a question (sometimes formally stated as a hypothesis). They marshal evidence to support various possible answers to the question. Finally, they attempt to persuade the reader of the truth of a particular choice of answers.

Review articles and case-series analyses, on the other hand, cover principally other scientists' discoveries rather than one's own. This is not to downplay their importance, nor to suggest that they are in any way "invalid" or second-rate. Reviews, such as those found in the *"Annual Review of . . ."* series, perform a valuable role by synthesizing the results of a search through literature or other records. Reviews can be particularly valuable to someone entering a subject for the first time, and for communication between scientists. They can also introduce new ways of looking at a topic, and point out flaws or gaps in scientific understanding or in the published literature.

The structure and format of reviews and other summary analyses are less standardized than those of a research article. If there is a "methods" section, it often states the manner and extent of the search. If a series of cases is being included, it often tells what records were accessed. The organizational sequence of these papers depends on the topic. Commonly, items are covered either in chronological order, from general to particular, or from frequent occurrence to rare. Both reviews and case-series analyses may yield new insights, hypotheses, and understanding, and in that sense they also constitute "valid" original research.

What is a "primary journal or other source document that is readily available within the scientific community"? Primary and secondary has nothing to do with quality or importance. Rather, a primary journal is merely one that details first-hand information reported by people directly involved with an action or event. A secondary journal presents information that does not come directly from people involved in the action or event. Rather, a person two or three steps removed from the source reports the information. Some of these publications are significant sources of communication among scientists and the educated public, particularly now that the Internet provides increased accessibility to them.

Popular articles – secondary accounts designed to entertain as well as to inform – may not adhere to the rigorous standards of regular scientific articles. They typically offer only a condensed overview of the methodology used and a summary of the major findings, without presenting actual data. For these reasons, popular articles do not generally constitute valid publication. However, writing or providing consultation for popular articles based on validly published scientific research should be an important part of a scientist's outreach activities to the wider community that supports his or her work.

Who will be most interested in my message?

Most of us have pretty healthy egos. We think our writing will merit the attention of far more readers than it will in fact attract. This nearly universal failing can lead to poor choice of a potential journal, and this poor choice can lead to delays, requests for major revision, or outright rejection.

Two closely related, bluntly asked questions can help a writer find the most appropriate audience.

> *So what?* This question could be cast less abruptly in any of several ways. What effect will my message have on concepts or practices? Why should readers pay attention to it? Will it lead to widespread changes in the way we view the world?
>
> *Who cares?* One could also ask this question more mildly. Who will be the most interested in this information? Will it be the specialists in a small field? Most practitioners? The scientific world in general?

Be realistic. Don't get caught up in contemplating a vast potential audience that "needs" to know your information. (In this information-filled world, no one should be expected to make brain-room for data simply because the facts are currently unknown to him or her.) The more accurately you can answer these questions, the more precise your journal publication options become. And the more precisely you can target a journal, the better the chances for publication.

Table 1.3. *Questions to ask when considering a journal for potential publication of a scientific research paper*

1. What type of journal is it?
2. Is the topic of my proposed paper within the journal's scope?
3. Is the topic represented in the journal frequently or only rarely?
4. What is the size and type of the journal's audience?
5. What is the journal's rejection rate?
6. What formats are acceptable to the journal?
7. How long does this journal take to publish papers? (How much is editing phase? How much is production phase?)
8. What is the quality of photographic (half-tones) and graphics reproductions?

So, where should this paper be published?

Even after all these considerations have been examined, a lot of choice remains. There are tens of thousands of refereed scientific journals in current publication. Within a single specialized area, they differ in such vital aspects as topic coverage, format, promptness of publication, acceptance rate, page charges, and presumed prestige. Their readership varies as well. For the greatest efficiency and the best chance of acceptance and prompt publication, search early and well for the best match of topic, journal, and audience you can possibly achieve. Some surveys suggest that 80–90% of papers that are rejected from the author's first journal choice will eventually find a home somewhere if the author perseveres. Nonetheless, one can only imagine how many hours are consumed during this rewriting/re-submission process.

Refer to those abstracting services or indexes that you used to begin a literature search, and use them to help identify potential avenues for publication. Did your literature search indicate that one or more journals were the principal sources of reports related to your research? At this point it is time to seek information about the most promising possibilities you have uncovered (Table 1.3). Examine current issues of periodicals in which others in your field have published. Note that some journals with scientific society sponsorship may require that an author or coauthor be a society member.

Evaluate journal suitability and impact

After you have identified a few promising possibilities, go to the library or Internet and scan some recent issues. Check the table of contents. Look inside the front or back cover. Nearly all will have two items of special interest – a statement of the journal's scope, and a variably titled set of editorial guidelines we've chosen to call *Instructions to Authors* or *ITAs*. Do they seem appropriate for the topic and type of paper you will be preparing?

Generally, if a journal is regularly publishing a number of papers on topics similar to yours, you stand a better chance of acceptance than if very few papers related to your topic have appeared. However, stay open to considering journals outside your field. Editors today increasingly seem to be accepting papers on the basis of their importance to the journal's audience, rather than on the basis of narrowly defined academic fields. If you feel your topic would be of more than peripheral interest to the journal's audience, it is quite appropriate to query the editor.

Will your colleagues still see your paper if you publish it here? One way to determine whether scientists in your field are reading this journal is to examine journal citation reports through various databases such as ISI Web of Knowledge (see Table 1.1). These reports indicate how many of a given journal's papers appeared in citations in other journals during a calendar year.

There is little doubt that the scientific community views journals as having various degrees of "prestige." Like beauty, much of this may lie in the eye of the beholder because, despite repeated efforts, this has been a difficult matter to assess reliably. It certainly is not simply a matter of circulation – some journals with a high reputation in the scientific community have relatively small circulation. Journal citation reports rank journals by their relative "impact factors." Comparing the impact factors for two or more journals in a particular field can give a sort of "reality check" in the form of a quantitative clue as to their relative intellectual influence.

A caveat is in order here: Most of us would like to think that the best choice for each of our publications would be a prestigious large-circulation journal. We pretty well know which these are, and we would love to build our reputation by publishing in them. This is natural. However, remember that the match of topic, journal, and audience is the critical issue. Because high profile journals often receive thousands of typescripts per year, their rejection rates can run as high as 90%. Subjecting a paper to these lottery-like odds means a fairly sizable risk of living in limbo for weeks (and probably months), before ultimately receiving a rejection notice.

If, after conscientiously going through all of these steps, you still feel unsure whether you have picked the right journal and the right format, it is acceptable to email, write, or call the editor and raise the question. Frame your query diplomatically. Don't ask, "Will you publish my . . . ?" or "Will you publish a review of the diagnosis and treatment of . . . ?" Instead, ask "Are you willing to consider for publication a 50-page detailed review of the diagnosis and treatment of . . . ?" You may learn that the editor has just accepted such a review, or that the journal never publishes reviews that long – a disappointment for the moment, but an answer that can save you time and work.

If information regarding publication time is not indicated in *Instructions to Authors*, it is also appropriate to query the editor politely about this matter, requesting average and range of time from submission to publication. Most editors take pride in their continued efforts to try to reduce the time from submission to publication.

Additional factors that might influence your journal choice include costs such as page charges and Internet access fees. These vary widely.

If you are still not sure where your document will ultimately be sent, prepare the typescript according to the requirements outlined in Appendix 2 while continuing

---

Exercise 1.2. Message, format, and audience

How would you answer these questions?

1. A 75-year-old woman brought to your clinic has contracted a rare form of viral infection previously known to be associated primarily with children. A quick library search shows that the oldest affected person in the published literature was 62 years old. Should you publish your new information?

2. Your supervisor suggests that you both review the records of the last 50 cases of canine heartworm disease referred to your clinic and coauthor a paper on the findings. You ask what question the paper is going to answer. He is not trying to answer a question, he says irritably. He just wants to report a summary of these data because colleagues elsewhere will be interested. Does the paper have a purpose? Does it have a message? What format would be most appropriate?

3. The two of you proceed to analyze those 50 cases of heartworm disease. Your analysis doesn't yield any new important findings, but does lend additional support to some previously published views. Is it still publishable? If so, in what form?

4. You've written a concise, clearly worded summary of the genetics of horn development in jackalopes. A series of examples from the literature, combined with your own laboratory analyses and a field-based population study, all point to the conclusion that a single gene controls this trait. You reason that geneticists, veterinary pathologists, and wildlife biologists all should know this important new information. How many papers could justifiably arise from your study?

5. You've gone back through psychiatric clinic records for the past 18 years, and made a startling discovery. Nearly 80% of all the children hospitalized for manic depression had been previously identified in school tests as being highly creative. Who might be the potential audience for your message?

---

to consider journal possibilities. When you make your decision, check the *ITAs* to see whether they specify acceptance of the Uniform Requirements.

Avoid salami-slicing science

One final caveat – as your search begins to uncover a variety of specialized journals, each may seem perfectly suited for reporting a different part of your data. Some studies do justify more than one report, particularly when different portions have given rise to differing messages of interest to different audiences. However, given the importance of publication in academic circles, one often can be tempted to carve clearly related aspects of a study arbitrarily into more documents than is really sensible. When all of the findings together yield a single message that can be presented in a paper of normal length for the intended journal, they belong together. There is no reasonable justification for what one writer (Lawrence, 1981) has called salami science. (We would add that salami science tends to produce baloney!)

Other ways to publish

In addition to the many new informal and formal communication channels mentioned earlier in this chapter, there have been changes in the way peer-reviewed formal research is presented. In recent years, the lag time between acceptance and appearance in primary publication has grown. A gap of one to three years now sometimes exists. For work in highly competitive leading edge areas, this is no small consideration. Variants such as research notes, short communications, and research briefs have arisen to address the need for quicker, but less comprehensive transmission of results.

Writing variants such as abstracts, transactions, conference proceedings, local bulletins, posters, newsletters, websites, and other such outlets are often viewed as commanding less prestige than classic journal articles, and thus may be considered less important to career advancement. Admittedly, they are not peer-reviewed, and can be ephemeral in nature. However, they offer much more immediate communication with fellow specialists, and can be particularly valuable in helping one stake an intellectual claim in a rapidly changing field of study.

At conferences in many fields of study, the use of posters to present new research has burgeoned in recent years. See Chapter 4 for more information on this important avenue of scientific communication.

Consider giving an oral presentation

Spoken presentations are overwhelmingly common in the scientific and technical professions. They take many forms, from conference presentations, departmental seminars, and job interviews to classroom presentations, brown-bag lunches, and public talks. Treat each opportunity with respect. Each has its own role to play in a scientist's life, equally valuable in its own way to communication through formal peer-reviewed publication.

At a point partway through your study, seek out an opportunity to present your research orally or in poster form at a public forum such as a laboratory meeting, a departmental seminar, or a scientific conference whose proceedings are limited to abstracts. The comments and questions you receive will help you determine where more work might be needed to fill gaps in your arguments and observations.

Oral presentations can be more than merely way-stations on the track to eventual publication of new information. A well-designed and well-delivered oral presentation of ongoing work can be one of the most effective forms of communication experiences available to both the speaker and the audience.

With the burgeoning popularity of computer-based presentation software such as Microsoft® PowerPoint®, temptation has strengthened to treat oral presentations as though they were simply spoken versions of a typescript. In its worst iteration, the speaker is simply a reader, parroting text directly from the screen as it is projected. Don't even consider such a route. See Chapter 4 for guidelines and tips on effectively presenting material orally.

PLAN TO SUCCEED

Failing to plan is planning to fail.

All of us, when confronted by a writing deadline, face the temptation to skip the organizational phases of writing. This is akin to leaving on a trip to unknown parts without a road map! Professional writers are quick to point out that organizing one's thoughts at the outset will save time in the long run, and will result in a more effective document.

Organize and plan your message

Whenever the subject of organization comes up in the context of writing, people picture an outline – the most widely used technique for placing ideas in linear sequence for a written document. However, organization has both a thinking and a writing stage, and half of any writing effort is taken by the thinking stage. At the thinking stage, outlining is actually less effective than any of a number of other, lesser-known activities, including brainstorming and clustering. You may wish to try out the procedures mentioned below, and see which best contributes to the unity of your document and eases the writing task.

If you find one or more of these techniques to be helpful, you will probably discover yourself using it freely and often. Some journalists use clustering to take notes during interviews, for example, developing a concept map as the responder talks. Technical writers report that these methods help minimize the edit–rewrite–edit–rewrite syndrome common in many commercial and academic situations. After capturing key points onto a concept map, issue tree, or cluster diagram, these writers translate the points into an organized list rather than a complete sentence draft. Only after approval of this version by supervisors do they go on to produce a full-sentence version.

To compile possibilities, consider brainstorming (random topic lists)

When you truly have no idea where to begin, try brainstorming. Brainstorming is a problem-solving technique in which one person or a group suggests as many ideas as possible about a given problem or situation, concentrating on quantity

Things to mention about laryngeal neoplasia:

It's pretty rare.

It causes breathing troubles.

I'm glad I don't have it.

Radiographs usually show soft tissue masses.

Surgery is usually used to correct it.

It can be malignant or benign.

Surgical techniques should be described.

My patient recovered from it.

About 10 cases have been described from companion animals.

Fig. 1.1. A list compiled by brainstorming includes a variety of ideas.

rather than quality; the result is a random topic list composed of brief notes compiled quickly without much concern for order (Fig. 1.1).

Ideas on a brainstorming list often overlap. Some are general and some are specific. Some may be earthshaking, others silly. This is not only acceptable, but necessary and desirable. Avoid making judgments during this stage. This powerful idea-generating technique works best when the brain functions in an unrestricted manner.

After an exhaustive set of ideas has been listed on paper, evaluation and organization can begin. Use arrows or numbers to suggest an appropriate arrangement such as chronological order or order of importance. Consider the points in light of the potential audience, desired outcome, and publication constraints. Now the list can be rearranged, edited, and structured into a functional outline, if desired or required.

To suggest organization, try clustering (concept maps)

When you know what ideas you want to include, but are unsure about how to put them together, consider the technique called clustering. Midway in complexity between topic lists and outlining, this approach has been developed and refined more-or-less independently by various information-management experts in fields such as computer software development and data processing. As a result, the approach has many names and variations, but all involve a process – generally called clustering, brain writing, or branching – that results in web-like charts called concept maps, pattern notes, idea wheels, or bubble charts. For the visually oriented person, these charts can be an extremely effective way to organize information.

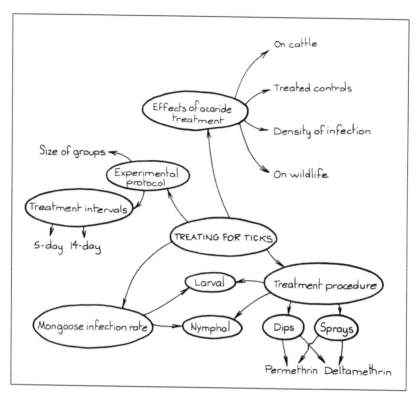

Fig. 1.2. The clustering process results in a type of concept map.

To begin clustering (Fig. 1.2), write the paper's main subject in the center of the page and circle it like the hub of a wheel. Think of major ways in which you could subdivide this subject, and write these ideas on the page at intervals around the circled main hub. Circle each of these second-level hubs (or bubbles, if you prefer that terminology), and draw lines or arrows connecting them to the central subject. Think about each of the second-level subjects. Near each one, add any details, examples, or further divisions. Circle these too, and draw lines connecting them to their respective subjects. Continue this process until you run out of ideas. When you see repetition, simply rearrange the pattern of spokes. If the pattern reaches the edge of the page, turn the spoke into another wheel hub, and start the process over to subdivide your ideas further.

After all of your ideas are clustered on the page, you may wish to go back and add numbers and letters to show the logical order. The numbered arrangement of these linked clusters can be used as a guide in organizing your writing and your final document.

To assess balance, develop an issue tree

An issue tree (Fig. 1.3) appears similar to an outline, and it looks more like the roots of a tree than its branches. These quibbles aside, an issue tree (Flower,

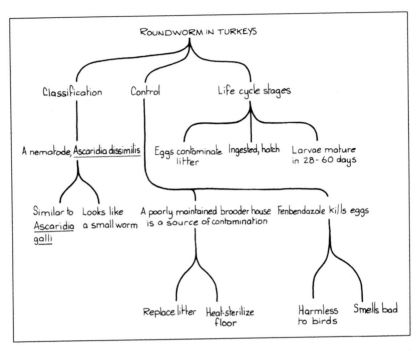

Fig. 1.3. An issue tree is a flexible tool for assessing balance in the treatment of a subject.

2000) can help check the balance of your treatment of a subject. Because it is more flexible than a formal outline, an issue tree is easy to rework during the organizing process and for a visually oriented person, it can seem less intimidating than other choices.

To develop an issue tree, write the main point at the top of a page. List sub-points under this main point. They may be phrased in any way that is comfortable, from single words to sentences or fragments. Then list sub-points below these, in decreasing order of importance. Connect all of these various levels with branching lines in a cascading manner.

As you explore topics, you may find that one branch begins to grow and spread across the page, almost excluding the others. Perhaps this material is an unnecessary digression. If so, this can be corrected at this early stage, before you have invested hours in drafting a narrative. Alternatively, the other branches may need more detail. Ask yourself questions about the subject of each branch: "How do I know this? Why is it important? Does it contribute to the whole picture? What evidence do I have for this?" Be as complete as you can.

To develop the paper's framework, consider an outline

Outlining is a time-honored technique, but it is important to remember that outlines serve two distinct purposes – to help organize one's thoughts, and to help organize one's written words. Some writers who find them useful for one of these purposes may find them less helpful for the other. Thus, the first decision should be whether to draw up an outline at all. You know your own personality best.

If you decide to use an outline, the next decision is what kind. Outlines come in many types, from sketchy affairs that are little more than lists to full-blown formal documents. Some extremely methodical writers first construct a topic outline to specify the order of the paper's sections, then develop a sentence outline to specify the order of the paragraphs within each section. Then and only then do they sit down to actually write. This is the time-honored formal outline system. Many of us subverted this process even back in English composition class, and wrote our required outlines only after the paper was finished. We either didn't know or didn't care that, when we treated the outline as an afterthought, we negated most of its potential usefulness as an organizational tool. However, we did intuitively recognize that a working outline differs from a final writing outline, and only a masquerade could make them appear the same.

To discard the entire outlining process is to throw the baby out with the bath water, however. You may wish to consider developing an informal working outline, for your eyes only. In the early 1970s, a survey of members of the Society for Technical Communication found that ninety percent of those who responded used such a topic outline of words, phrases, and sentences. Only five percent used either a formal sentence outline or no outline at all. Likewise, some organizations require formal topical outlines for their publications. Even in the absence of specific requirements, formal topical outlines often turn up as tables of contents in finished typescripts. With no apologies, these are produced after the document is written, revised, and edited.

Outlining is a fairly mechanical process, and most word processing programs have this capability. With automatic outlining, it will be dynamically updated each time the document is restructured. When the typescript is finished, this outline can be used to generate a table of contents and/or index, if needed. (Without an outline, headings still can be marked in the document so that a word processing program can compile a table of contents from them. This is more tedious than the outline-based method, but it still is faster and more consistent than compiling such a table by hand.)

A typical topic outline consists of short phrases linked in a way that shows the sequential order and relative importance of ideas. The alphanumeric system (Fig. 1.4) alternates numbers and letters, and usually also uses degrees of indentation to indicate descending levels of headings.

Another type of outline is based on a numeric or decimal system (Fig. 1.5). Entries may be indented sequentially or all placed flush left. Decimal outlines are widely used in government and military publications. However, they can appear pretentious, and alphanumeric outlines are generally easier for readers to grasp.

Standard grammar books usually present specifically prescribed heading styles and rules of indentation. If your outline must pass outside review and critique, careful attention to such outlining conventions will help you gain approval. With either alphanumeric or numeric outlines, strive for consistency and balance. Use

Sonographic Evaluation of the Cranial Mediastinum in Small Animals

I. Introduction

   A. Two techniques were previously used to assess mediastinum condition.

      1. Radiography was the first technique developed.

         a. Its advantage lies in its widespread use.

         b. Its disadvantage is that it is an insensitive technique.

      2. Computed tomography (CT) was the next technique to be developed.

         a. It has two significant advantages over radiography.

            (1) The technique clearly defines margins.

            (2) It indicates the relative opacity of masses.

         b. Its clinical disadvantage is that it is not widely used.

   B. Sonography is a powerful new technique now being tested in clinical trials.

Fig. 1.4. An alphanumeric system is evident in this excerpt from a detailed, sentence-based outline.

Pathogenicity of Two Field Strains of Infectious Bursal Disease Virus (IBDV)

1. (or 1.0). Description of IBDV

      1.1. Causative agent of Gumboro disease of young chickens

            1.11. Produces severe changes in Bursa of Fabricius

            1.12. Results in immunosuppression

      1.2. Classification

            1.21. Member of Birnavirus group

            1.22. Nonenveloped icosahedral virus

            1.23. Two serotypes (I and II)

2. (or 2.0). Timeliness of IBDV research

      2.1. IBD emergence as a major poultry disease problem

      2.2. Increase in subclinical IBD cases

      2.3. Many broiler farms losing money to this disease

Fig. 1.5. A decimal-based numeric system, such as the one in this selection from a phrase-based outline, is often used in government and industry.

Exercise 1.3. Organizing ideas

Reorganize the following outline of ideas, using a concept map or an issue tree.

ABUNDANCE OF SAND FLIES

A. Determining population dynamics
   1. Aspirating flies from resting sites
       a. 6 ft high tree holes (most were here)
       b. Ground level
   2. Light traps at different levels

B. Determining offspring age
   1. Laboratory studies
       a. Maximum age, 5 weeks
       b. 50% mortality by 2 weeks
   2. Field studies
       a. Most were 2–3 weeks old
       b. Youngest found, 1 week old

---

either complete sentences or just phrases or words, but never mix them. Each level also should always have two or more parts. If only one element appears, incorporate its information into the heading immediately above it.

Avoid plagiarism

Countries and cultures differ as to whether the tangible expressions of an author are "intellectual property" requiring permission and acknowledgments for the use of them. In Chapter 8, these issues are discussed more fully.

Here, let us just note that, if you are accustomed to using other sources freely without clear documentation or permission, you need to be very careful to adjust to the system of documentation used in the United States. Use of intellectual property by others can be considered theft. It is unethical and even illegal if it is not clearly documented or if permission is not obtained.

It is also unacceptable to use too much information from a single source, copy material directly from the Internet, or to use a great many of your own words from an earlier paper without referencing that paper. These uses are also considered plagiarism.

Use the Process Approach to take charge

Has this ever happened to you? Under pressure of a deadline, you must write a paper, but you just can't quite get started and aren't sure quite where to begin anyway. Days pass, and your guilt increases. Finally, a couple of days before the deadline, your adrenaline kicks in . . . you throw words together in whatever way you can, writing into the wee hours of the morning, then print a copy and hurriedly send it off or turn it in. Not your best effort, you mutter, but considering how little time you had, not too bad, either!

This is an old, sad story. We all have fooled ourselves like this at times. We know in the back of our minds that time spent on revision would have improved that hastily written paper immensely. But . . . it might take more work, and we're not even quite sure where to begin. What if fiddling around just made the paper worse? What if we ran out of time half-way through? What if . . . ? Maybe it would be easier to keep on making excuses.

There is a way to win new control over your writing. It's called the Process Approach. A process is a directed activity in which something changes. Something is always happening – work is being done, a product is being formed, an end of some kind is being achieved. To describe or organize a process, you must analyze its stages.

Applied to writing, the Process Approach involves methodically breaking the task into discrete stages, and tackling each stage in the most systematic, efficient, and effective way you can determine. We believe that this way of approaching the task will make the writing process more efficient, effective, satisfying, and perhaps even enjoyable, compared with your previous scientific writing efforts. (For this reason, you'll notice that this book follows a Process Approach, as well.)

You have already met the initial steps in the process. The first is planning, gathering, and organizing information. The next stage includes organizing your thoughts with such devices as outlines, bubble-charts, and (perhaps surprisingly) tables and figures.

Chapter 2 will help you begin the "real" writing, guiding your first draft. To help you do this efficiently, we'll discuss productivity tools and their pitfalls. We recommend that you write the first draft in a standard format and fairly conversational style, working as continuously as possible, without stopping to fine-tune anything. Then it should be set aside to "cool" for a bit, so that it can be revised more dispassionately.

Visual aids such as tables, figures, graphs, and other artwork take the stage early and play a strong part in this approach. The writing pause that occurs between the first and second draft is an excellent time to pay further attention to their creation and use. Chapter 3 details ways to develop strong visual support for the classic research paper, and Chapter 4 suggests approaches to create and deliver a strong visually supported oral presentation.

Revision, an essential part of the process, follows. Although word processing has softened the distinction between writing and editing drafts, it still is helpful to think of the revision process as a series of tasks of successively smaller scale. The first revision (Chapter 5) concentrates entirely on organization, logic, and broad matters such as clarity, readability, and brevity. Only after these matters have been considered do we finally pay attention (Chapter 6) to word choice and style, and then (Chapter 7) to the fine points of grammar, punctuation, and such.

Finally (Chapter 8) we give the typescript its last polish and send it off to the journal editor or publisher.

Know when to stop

Writing is only one part of a scientist's work. There comes a time when a writing project must be declared finished so that life can move on.

Revision can be taken too far. We knew a successful artist who would occasionally become so possessed by the urge to "touch up flaws" that we learned to hide the brushes so she couldn't completely obliterate her artwork! The same thing can happen with scientific papers.

When in doubt, apply a cost–benefit analysis – a well-known maxim that seems to apply to a great many endeavors, including revision, states that 20% of the effort is responsible for 80% of the results, and the remaining 80% of the effort only produces an additional 20% of the results.

Keep tasks in perspective

Each chapter in this book presents suggestions and guidelines for dealing efficiently with another of these sequential stages. However, along the way, even a relatively brief handbook like this one presents what can seem like an overwhelming myriad of details. A checklist may help keep you from losing sight of the forest among the trees. Consider adding additional columns with target dates for finishing each step and for the dates of their actual completion.

We can't resist one final word of advice . . . Above all else, keep both your sense of perspective and your sense of humor. Important as they may be, don't let the mechanics of writing the paper overbalance the intellectual challenge of pursuing a question that truly interests you and analyzing the science that forms the basis of your research. The excitement of pursuing, developing, and expressing ideas is one of the finest satisfactions of research and scholarship.

B.C.   by Johnny Hart

By permission of John L. Hart and Creators Syndicate, Inc.

2

Composing a first draft

> Writing is an adventure. To begin with, it is a toy and an amusement. Then it becomes a mistress, then it becomes a master, then it becomes a tyrant. The last phase is that just as you are about to be reconciled to your servitude, you kill the monster and fling him to the public.
>
> *– Winston Churchill*

Writing is usually portrayed as hard, mindless, joyless work. Great authors, it is said, must suffer from a sort of "creative madness" and work in mindless binges under endless pressures of deadlines, exhaustion, and criticism. Writing is said to be stressful, unpleasant, and disliked. Yet, if this were really the sole route to successful writing, why would anyone choose it?

Yes, it is true that stress is associated with writing that is delayed and then forced under deadlines. However, there are more attractive and productive alternatives to writing in tedious, joyless ways. In this chapter we'll guide you along. We'll help you deal promptly with matters of authorship, both to minimize the potential for misunderstandings and to guide collaboration and any division of responsibility. Recommendations for ways to use word processing tools will help you write more proficiently, avoiding pitfalls while becoming adept at using efficiency-enhancing features. We'll show you how to ease the writing task by paying attention to standard format conventions. We'll share tips on ways to build your writing momentum and deal constructively with the dreaded writer's block.

Soon, your hardest work will be finished. You'll have successfully completed a very effective first draft!

DEAL WITH MATTERS OF AUTHORSHIP

Increasingly, scientific research involves collaboration, often across several disciplines. All contributors should receive credit for their particular contributions to the research, usually by being included as a coauthor. Joint authorship can be either a blessing or a curse, however, depending upon when and how it is approached (LaFollette, 1992).

Discuss authorship before starting the first draft

Reach an explicit consensus on authorship as soon as you possibly can. Except possibly for the issue of plagiarism, nothing in the world of scientific publication

31

is more likely to breed hard feelings and wreck friendships than a disagreement over authorship.

As defined by the International Committee of Medical Journal Editors (2006), decisions on authorship should be guided by a simple ethical principle – any author listed on the paper's title page should take public responsibility for its intellectual content. No one is likely to be able to take such responsibility unless they have taken part in the research *and* in writing the paper or revising it for accuracy of content. Participation solely in data collection or solely in the writing of the grant that funded the research does not necessarily justify authorship. Nor does general supervision of the laboratory group qualify one for authorship unless the supervisor contributed to the conception and design of the research or to the analysis and interpretation of the results. Don't lose your job over this issue, however! Most research today is necessarily done by teams, with some contributions being intellectual and others practical. Often, all contributors are listed as authors.

Check the *Instructions to Authors*. Some *ITAs* require an explicit statement, signed by all the coauthors, to the effect that each author has contributed significantly to the paper, understands it, and endorses it. Further discussion of authorship can be found in the on-line version of "Uniform Requirements for Manuscripts Submitted to Biomedical Journals" (excerpted in Appendix 2).

Agree on the order of authors' names

Why does it matter in what order names appear on the title page of a typescript or published paper? One reason is that the order implies the authors' relative contributions. The first name to appear is generally assumed to be the individual who played the largest part in the study. This person is called the senior author. In some laboratories, the head of the laboratory, department, or research team is automatically included on any paper coming from the laboratory. In various science disciplines, the last author by convention is the head of the laboratory where the research was done.

Visibility is a second reason. If several people have worked together on a project, and you are not one of the first three authors named, be prepared for your name to be invisible in other authors' articles. In reference lists (and sometimes in text as well), journals typically print all the names up to some arbitrary number (three or six are common choices). Beyond this number, they usually include only the first one or three names, and use *et al.* for the rest.

When many people all have contributed more or less equally to the research, alphabetical or reverse alphabetical name order is sometimes used. Alternatively, if more than one paper logically comes from a cooperative project, authors sometimes rotate as first author on successive publications.

Many research reports result from the efforts of large cooperative teams. Perhaps the greatest number of coauthors on a single publication to date is the 488 individuals from 39 institutions for an article in *Physical Particle Physics*! For other examples of unwieldy multi-authorship, see Yang (1995).

Although authors generally would like to see their individual names appear, when this many people are involved, editors may like to see authorship credited by group titles. Rather than listing the names of individuals, none of whom can really take responsibility for the whole, the group could coin a designation, such as "The National Cooperative Atherosclerosis Study." A footnote would list group members, and each could legitimately list the paper on their personal résumés.

Let authorship guide collaboration, and vice versa

An early decision about authorship allows the work of writing to be divided accordingly. When several people are collaborating on a typescript, one's first temptation may be to simply assign a section to each and compile the sections. This poses potential problems – including illogical strategy, weak transitions, and inconsistencies in language, to name a few of the more common.

An alternative method of dividing responsibility that often works better is to designate the best writer in the group as coordinator. Assign this person the responsibility for the outline, introduction, summary or abstract, and conclusions. Divide responsibility for the other sections among the remaining authors. Set clear deadlines for each step of the writing. Communicate often and clearly, using email for speed and efficiency if possible.

When the rough drafts are collected, give the coordinator the license to change any section in order to make it flow smoothly into the whole. Then give all contributors the opportunity to comment on the collated draft. Before submitting the final version to a journal, be sure to have all coauthors read and approve it.

PRODUCTIVITY TOOLS AND PITFALLS

My computer is down. I hope it's something serious.
– *Graffito*

Word processing programs have become incredibly sophisticated, with all manner of developments that at least theoretically ease the mechanics of writing. At the same time, however, they have robbed reluctant writers of some of their best, most time-honored excuses, and introduced new pitfalls for the unwary. Think about them as you write your first draft; once again, knowledge is power.

Use word processing to write more efficiently

The words come out of you like toothpaste sometimes.
– *Garrison Keillor*

With a computer and appropriate word processing software, even young children can type, revise, and print text with minimal effort. By all means, use the computer to compose your scientific paper, right from the beginning. While the typescript is on the screen, insert and delete words or passages and rearrange text without repetitious retyping. With a single command, change a word or a spelling throughout the manuscript. From the first draft to the last, word processing will save hours of time. In addition, most journals are now accepting electronic submissions, either as disk copy, through an email attachment, or directly downloaded to a website. This is a welcome development for everyone involved, saving time and money and decreasing the probability of errors creeping into the final publication.

Master the tools that will make your writing life simpler

Human beings are creatures of habit, but new habits can be surprisingly difficult to cultivate. Each of us has our private glitches in this regard. You may know that almost nothing in a word-processed typescript need be numbered, alphabetized, or sorted manually – yet you persist in typing in the numbers manually in your lists. Or you may be aware that the software includes a thesaurus, but you've never bothered to use it.

Stepping outside your comfort zone to master new techniques is a matter of attitude. In general, these features are included because a great many people have found them useful. Will you be one of them? Probably, but you will never know unless you take the time to try them.

Use automatic formatting to save time and ensure consistency

When mastered, features such as automatic formatting, styles, and templates can be used to design a look for almost any purpose, from a letter, typescript, or journal article to an address list. Merrily type away and the computer will format the material, automatically handling such mundane details as paragraph indentation, hyphenation, pagination, and heading styles.

Automatic formatting can save considerable time when used on lengthy reference lists, in particular. An additional advantage of automatic formatting becomes evident if that format later must be modified. One simple change to the document style sheet will update all occurrences of text formatted with a given style.

Some journals require that lines of text be numbered in the left margin to allow editors to refer authors to specific passages. In the past, this required the use of special paper, and changes in text necessitated retyping the entire typescript. With the proper command, word-processing programs now will number lines automatically as the document is printed, either page by page or from the beginning of the typescript to its end.

Use hidden text for notes

Using this feature can speed the writing of a first draft because it allows the equivalent of secret parenthetical notes throughout the typescript. Characters formatted as hidden text do not appear on the screen (or in print) without a specific command. They are equivalent to notes jotted in the margin. The hidden text feature is also extremely useful for dialog between coauthors that does not affect the typescript itself.

Hidden text can be used for special commands that mark entries for a table of contents and index. This can be especially useful when one wishes to index a concept rather than specific words. (An index also can be based directly on a search for the occurrences of specific words, a less powerful technique but one that is still faster than the old handwritten index-card method.)

Use special features to make sweeping changes easily on the screen

For example, become familiar with the "search" or "find" feature. Not only can you find and change words or characters throughout the typescript with a single keystroke, you can also use these features to standardize format and to instantly locate and scroll to specific sections of the typescript.

This feature is often combined with a "replace" option, which can be very handy but needs to be used with care. For example, suppose you wished to replace the word "one" with "two" throughout your typescript. Since such a short word often happens to be part of another word, you would find all sorts of interesting but nonsensical words peppered throughout the text. Questioned would now be *questitwod*; telephone, *telephtwo*; done, *dtwo*. This predicament can be largely avoided by specifying "whole words only" or typing a space before and after the word in the "find" box. (However, with the spacing option, if the word begins a paragraph it may now be missed.)

If your word processor has a thesaurus feature, use it to help make your prose more varied and interesting. Turn to it if you experience a mental block and can't come up with the right word. Try a possible synonym and let the thesaurus suggest and substitute alternative choices.

Resist premature cosmetic work

Because it is so easy to make superficial changes, it is tempting to make each draft technically perfect, with every comma in place, every word spelled correctly, every margin perfectly aligned. Then, because the paper looks so good, one becomes rather hesitant to change it further, even though the basic structure may need a major overhaul. A paper like this can be compared to a beautifully painted house with termites – lovely outside but unsound within. Trust us – it's unlikely to fool editors and reviewers.

Furthermore, because the manuscript looks so good, many people find it difficult to throw away unnecessary material. If you find you've strayed off course, and ended up with more verbiage or material than you really need, cut out the extra, no matter how hard you worked at it. Some writers save their trimmings in a separate "orphan" file. Adopting a similar approach could be useful in case you change your mind later.

Use tools that ease collaboration

Much of modern day science is collaborative, resulting in typescripts that pass through many hands. Coauthors may work on the same draft concurrently or write different sections that are then circulated among them. Insist that everyone "track changes," a feature that will clearly mark suggestions and revisions, as well as identifying their source should it be necessary to revisit them.

There will also be times when you will want to write-protect a document with a password so that permanent changes cannot be made. Even so, always save a backup copy of the original draft before sharing it among collaborators.

When several individuals independently suggest revisions, it used to be necessary to manually transfer such changes from paper to computer. Most word

PEANUTS   by Charles Schulz

© United Feature Syndicate, Inc. Reprinted with permission.

processing programs have the ability to merge hidden text annotations and revisions from different file copies of the manuscript onto a single master copy.

The ability to send even lengthy documents as attachments to email messages
makes collaborative typescript preparation easier than it has ever been. You can
correspond rapidly with colleagues around the globe, seek and give advice and
suggestions, and work together more closely than has ever been possible. Even
when you work on collaborative writing projects with the person across the hall,
you can send drafts back and forth between team members for comment, and
can receive and incorporate those comments electronically.

Save your work often, and always make backups

Computers do lose material – both during and after you've worked on it – and
you must take extra steps to safeguard yourself from this catastrophe. During every working session, save your document at regular intervals. If a power
failure or other problem causes the program to shut down while you are working, you can recover everything entered before the last save command. If your
program has the option of automatically saving documents, learn about this
feature.

For extra security, keep a backup copy in a separate location, or consider
emailing the file as an attachment to a colleague or yourself. Remember, there
are only two types of computer users – those who have lost files, and those who
will.

Spellcheckers, grammar and style analysis programs

> I now can quickly spell hors d'oeuvres, which grates on many people's nerves.
> – *Unknown*

The incredible capabilities of modern word processing programs can have a
profound psychological effect, particularly because changes are relatively easy to
make, and mechanical aids such as spellcheckers and style checkers save a lot of
tedious effort. However, be somewhat wary and not too easily seduced by bells
and whistles. Some new tools can be a tremendous productivity booster, while
others can seriously distract one from the writing task at hand.

Use computerized grammar checking programs wisely, if at all

Grammar checking or style analysis programs are now widely available either as part of word processing programs or as separate software. However, unlike a spellchecker, which is fairly mechanical and straightforward, a grammar checker requires a great deal of personal judgment. Each word, phrase, or passage that it questions must be considered individually to decide whether the program truly has flagged an error. Sometimes, this is more time-intensive than relying upon the grammar checker built into one's own neural anatomy.

Style analysis programs are most helpful for picking up simple mechanical problems, such as a missing parenthesis or quotation mark. Some will alert you to commonly misused words such as affect and effect. They will identify redundant, overworked, wordy, or trite phrases, and can help you detect noun-heavy passages by counting prepositions. They also can pick up writing quirks, such as too many short sentences or overuse of "to be" verbs. However, they flag only items that can be detected by pattern-matching. For this reason, errors such as subject–verb agreement – a particular problem in scientific writing – sometimes slip by. Logic is completely beyond them, and they will approve a completely incomprehensible document if it appears in a form that passes for Standard Written English.

To date, style analysis programs are not very closely targeted to biomedical writing. They tend to flag a great many passages that do not need revision. For example, they may question every instance of the passive voice, even when used appropriately in scientific writing. Some programs allow you to disable the passive voice rule and certain other rules, but many idiosyncrasies inherent to the topic of your scientific paper will probably be questioned over and over again.

Writing experts stress that organization and coherence are the main determinants of writing quality. These are beyond the scope of any available editing program. Trying to use one of these programs while composing a first draft wastes time and promotes writer's block. The most efficient time to use a grammar checking or style analysis program, if at all, is near the end of the writing process, after the document has been shuffled into a reasonable organization and polished to a reasonable degree of coherency, style, and grace. At this point, a grammar checker can provide one more way to ferret out undetected mechanical errors.

Use a spellchecker but never entrust it with everything

The ability to check spelling is one of the strengths and blessings of word processing. Take advantage of it. More than that – make its use a regular habit. Professional writing requires perfect spelling. Many people view misspelled words and typographical errors as signs of carelessness, lack of professionalism, or limited intelligence – hardly the impression one wants to make on an editor or reviewer!

Run a spellchecker on every document that will leave your computer. It will speed your work, improve its accuracy, and spare you from becoming delayed by manual dictionary searches to check the spelling of seldom-used words. Most spellcheckers have several built-in dictionaries in various languages. In the United States, the main dictionary usually is called English Dictionary. However, there

---

Exercise 2.1. Spelling and grammar programs

A. Enjoy these examples inspired by *Anguished English* (Lederer, 1987). Then rewrite the sentences to correct the errors a grammar checker would miss.

1. Migraines strike twice as many women as do men.
2. Wanted: Worker to take care of cow that does not smoke or drink.
3. As a baboon who grew up wild in the jungle, I realized that Wiki had special nutritional needs.
4. The patient was referred to a psychiatrist with a severe emotional problem.
5. In the photograph, veterinarian Joe Mobbs hoists a cow injured while giving birth to its feet.
6. About two years ago, a wart appeared on his left hand, which he wanted removed.
7. People who use birth control methods that smoke are in danger of having retarded children.
8. The woman wants to have the dog's tail operated on again, and if it doesn't heal this time, she'll have to be euthanized.

B. Find the errors that the spellchecker missed.

1. The young of the hoatzin, curious foul native to South America, are remarkable in having clawed fingers on their wings, by moans of which they are able to climb about trees like quadruplets.
2. These imported trees are so profligate they are crowding out the more fragile naive species.
3. The client has a congenial hip disease.
4. His prostrate gland problem had persisted for many years.
5. The animals that normally inhabit the pond were dyeing because it had too much green allergy.
6. The experimental group included three Great Dames and eight puppies from a German Shepherd and an Alaskan Hussy.
7. She had a seizure, fell, and went unconscious. She was in a comma, and she never woke up.
8. The pistol of a flower is it's only protection against insects.
9. The doctor advised the patent to rest until the stitches were out and that there would be a permanent scare.
10. Our Spellwriter has the power to check wards within a document in as many as eight different languages, and this is only the tap of the iceberg.

"GARFIELD, I THINK I KNOW WHY WE'VE BEEN RECEIVING SO FEW COMMISSIONS."

ScienceCartoonsPlus.com. Reprinted with permission.

are many differences between American, Australian, and British spellings of English words. The customization feature will allow you to open one or more of these variant dictionaries, either singly or simultaneously.

Spellcheckers can be used for more than their name suggests. Faced with a word that is not in their dictionary, most spellcheckers will display a list of one or more potential choices. This feature can be a tremendous time-saver when one knows only approximately how to spell a word or when trying to think of a word one cannot quite remember. Make a best guess, and count on being able to recognize the word when it appears on the list.

At a command such as "change all," most spellcheckers will correct a word's spelling throughout the entire document without further need for confirmation. This feature can also be used like a "find and replace" command to change one word to an entirely different one. (However, remember the potential for problems will be the same.)

Use a spellchecker to catch repeated words or errors in spacing. The best spellcheckers will do this automatically. This can be an important advantage, for repeated words (such as *this this*) and run-on words (such as *thisandthis*) are easy to overlook during proofreading.

Ode to a Spell Checker

Eye halve a spelling chequer
It came with my pea sea
It plane lea marques four my revue
Miss steaks eye kin knot sea.

Eye strike a key and type a word
And weight four it two say
Weather eye am wrong oar write
It shows me strait a weigh.

As soon as a mist ache is maid
It nose bee fore two long
And eye can put the error rite
Its rare lea ever wrong.

Eye ran this poem threw it
Your shore reel pleased two no
Its letter perfect awl the weigh
My chequer tolled me sew.

—*Arthur on Gnome*

*(Shamelessly hybridized
from several versions
circulating online)*

At the same time, recognize a spellchecker's limitations. First, spellcheckers don't really check spelling. Instead, they compare the words in a document with correctly spelled words that are stored in the program's dictionaries. If the computer cannot find a match, it flags the word as unknown. Because it operates in this way, a spellchecker will not catch correctly spelled words used in the wrong context. A word can be correctly spelled and still be wrong – as in the case of homonyms, or the use of a correctly spelled word with the wrong meaning or tense. One cannot expect it to catch such errors as using *their* for *there*, nor can it catch misspellings that form other words. For example, omission of one letter changes *underserved* to *undeserved*, significantly changing the meaning. Nothing can substitute for a final human proofreading.

Second, a spellchecker is only as good as the words entered in its dictionary. Specialized terms, most names of people and places, and many commonly used scientific abbreviations and acronyms are generally absent. The words in the main dictionary of a spellchecker cannot be accessed; they are stored in a special, compressed file format. (Furthermore, if an incorrectly spelled word were added to this dictionary, the error could not be repaired.)

Building a user-accessible custom dictionary lessens the number of flagged words that appear. Because searching a custom dictionary may take longer than searching the main dictionary, savvy writers keep custom dictionaries short by building them by subject. One for general correspondence might include proper nouns such as street and city names; one for grant writing might contain common governmental acronyms and agencies; still another might contain the technical terms, Latin binomials, and proper nouns needed to spellcheck a research typescript.

When you build a custom dictionary specifically for your scientific writing, be sure the words are spelled correctly when you enter them. Useful authoritative resources for specialized biomedical vocabulary include *Stedman's Medical Dictionary* (1995), *Dorland's Illustrated Medical Dictionary* (2003), *Handbook of Current Medical Abbreviations* (1998), and *Medical Terms and Abbreviations* (2002). See also Smith *et al.* (2001), Campbell and Campbell (1995), Holt *et al.* (1994), and Jablonski (2004). If you regularly write papers replete with specialized medical terminology, consider investing in medical dictionary software, which includes both definitions and specialized spellchecking.

Proofread the final version on paper

Spellcheckers assume that if a word is correctly spelled, it is the correct word. However, you may have chosen the wrong word. Thus, the last step should be your own careful proofreading of a paper copy, and a read-through by the most finicky person you know!

It is not easy to proofread your own material well. By the time you have worked on the paper for awhile, you are no longer as observant as you might be. You will tend to read what you think is there, not what is actually on the page. One way around this is to pair up with someone else. As one of you reads aloud from one copy of the paper, the other should follow along on a written copy. If you must go it alone, it is best if you can lay the material aside for a period of time before proofreading it. A fresh start makes it more likely that errors or stylistic flaws will be detected.

Guard your investment

Continue to save work frequently and make backups. The more time and energy you have invested in a document, the more important it is to protect that investment. A bit of paranoia can be healthy. Keep a duplicate copy. Remember to update the backup file each time you make significant changes.

FOLLOW STANDARD STRUCTURE

By this point in life, you've undoubtedly seen enough scientific documents to recognize that almost all of them follow a quite similar pattern, the so-called IMRAD format – an acronym for Introduction, Methods, Results And Discussion (Day and Gastel, 2006). Each main section is structured to address certain questions, and together they shape a critical argument.

Happily, this fairly rigid structure usually makes scientific writing easier, not more difficult. The next few pages offer a brief overview of what will be required. When you plunge in and begin to write, refer back here as necessary for inspiration and to stay on track.

Introduction

What is the problem, and why should anyone care? In other words, why was this work done? Deal with these questions briefly, interestingly, and as simply as possible. A well-written introduction should persuade colleagues and even non-specialists to begin reading the paper's text after their attention has been attracted by the title, abstract, tables, and figures.

A three-part introduction works well. First state the general field of interest. Concisely present what is already known about the subject of your investigation, referencing the most important publications. Don't try to mention everything, unless you are writing a review article or a thesis. One to three paragraphs should be enough for most journal articles.

Next, present others' findings that will be challenged or expanded. Explain how you are hoping to extend or modify what is already known or believed. Provide support for your argument.

Finally, specify the question that the paper addresses, and how it does so. This sentence is often phrased in hypothesis form. Indicate your experimental approach. Point out what is new and important about your work. When appropriate, briefly summarize the answer(s) you found.

Materials and methods

This section may have any of several names. Materials and/or Methods, Experimental Design, Protocol, and Procedure are some of the common ones. Sometimes it is divided into separately titled subsections, as well. Overall, it answers a simple question – how was the evidence obtained?

Begin by listing the supplies that were necessary for your work, including both animate materials such as experimental animals and inanimate ones such as chemicals. Explicitly note that use of animals and human subjects conformed to the legal requirements for the country in which the research was conducted.

Next, specify what was done, and for what purpose. Chronological order is a common way to proceed through this segment. Alternatively, parallel the sequence in which you present results. A flowchart may be useful for readers. Conclude with a discussion of any statistical procedures employed (but not the tests' outcomes, which belong in Results).

The key to a successful Methods section is to include the right amount of detail – too much, and it begins to sound like a laboratory manual; too little, and no one can determine what you actually did. For publication of a new discovery to be "valid" or scientifically accepted, it must appear in a form so that a reader could repeat the experiment. However, this really means not just any reader, but a trained investigator with considerable experience. Once again, it is important to know one's audience. As an additional guide, frequently refer to examples published in your chosen journal.

Increasingly, federally funded research in the United States is requiring studies to be conducted in accordance with Good Laboratory Practice (GLP) guidelines (Benson and Boege, 2002). The guidelines require preparation of standard operating procedures for all aspects of a project. Referring back to these procedures can be very helpful, both when preparing Materials and Methods and when documenting the data that were collected. Even when GLP guidelines are not required for a project, using this research approach can facilitate the writing task.

If you have followed a widely known method, simply name the principles on which it is based and cite the original publication or recent textbooks or handbooks that give full details. If you made changes to a published procedure, describe only the changes and reference the rest. Only if you have employed an entirely new process or technique must you describe it in full. In this last instance, you may wish to test the adequacy of your description by asking a colleague to do an experiment while following the technique as your text describes it.

Results

This section should be relatively easy. What was found or seen? Decide on a logical order for presentation (see Table 2.1). Present the results that have a bearing on the question you are examining, but do not interpret them here unless your journal combines Results and Discussion. Exclude irrelevant findings, but never omit valid results that appear to contradict your hypothesis. Suppressing such data is unethical, but when presenting them you may explain why you feel they are anomalous.

Tables and figures are usually an integral part of this section. Don't use the text to parrot the information they contain. Readers can see the data for themselves. Instead, point out salient features and note relationships between the various results.

Discussion and conclusions

What do your findings mean? Why are they important? Discussion and Conclusions sections exist to answer these questions. Often combined with each other

Table 2.1. *Common patterns for organizing material*

Pattern	Basis
Categorical	Groupings of like items
Chronological	Time sequence
Spatial	Physical arrangement of entities
Functional	How parts work
Importance	Usually with elements in order of decreasing consequence
Problem-solutions	Predicament, possible answers, why each will/won't work, usually followed by specific recommendation
Specificity	General to particular, or particular to general
Complexity	Usually from simple to complex
Pro and con	Both sides of an issue or decision
Causality	Cause and effect
Deductive	Conclusion first, then background leading up to it
Inductive	Individual facts first, leading to conclusion

and sometimes with the Results as well, these sections generally parallel the organization used in earlier sections of the paper.

Your task here is to interpret your results against a background of existing knowledge. Explain what is new in your work, and why it matters. Discuss both the limitations and the implications of your results, and relate your observations to other relevant studies. State new hypotheses (clearly labeled as such) when they are warranted. Include recommendations when appropriate.

When writing this section, watch for symptoms of megalomania. Avoid exaggerated or extravagant claims for your work. Carefully distinguish between facts and speculation. Be wary about extrapolating your results to other species or conditions. Rein in the natural human tendency to want to point out the shortcomings of another investigator's report. Indicate what the next steps might be to resolve any apparent conflicts. Frankly admit anomalies. Discuss any possible errors or limitations in your methods and assumptions. And finally, don't stack in so many alternative hypotheses to explain the results that readers become buried in the pile. Hailman and Strier (1997) state that as a general rule, the discussion should never be the longest section in a paper.

Acknowledgments

Acknowledgments usually appear between the Discussion and Reference sections. (Note that some journals spell the title of this section with two "e"s, others with three.) Include any substantial help received from organizations or individuals, whether they provided grants, materials, technical assistance, or advice. (Some journals specify that funding bodies be named on the title page instead.) Concisely thank those who went out of their way to help, and describe their contribution. Do not list people who did not contribute directly to the reported work or those who did no more than their routine laboratory, secretarial, or office work. As a courtesy, ask consent from anyone you name; some journals require signed permissions from everyone who is acknowledged.

References

In this section, include all the references you cited (specifically referred to) in the text, tables, and figures, but not references that were only useful background reading for you.

For your first draft, use the name-and-year (Harvard) system for citations rather than a consecutive number (Vancouver) style. It is easier to compile a final reference list from names than from numbers, and the Harvard system minimizes the chances that reference citations will become scrambled during reorganizations of the text.

There are literally hundreds of variations of literature reference style. Some excellent computerized bibliographic programs are available to help you consistently apply proper formatting to your final draft.

Note that some journals limit the number of references you can cite; check the *Instructions to Authors*. One common restriction is 40 references for full articles and 10 for brief communications, but some journals specify even fewer.

Abstracts and summaries

Abstracts are usually inserted right after the title page in the completed document. They are easier to prepare when your document is finished, but a first draft now may help you stay focused.

Some journals use the term "summary" to describe abstracts of their articles, but a summary is not the same as an abstract. An abstract is an abbreviated version of the paper, written for people who may never read the complete version. A summary restates the main findings and conclusions of a paper, and is written for people who have already read the paper. Include a summary only if the journal requires it.

Abstracts come in several varieties. Informative abstracts include some data and are commonly used with documents that describe original research. They address the same questions as the body of the paper, but briefly and without supporting tables or figures. Indicative abstracts (also called descriptive or topical) contain general statements about the subjects covered. Often used for review articles or books, they usually can be created simply by turning the table of contents into sentences.

Both informative and indicative abstracts are typically limited to between 100 and 250 words, and different points are emphasized in proportion to the emphasis they receive in the text itself. They are generally written as a single paragraph.

Structured abstracts are often longer, sometimes allowing as many as 400 words. These abstracts group series of points below headings such as Objective, Design, Setting, Patients, Treatment, Results, Conclusions, and Clinical Relevance. Experts disagree whether structured abstracts are on the way to disappearance or are evolving into a new kind of publication, with the main text available only in electronic form.

Staying within an abstract's word count specifications is a challenge for almost every writer. Be as brief and specific as possible, but write complete sentences that logically follow one another. Use the third person, active verbs, and the past tense unless it becomes unacceptably awkward to do so. The title and abstract are always read together, so there is no reason to repeat words or paraphrase the title in the abstract.

Write the abstract so that it can stand on its own merits, because many readers of your abstract will never see your entire text. If possible, avoid citing others' work here; when a citation is essential, include a short form of the bibliographic details. Likewise, avoid unfamiliar terms, acronyms, abbreviations, or symbols; if they must be used, define them at first mention in the abstract, then again at first mention in the text. And finally, never introduce information in the abstract that is not covered in the paper.

The title

From the moment when the first words are written, every document needs a rough working title for identification purposes. However, a working title is rarely suitable for the final paper. Refine it now. Is it interesting, concise, and informative? Is it accurate enough for use in indexing systems and bibliographic databases? Will potential readers be able to judge your paper's relevance to their own interests on the basis of the title alone?

Once again, it's time to check your journal's *Instructions to Authors* and to look over the publications in recent issues. Note capitalization style, title length, and general form. For journals in some fields, writers are being encouraged to use a declarative title written as a sentence or fragment that includes what the paper says, not just what it covers; in other fields, neutral descriptive titles remain the norm. Sometimes, they coexist. For example, in the international weekly journal, *Nature*, one can find both:

> *Declarative:* Selective elimination of messenger RNA prevents an incidence of untimely meiosis
> *Descriptive:* Mechanism of DNA translocation in a replicative hexameric helicase

Most journals prefer short titles, typically not over 100 characters (and sometimes considerably fewer), including the spaces between the words. This usually works out to only 10–12 words. Delete trivial phrases (such as "Notes on" or "A study of"), but do not use uncommon abbreviations or stack nouns and adjectives together without their prepositions.

> *Poor:* A Study of Chipmunk Muscle Tissue Ion Channel Amino Acid Activation Parameters
> *Better:* Amino Acid Activation of Ion Channels in Chipmunk Muscle Tissue

Most editors frown upon fanciful titles. Some also object to two-part titles, with a main title and a subtitle. Titles that end with a question mark are seldom acceptable.

Risky choices:
German Saxifrage Pollens are Superior to Those in Austria.

Does *Saxifraga* Pollen in Germany Resemble That in Austria?

Pollen Between a Rock and a Hard Place: German and Austrian Saxifrages

> *Widespread acceptability:* Pollen Morphology of German and Austrian *Saxifraga* Species

When writing a series of papers on a subject, title each separately. Numbered series with the same title and differing subtitles are a headache to everyone, especially if the papers have slightly different sets of coauthors. Editors are unhappy with the implication that acceptance of one paper obligates them to publish successive ones. Readers, librarians, and cataloguers deal with unnecessary confusion, especially if Part 4 is published before Part 2, or Part 3 is rejected entirely. If you feel it is vital that everyone knows the papers are a series, link them by mentioning the others in a footnote on the title page or by citing them in the Introduction. If the typescript on hand is interdependent with another unpublished paper, remember to include copies of that other paper for reviewers when you send the document to an editor.

Exercise 2.2. Title choices

How could the following manuscript titles be improved? Explain the reasons for your choices.

1. Plantar's Wart Removal: Report of a Case of Recurrence of Verruca after Curative Excision

2. Characteristics of Columbine Flowers are Correlated with Their Pollinators

3. Panda Mating Fails: Veterinarian Takes Over

4. Gleanings On The Bionomics And Behavior Of The East Asiatic Nonsocial Wasps. III. The Subfamily Crabroninae With A Key To The Species Of The Tribe Crabronini Occurring In Formosa And The Ryukyus, Contributions To The Knowledge Of The Behavior Of Crabronine Fauna, And Changes In The Taxonomic Position Of Three Species Of Crabronini Occurring In Japan

5. Report of New Health Data Results from the 1999 National ASAP-FYI-ERGO Health Study: Lung Cancer in Women Mushrooms

Other title page items

The title page really doesn't need to be compiled until the final document is assembled. However, for a psychological sense of completeness, writers often like to put one on the first draft. Most journals specify what information should appear – commonly, authors' names, degrees, job titles, and the name and addresses (postal and electronic) of the author to whom correspondence, proofs, and reprint requests should be sent. Keywords and funding sources may be mandatory, and some journals request a text word count.

Keywords or key phrases serve as reference points to indicate document contents for indexing and cataloguing. Check your journal's *Instructions to Authors* for their location in the typescript. The number of keywords that can be included is usually specified; three to ten are common limits.

If guidance from the journal is lacking, it is generally prudent to choose keywords and terms from the Medical Subject Headings used in *Index Medicus*, or from lists such as those published in *Biological Abstracts* and *Chemical Abstracts*. Choose the most important and most specific terms you can find in your document, including more general terms only if your work has interdisciplinary significance. Unless the target journal specifies otherwise, words that appear in the title do not need to be included among the keywords.

USE TENSE TO SHOW THE STATUS OF WORK

The use of present or past forms of verbs has a very special meaning in scientific papers. Proper tense use derives from scientific ethics. The use of past or present verb forms is a way of indicating the status of the scientific work being reported.

Because of these conventions regarding tense use, a scientific paper usually should seesaw back and forth between the past and present tenses. An Abstract or Summary refers primarily to the author's own unpublished results, and uses the past tense. Most of the Introduction section emphasizes previously established knowledge, given in the present tense. Both the Materials and Methods and the Results sections describe what the author did and found. They appear in the past tense. Finally, the Discussion emphasizes the relationship of the author's work to previously established knowledge. This section is the most difficult to write smoothly because it includes both past and present tenses.

Use the present tense when a fact has been published

Generalizations, references to stable conditions, and general "truths" should be given in the present tense. When scientific information has been validly published in a primary journal, it likewise becomes established knowledge. Therefore, use the present tense when writing about it. In this way, you show respect for the scientist's work. Similarly, when previously published work is mentioned, and the author is cited parenthetically or by footnote number, the sentence usually should be written in the present tense.

> Serological tests commonly *are used* for the diagnosis of *T. cruzi* infections.
> Several recent reports (2, 3, 6) *describe* similar findings.
> This phenomenon *determines* the absorption coefficient of the tissue (Christensen *et al.*, 1978).

In giving the author's name non-parenthetically as a source of the information, one can use either past or present tense for the verb that is linked to the author. However, the part of the sentence that refers to the scientific work itself is still given in the present tense.

> Smith (1975) *showed* that streptomycin *inhibits* growth of the disease organism.
> The investigations of Graff (1932) *show* that the structure *is* a true perithecium.
> Jones (1978) *does* not *believe* that streptomycin *is* effective.
> Boice (1912) *did* not *believe* that Diplococcus *exists*.

Use present perfect tense for repeated events

The present perfect tense is appropriate when observations have been repeated or continued from the past to the present.

> Nesting behavior *has been studied* under many environmental conditions.
> These drugs *have been shown* to produce significant elevations in blood pressure.

Use past tense to discuss results that cannot be generalized

Some results have been obtained under such specialized conditions that they pertain only to the particular study being reported. Numerical data sometimes fall into this category. Use the simple past tense of the verb that refers to the scientific work.

> Barber (1980) reported that 28% of the 396 wasps in his study *showed* signs of parasitism.

It also would be correct to say "Barber (1980) *reports*," but using past tense for both verbs is somewhat smoother and more consistent.

Use the past tense for unpublished results

By this line of reasoning, the research being reported for the first time in the paper you are writing will not be established knowledge until after it has been published. Therefore, use past tense to describe what you have done.

> In the study presented here, the drug killed 95% of the *M. tuberculosis* bacilli.
> Our data showed that few monarch caterpillars survived.

When your paper is published, the results become established knowledge. Thus, in citing your own previously published work, use the present tense, just as you do for others' work.

Use the present tense to refer readers to your figures and tables

Even though these are new and unpublished material, they are explanatory aids, not research itself. Discussion of the research itself remains in past tense, but directives appear in present tense.

> Antibodies occurred in 11% of our mice, as Table 1 indicates.
> See Figure 3, which illustrates the six-fold increase in leukocytes found in the study population.

BUILD MOMENTUM – AND KEEP IT!

> There ain't no rules around here! We're trying to accomplish something!
> – *Thomas Edison*

Ready to begin "really" writing? It's time to work with – not against – your natural habits, for you'll find that the key to success is building up a head of steam with a steady sense of progress that propels you on toward completion.

Start in the place that makes sense for you

When it comes to writing style, are you basically a rabbit or a turtle? As Michael Alley explains:

Rabbits hate first drafts. They despise juggling the constraints of writing with all the elements of style. So, in a first draft, they spring. They write down everything and anything. Rabbits strap themselves in front of their computers and finish their drafts as quickly as possible. Unfortunately, their first drafts are horrendous, sometimes not much better than their outlines. Still they've got something. They've put their ideas into a document, and they're in a position to revise.

Turtles, on the other hand, are patient. Turtles accept the job before them and proceed methodically. A turtle won't write down a sentence unless it's perfect. In the first sitting, a turtle begins with one sentence and slowly builds on that sentence with another, and then another. In the second sitting, a turtle then goes back to the beginning and revises everything from the first sitting before adding on. It usually takes a turtle several sittings to finish a first draft, but the beginning and middle are smooth because they've been reworked so many times. Revision then entails looking at the document from an overall perspective and smoothing the ending.   (Alley, 1996, pp. 241–242)

Few writers are strictly one or the other, of course, but you'll be most efficient if you determine which approach best fits your general style and personality. If you have turtle tendencies, ease into the first draft by starting with the section you feel is the most straightforward. (For many people, it is Materials and Methods.) If you are a rabbit type, begin with the Introduction and just plow right on, quickly getting as much information written as possible.

Exercise 2.3. Tense use

Indicate preferred tense use in the sentences below. If you feel that a sentence is correct as it stands, simply note the fact.

1. Work by Matthews (2007) showed that *Vespula* nests readily in the laboratory.

2. Bird size shows an increase in our study with width of wooded habitat, as Figure 2 indicates.

3. Beal (1960) also observed that size increased with meadow width.

4. In our study we find that there are significantly fewer antibody-producing cells in copper-deficient mice than in copper-supplemented mice (see Fig. 3).

5. In a study by Sengelaub and Finlay (1981), the average costal width for normal animals was 0.81 mm.

6. Conover and Kynard (1981) reported that sex determination in the Atlantic silverside fish was under the control of both genotype and temperature.

7. Recently published work by Fruchter *et al.* (1) characterizes the ash from the Mount St. Helens eruption of 18 May 1980.

8. Many researchers have confirmed that the balance of hydrostatic and osmotic pressures in the capillaries is a very delicate one.

9. ABSTRACT: The cell-to-cell channels in the insect salivary gland are probed with fluorescent molecules. From the molecular dimensions, a permeation-limiting channel diameter of 16–20 angstroms is obtained.

10. SUMMARY: Germinal and somatic functions in *Tetrahymena* are found to be performed separately by the micro- and macronuclei, respectively. Cells with haploid micronuclei are mated with diploids to yield monosomic progeny.

Set a realistic goal for each sitting. Don't stop until you've reached it, even if you become pressed for time and must "cheat" by finishing the section in outline form. Reaching a goal is almost guaranteed to give you a feeling of accomplishment that will help keep your momentum going. But don't stop here. Before you finish, write a few sentences of the next section. Psychologically, this makes it easier to start writing next time. Some writers claim it even helps to stop in mid-sentence or mid-thought!

Minimize distractions any way you can

While you are writing, it is worth making the effort to remove or escape from as many distractions as possible. Because each sentence in a scientific paper depends so much upon those around it, losing momentum usually leads to losing one's train of thought. Try to find a time and place when you can be relatively undisturbed.

Inevitably, from time to time your thoughts will tend to fly off in surprising directions while you are immersed in your work. Don't try to remember one set of ideas while working on another. They will either sidetrack you, or flutter off and never be recaptured. Keep a note pad near your work. Pen unrelated ideas onto a list when they occur, and deal with them later.

Watch what you eat. This tip may seem frivolous to those who have never been involved in a really lengthy writing project. However, as Alley (1996) points out, writing makes people restless, and that often makes them hungry. The wrong choice of snacks can derail your writing momentum. If you must eat, choose foods that require only one hand, don't stain papers, and don't make you thirsty or (worse yet) sleepy.

Keep the text simple, but somewhat organized

Write as simply and conversationally as possible. Remember those readers who will not be specialists in your area of research, and may not be reading in their native language. Imagine that you are describing your work to an interested friend in another scientific discipline. At this stage, don't worry too much about details of style or grammar, however. These things can be fixed at the revision stage.

Readers need a story line – a beginning, a middle, and an end, with clear links between each step. Insert headings to guide the way, especially if the paper is long. Follow your outline or other organizational aid, but treat it as a life jacket, not a straitjacket. As you write, new insights may come to mind and some previously identified topics may become irrelevant.

When really pressed for time, spend more time on the first draft, not less

A caveat is in order here. When you are in a hurry, be conservative. Take the extra time to develop a first-draft structure your coauthors or other readers can easily follow. Work steadily and quickly, and get the whole thing on paper in as rational an arrangement as you can. There may be no time to cut, paste, and rearrange. There may not even be time to polish. It's admittedly a horrible thought, but it would be even more horrible to have the paper in bits and pieces when the clock strikes!

Write around missing information

A common cause of lost momentum is the missing word. It's on the tip of your tongue, but after five minutes spent looking in the dictionary you still can't find it, and you've ground to a halt as a result. Write the name of your favorite sports team, your significant other, or simply "???" in its place, and keep on going. Your subconscious will bring it to the surface later. When that happens, don't forget to use the "search and replace" command in your word processing program to find your space-holder and insert the word where it belongs.

If you can't find the sentence to express an idea, you may not have fully formed the idea yet. Again, leave a space-holder, and keep on writing. Think about it later, perhaps when you are exerting yourself physically; many writers and researchers feel that exercise sharpens their processing of ideas.

Recognize the signs of bogging down

At some point in the writing process, you may feel overwhelmed. It can be an intense emotion, but be reassured that most writers experience these feelings as a very natural reaction to the magnitude of their task. Words rarely flow effortlessly all the time for anyone. Professional writers struggle, just like you do. Everyone also experiences times when their writing efficiency seems to decline or die.

Instead of quitting altogether when such feelings strike, switch to writing a different section. Alternatively, begin to write (or talk) about precisely why you are bogged down – surprisingly, this exercise often will free you. If you stop when you are stalled, it can become an excuse to avoid starting up again.

Deal constructively with writer's block

It's a writer's worst fear. The deadline is fast approaching. You sit down to write and absolutely nothing useful happens . . . You chew your pencil or tap a rhythm on the computer console, stare out the window, get up for a drink of water, decide to run an errand or shop for groceries . . . The inspiration to write has vanished. You have writer's block. Or do you?

Those who write about writing debate whether writer's block – particularly in scientific writing – is a real phenomenon or just a bit of folklore used to explain garden-variety distraction and provide an excuse to stop working. Whatever may ultimately be decided, a great number of solutions fortunately have been suggested. Many of them sound like the ideas we've already mentioned. Here are a few other imaginative suggestions:

- Alley (1996) suggests that writer's block can arise because many of us are inhibited by hidden voices, such as criticism from our eighth grade English teacher or our department manager. He proposes drowning them out with classical or jazz music.
- Even when you can't get a word down on paper, Shortland and Gregory (1991) point out that you might find that you could easily talk to friends about your topic. Write down what you would say, much in the manner of a rambling letter to a close friend. (Or, as a colleague suggests, record your conversation, and listen to it for ideas.) It will become easier to keep going once you have words on paper instead of still in your mind, and you may even make your story more understandable to your audience than it would otherwise be.

For Better or For Worse

FOR BETTER OR FOR WORSE © 2000 Lynn Johnston Productions. Dist. By
Universal Press Syndicate. Reprinted with permission. All rights reserved.

By permission of Universal Press

- For particularly severe cases, Mack and Skjei (1979) recommend a technique called "kitchen-sinking it," in which one repeatedly sits down and writes nonstop for a fixed but short time (such as 15 minutes) about any aspect of the paper's topic. One ends up with "everything but the kitchen sink," but these bits can be revised and pieced together for a first draft. It may be crude but it is a start, and this is often enough to get the writing process flowing once again. Reading over this mixture helps promote a focus on ideas.

- In an interesting turnaround, Nelson (1993) suggests that, rather than treating the symptoms, an author should view writer's block as an asset – the creative mind's healthy response to an inner imbalance – and use it as a stepping stone to new levels of creativity and artistic growth. Presenting writer's block as a constellation of problems with different causes and treatments, Nelson offers ideas tailored to such situations as beginner's block, perfectionism, notes and plans that refuse to make a book, and obsessive rewriting.

- If you feel the need for the structure and directedness of an entire program with both short- and long-term solutions, see the Four-Step Plan and Nihil Nimus approach developed by Boice (1990, 2000), a psychologist who has spent most of his professional life coaching academic writers in moderate but productive ways of writing.

Perhaps the most important defense against writer's block is simply to keep in mind that a first draft is a first draft. It will not go to the editor, the typescript consultants, the printer, your department head, or perhaps not even the coauthors. You are the only one who ever needs to see it. A first draft will have intellectual faults and flaws in prose. You will have many chances to correct these later. Instead of worrying about its imperfections, congratulate yourself. With the first draft in hand, you have successfully completed the hardest parts of scientific writing! Now, if at all possible, set it aside to "cool" a bit, and go work on something else.

3

Visual support for the written word

Art, like morality, consists of drawing the line somewhere.
                                                    – *G. K. Chesterton*

Whether or not one is prepared to call them art, visual aids can be vitally important in presenting a scientist's message. They summarize and emphasize key points and reduce narrative length. They simplify information, and in this way enhance understanding. They improve the conciseness and clarity of the narrative. And finally, when carefully crafted, they add visual appeal.

Visual material supports the printed message. Picking up a classic research paper, scientists often scan graphics such as tables and figures to see whether the rest of a paper is worth reading. While they may not go on to study every sentence, they almost always look at every illustration. For this reason, each visual aid must contribute an essential part to the written or spoken story, and each must be capable of standing on its own without reference to the text.

For two major reasons, it pays to start preparing visual aids as early as possible in the writing process. First, because tables and figures present data in condensed form and help clarify and support ideas, they make writing easier. Second, sooner than you think, you'll be asked to give an oral presentation on your research. While the visual aids for a written document seldom are suitable for direct transfer into a slide presentation, they undeniably will form the basis for that presentation.

In this chapter, we'll present guidelines for various types of graphic aids for the traditional research paper. In the next chapter, we'll discuss ways to adapt them for oral presentations and posters.

CHOOSING AND USING VISUAL AIDS

In the parlance of an editor, all illustrations in scientific writing are of two types, tables and figures. Tables are familiar to just about everyone, being the most used (and many say, overused) visual aid. Figures are anything that isn't a table. They may be numerically based (the many kinds of graphs), documentary (photographs, machine print-outs), or explanatory (drawings, diagrams).

Paradoxically, while figures themselves are often overused, many types are underutilized. Each type of figure has its own strengths and weaknesses. The brief checklist given in Table 3.1 can help you determine which types of illustration will be the most appropriate for a particular purpose, and this chapter presents

Table 3.1. *Choosing the most effective type of illustration for a given goal*

To accomplish this	Choose one of these
To present exact values, raw data, or data which do not fit into any simple pattern	Table, list
To summarize trends, show interactions between two or more variables, relate data to constants, or emphasize an overall pattern rather than specific measurements	Line graph
To dramatize differences or draw comparisons	Bar graph
To illustrate complex relationships, spatial configurations, pathways, processes, or interactions	Diagram
To show sequential processes	Flowchart
To classify information	Table, list, pictograph
To describe parts or electric circuits	Schematic
To describe a process, organization, or model	Pictograph, flowchart, block diagram
To compare or contrast	Pictograph, pie chart, bar graph
To describe a change of state	Line graph, bar graph
To describe proportions	Pie chart, bar graph
To describe relationships	Table, line graph, block diagram
To describe causation	Flowchart, pictograph
To describe an entire object	Schematic, drawing, photograph
To show the vertical or horizontal hierarchy within an object, idea, or organization	Flowchart, drawing tree, block diagram

some tips for effective ways to use them. When you are considering a potential visual aid, keep two questions in mind.

1.   Does the form of this illustration suit its purpose?

Many illustrations transform numerical data into other shapes. Graphs and histograms are examples. Developing these visual aids takes more conscious effort than tables do, but they are often the most powerful way to express relationships. They can illuminate ideas and trends that would be all but invisible to readers if the same data were presented in conventional table form.

Documentary illustrations such as instrument tracings, photographs, and micrographs offer primary evidence of the scientific observations presented in the text. When carefully chosen for clarity and relevance, these visual aids can be literally worth a thousand words.

Another category of illustrations includes explanatory materials such as maps, charts, and line drawings. The less familiar with your work your potential audience is expected to be, the more strongly you should consider including these.

2. *Does the illustration fit the audience?*

Deciding which illustration format would be most appropriate or most informative is not only a matter of its purpose. One's scientific discipline, the particular dataset, and the intended journal and audience will also influence this decision.

Information that will be presented on a poster or presentation slide should be prepared differently from that for a traditional research paper, for example. For a fast-paced talk at a research meeting, simple tables showing small amounts of numerical data would be desirable, whereas numerically complex tables would be overwhelming. In a written document, however, that same data might be summarized in the text or included within larger, more complex tables because readers could examine them in a more leisurely fashion.

Tables

Everyone has seen scientific tables – not surprisingly, for they almost always are a scientist's best choice for complex data or parallel descriptions. Tables range from informal in-text presentations hardly more complicated than a word list to complex formal compilations spanning several pages. Tables are, in fact, the single most over-used form of visual aid in scientific writing. Their use is so widespread in most scientific and technical fields that some beginning writers judge them to be an indispensable part of every scientific paper. Although most of us find tables to be the easiest graphic aid to compile, they are not necessarily appropriate for every paper.

Have the courage to prune extraneous material

In the process of conducting research we tend to construct rough tables to consolidate data or to summarize relevant information. The urge can be overwhelming to import these tables wholesale into the document. Resist this temptation. The fact that a table has been a useful organizational tool is not sufficient justification for its automatic inclusion in the text. Nor should numerical data be included solely because they were collected. Every study involves a certain amount of effort spent in gathering data that later turn out not to be needed. Careful planning can minimize this fact, but never eliminate it entirely.

At some point between the first draft and the final typescript, make a concerted effort to decide which tables might be combined, which tables would be better replaced by other illustrative materials, and which tables should be discarded in favor of summarizing the data in the text.

Word tables and numerical tables have their place

All this having been said, we must stress that tables are sometimes the best illustrations for a scientific paper. Word tables present parallel descriptions concisely. In medical writing, tables that appear in case series analyses provide a good example of their appropriate use. In an oral presentation, a teaching article, or a review, small tables of text (which function like figures) also may be used to emphasize the main points or included as a handy reference like the example in Table 3.2.

Table 3.2. *A helpful word table*

Cloned human gene products	
Protein	Used in treating
Insulin	Diabetes
Growth hormone	Pituitary dwarfism
Erythropoietin	Anemia
Factor VIII	Hemophilia
Interleukin-2	Cancer
Tissue plasminogen factor	Heart attack, stroke

Numerical tables provide a compact way of presenting complex information in a format that invites comparisons that would be lost or incomprehensible in narrative form. A useful rule of thumb (Bjelland, 1990) is to use a table when putting data in the text would take at least three times as much page space as presenting it in tabular format. This usually occurs when four or more sets of data are to be presented.

However, thoughtful preparation makes the difference between a numerical table that confuses and one that informs the reader. Tables that communicate the quantitative aspects of data are effective only when the data are arranged so that their significance is obvious at a glance.

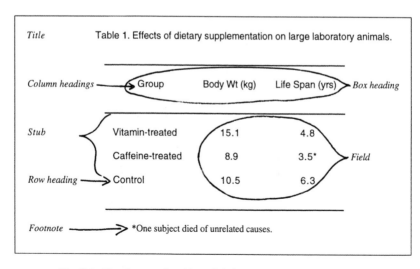

Fig. 3.1. Usual parts of a table and their names.

Understand how tables are constructed

In order to discuss table organization, it helps to know how table parts are named (Fig. 3.1). The column headings are known collectively as the *box heading*, and the group of row headings is called the *stub*. The *field* is the set of cells or spaces in

Table 3.3. *Wide table that would fit on a single-column page*

MAb	Assay scores (range 0–4) determined for various MG strains						
	A5969	F	6/85	tS-11	R	S6	K503
8F7/F	4	4	4	4	3	3	0
4G1/F	4	4	3	3	3	3	0

Table 3.4. *Modification of Table 3.3 to fit one side of a double-column layout*

MG strains	Assay scores (range, 0–4)	
	Mab 8F7/F	MAb 4G1/F
A5969	4	4
F	4	4
6/85	4	3
tS-11	4	3
R	3	3
S6	3	3
K503	0	0

the table's body that carries the numerical data, descriptive terms, or phrases that illustrate the message carried by the table. A *spanner* or *straddlerule* is a horizontal line used to indicate secondary column headings. A heading set above a spanner subsumes the subheads set under the spanner. Numbers in table columns are aligned on the decimal point. This is true even if the decimal point is implied rather than actually being included.

Unless your journal regularly publishes tables on grids, forego this option. A scientific table generally uses no vertical lines. Three horizontal lines run the full width of the table – one beneath the title, a second beneath the headings for the stub and the field, and a third below the field and before any footnotes.

Items are most easily compared reading down

In general, the independent variables in a table should be placed across the horizontal rows, and the items in columns should be the dependent variables. This rule is based on the simple precept that it is easier to compare like elements or work with numerical data when reading down, rather than across. (Try subtracting one number from another horizontally rather than in the usual vertical format, if you need first-hand proof.)

Data in columns are usually more concise as well. For example, when a wide table such as Table 3.3 is flipped so that the dependent variables are in columns, the result (Table 3.4) is visibly more compact.

Use space efficiently

Word processing software provides various table templates that greatly facilitate table formatting. Take the time to experiment with table shapes. Provide enough spacing between rows and columns to create a perceptual order to the data.

Most journals are printed in either a one-column or two-column format. Publications with a one-column format usually handle wide tables better than those with a two-column format; the latter will generally try to fit smaller tables into the width of a single column. Whenever possible, design tables (and figures, see below) to fit the width of a single column of text. In most scientific publications, narrow tables will stand a better chance of being printed close to the corresponding text.

Straightforward but often overlooked strategies for minor condensing include eliminating repeated words and economizing on heading lengths by judicious use of abbreviations. The key word is judicious, however. If abbreviations are overused, the table will no longer be understandable as a stand-alone product. Tables 3.3 and 3.4 are cautionary examples.

When all entries in a column or row are identical, it is nearly always advisable to drop that column or row. Instead, note the identical value in the text or in a table footnote.

If major condensing seems to be needed, instead consider dividing the material into two or more smaller tables. Consider whether the material in a complex table really must be presented as one unit.

Steer clear of grossly oversized tables

Broadside tables – tables so wide that they must be printed at right angles to the text – are an inconvenience to readers who must turn the journal sideways to read them. Likewise, lengthy tables that spill over from one printed page to another are difficult for printers to align and difficult for readers to use. Some journals flatly refuse to print such tables.

Large compilations of data often include information that is nonessential to the paper's real purpose. Before altering the table's format, ask (1) whether all the information in the table actually is necessary, and (2) whether it must be presented in its current form. Does the reader need to know individual test results, or might summary statistics (such as mean, standard deviation, range, or median) be sufficient?

Data are not sacred simply because they have been collected, no matter how much work was involved in that collection. If you feel strongly that some readers of your condensed table will be vitally interested in more details long after you are able to provide them personally, consider placing your reams of data in permanent storage. The editor of the journal in which reference to the deposited material will be made can suggest arrangements for the deposit of such material. Detailed information on how to access this adjunct material must be clearly given in the acknowledgments section or as a table footnote.

Draft concise table titles

Unlike figure legends, which usually are listed together on a separate page from the text in a typescript, table titles often are placed directly above each table. An effective table title should include both the general subject and enough detail to make sense without the text.

Too vague: Deer deaths in Wisconsin
Better: Incidence of white-tailed deer fatalities in Wisconsin, 1995–2000

Some journals allow or require brief descriptions of methods, experimental design, or statistical analysis after the table title; others treat such information as a footnote below the table. In either case, keep them brief. They are generally printed in smaller text and when lengthy are difficult to read.

When including a number of tables in one document, use the same terminology and similar titles and headings. Sometimes, as in many clinical papers, the title of the first table can be used to identify the main component of the results for the sequence of tables, with shorter titles for the tables that follow. For example, the first table in your review of 25 cases of puncture wounds might be titled "Puncture Wounds of the Canine Abdomen: Clinical Features." The second table could be titled simply "Operative Findings and Postoperative Course."

Help readers make comparisons by organizing tables logically

Remember, the reason for using tables is to help readers compare data, both within and between tables. We've already noted that, because items can be more easily compared down a column than across a row, it is best to place independent variables in rows and dependent variables in columns.

To facilitate comparison between tables, be consistent in table presentation. When the reader scans the column headings from left to right, and the stub headings from top to bottom, some sort of order should be apparent in both. Pre-treatment measurements, for example, might precede post-treatment ones; disease symptoms could be arranged from mildest to most severe. If there is no compelling reason for some other type of order, even listing material in rows or columns by the size of the numbers will help readers make mental comparisons.

The poorest sort of arrangement appears in analyses where data are arranged by arbitrary numbering of experimental subjects. Unless the numbers are truly relevant to understanding the results and some sort of explanatory code is included, experimental designations *(A-307, D-10,* and *PC-2069)* mean nothing to anyone but the investigator. In most cases, one can number the subjects by a conventional numeric system if they must be noted individually in the text. If they do not need individual mention in the text, omit subject numbers entirely in the accompanying table.

Research on illustration effectiveness (Macdonald-Ross, 1977a, b) suggests giving row and column averages as reference points. These averages can provide a visual focus that allows readers to inspect the data easily. However, do not clutter up a table with columns of numbers that could easily be derived from other columns by simple arithmetic.

Watch the details!

An effective table results from attention to a myriad of details. Study the format used by your journal. Consult *Instructions to Authors* and recent journal issues for table style, and mimic this style carefully. If the journal doesn't specify details of table style (and many do not), these details can usually be deduced from tables that have appeared in recent issues.

Note the style of table numbers and titles, box headings, subheadings, field entries, and footnotes. Check the use of horizontal and vertical rules. See where and how sample sizes ($n = 230$) are reported, and remember to include them. Without sample size information, your study may have little worth to others.

For numerical data, use decimals rather than fractions to express parts of a whole number. Do not switch units of measure within a column. Instead, restructure the table so that the second kind of unit and accompanying data appear in another column. Alternatively, change one of the units to an equivalent number of the other so that a single heading can apply to all.

Indicate units in column headings. If row headings designate numerical data, include the appropriate unit of measure immediately after or below the headings, either within parentheses or after a comma, depending on the journal's style.

Fill all cells in the field. This can be done in various ways. One system is to use ellipses (. . .) instead of dashes for a missing entry, *ND* for "not done," and *NA* for "not applicable" or "not available." For maximal clarity, some writers also append a footnote to the table to explain these abbreviations.

Finally, remember that with the exception of certain camera-ready productions, print journals generally require that you double-space the entire table, including headings and entries in the text body. This requirement originally arose to aid beleaguered typesetters, who also appreciate not receiving photocopied reductions. Electronic journals, by contrast, often make you essentially become the typesetter; the final copy of the table will appear in whatever format you submit, complete with any errors.

Figures

The general term "figures" encompasses all the graphic aids that are not tables. Figures should be included in a scientific paper when they are needed for one of three E's: evidence, efficiency, or emphasis. Evidence is easy. If something of visual interest occurs during a clinical trial or a case study, one naturally wants to document it with a photograph. During a taxonomic study, an unusual structure or notable range in a character's expression seems to beg for illustration.

Efficiency implies that the figure is the most succinct and effective way to make a particular point. In a scientific paper, for best efficiency one should generally combine material rather than presenting a repetitive series of similar figures. Draw several curves on a single graph. Combine diagrams to illustrate steps in a procedure. Illustrations well prepared for an oral presentation generally present a relatively limited amount of information; they usually can and should be combined for publication.

Emphasis, the third E, is a major reason for using illustrations in a spoken talk. However, journal editors may consider emphasis alone to be insufficient for a published paper. Most editors will stringently assess each figure's usefulness in communicating the message of the paper.

Prepare attractive figures, but beware of "glitziness"

Even a cursory look through the scientific literature will reveal that published illustrations differ widely in their quality. Many details in format lettering and labeling call for careful attention, and seemingly small things can make the difference between a so-so illustration and an excellent one. If professional graphic artists and photographers are available, consult them, and provide them with samples from the journal.

Increasingly, scientists are using their computers (with associated peripherals such as scanners and laser printers) to prepare their own graphic illustrations. If you decide to prepare the illustrations yourself, investigate the latest software and printer requirements and learn how to use them.

Finally, watch out for what Peterson (1993) calls "glitziness." It is easy to become caught up in the capabilities of sophisticated graphics software. Some truly beautiful illustrations are possible. However, be aware that they can present a new set of communication pitfalls.

Pay attention to size and scale

Even when there is no overt attempt to deceive, it is possible to present a compelling visualization that through choice of perspective can obscure or distort data. For example, reducing the size of artwork for publication can do strange things to scale. Reduction minimizes some flaws, but accentuates others. Use computer software capabilities or a photocopier with reduction abilities to check what a figure will look like after reduction.

A horizontal rectangle, with a longer horizontal than vertical axis, will usually fit within the layout of a journal's page. (A ratio of 2 vertical units to 3 horizontal units is considered especially pleasing.) Vertical rectangles often need reduction; whenever possible, reformat them to a square or horizontal rectangle.

After reduction of the illustration for publication, experts suggest that the capital letters in written material on the illustration should be about 2.0 mm in height. Lines for the x- and y-axes and trend lines in graphs should be no wider than the width of the lines making up the letters. Points on curves in graphs should not be so large as to merge upon reduction.

If the size of the subject of a photograph is important, include a short scale line to indicate dimensions. If possible, lay a centimeter–millimeter rule in the field so that it will be visible in the finished photograph. Apply a scale to a photomicrograph.

Write and position legends carefully

Legends (explanatory titles or captions) are a vital part of every figure, not a tacked-on afterthought. When readers turn a page, they look first at illustrations, then at the legends. Each title should orient the readers toward the figure's meaning and enable them to identify its components without referring to the text. It should also differentiate that particular figure from all other illustrations in the paper.

Like a table title, a figure legend should be brief – 8 to 12 words, as a rule of thumb – and need not be a complete sentence. A good legend should contain only enough detail for readers to understand the illustration; consign the necessary minutiae to the text.

> *Too vague:* Fig. 1. Graph of Relevant Data.
>
> *Over-specified:* Fig. 1. Outcome of Multifactorial Analysis of Relation- ship Between Symptoms, Chronology of Appearance, Diagnostic Signs, Blood Work Constants From The Literature, Health Out- come, and Other Parameters For Selected Group of Fifteen Adult Ostriches.
>
> *Better:* Fig. 1. Multifactorial Analysis of Health Records of Fifteen Adult Ostriches.

For a classic research paper, the legend for a figure should never be included within the figure itself. In the final version of the typescript, list the figure legends (double-spaced) on a separate page at the end of the text. For a verbal presentation, place the legend directly on each figure.

Graphs

Tables present results; graphs promote understanding of results and suggest interpretations of their meaning and relationships. Most graphs are based on a set of numbers, just as most tables are. But, because graphs are fundamentally pictures rather than a set of numbers, information generally is easier for the reader to grasp than if it were printed in columns.

Consider graphing data when you feel that the relationships are more vital to your message than the actual numerical values themselves. Thus, you might use a graph to present trends dealing with two related variables, one or more variables changing through time, or data interesting for the magnitudes of differences which might be related to unknown factors or experimental manipulations.

A graph always shows how one parameter varies relative to changes in another. One factor may be controlled and varied (temperature, for example) while some effect of this change is measured. Alternatively, the effect of changes in some uncontrollable factor such as time may be measured. Temperature and time in these examples are independent variables, which are usually plotted in relation to the horizontal (x)-axis. The effect these changes have on some- thing else (the dependent variable) is normally plotted in relation to the vertical (y)-axis.

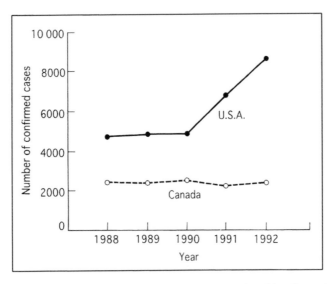

Fig. 3.2. This effective line graph shows changes in rabies disease incidence over time.

A range of software programs can produce sophisticated graphs with the touch of a finger. Use them initially to construct various graphic presentations of the data and consider the alternatives. Then modify such aspects as fonts, type size, shadings, and symbols to produce visually dynamic illustrations. Remember, however, that legibility and comprehensibility should remain the most important criteria. For further help, see Robbins (2005).

Keep line graphs simple

Line graphs (Fig. 3.2) visually show continuous variables such as movements over time. They range from straightforward visual representations of trends to depictions of complex advanced statistical analyses.

Line graphs are probably the most popular of all graph styles in scientific writing. Unfortunately, studies have shown that many readers lack the skills to interpret them (Macdonald-Ross, 1977a). If you decide to use line graphs, keep them as simple as possible. Limit the number of lines in any one graph. Visually distinguish different lines by using different symbols, and label each line carefully.

Note that line graphs are appropriate only for continuous data. A false impression may be given if successive discontinuous data points on a graph are connected. It is better to present such information as a bar graph or to leave the points on the graph without connecting lines.

Reveal general relationships with bar graphs

Bar graphs (Fig. 3.3), also sometimes called column graphs, are used to present discrete variables in a visually forceful way. They are a single axis graph used

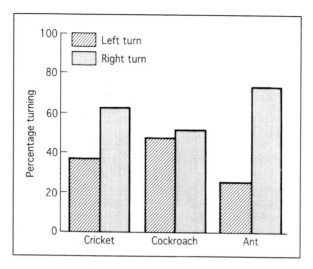

Fig. 3.3. This effective bar graph relates insect type to left and right turning choices.

to compare size and magnitude of discontinuous data. They are superior to circle and line graphs for showing relationships, magnitudes, and distributions (Macdonald-Ross, 1977b). On the negative side, bar graphs generally provide a relatively small amount of information while taking up a fairly large amount of space.

The bars may run either vertically or horizontally, but are most effective when they run in the direction in which people expect to see them. Thus, vertical bars are usually used for such data as temperature and weight, horizontal bars for distance, time, and speed. Whatever type of bar graph you choose, make the bars the same width, and the space between bars or bar groups one-half of a bar width.

Subdividing bars by shading or cross-hatching adds another dimension of information. Divided bar graphs, for example, can compare percentages of a whole rather than relative size. In this, they function much like pie charts but are less effective. Superficially similar to bar graphs, histograms are two-axis graphs that typically show frequency distributions by use of a series of contiguous rectangular bars.

Illustrate the relationship of parts to a whole with divided-circle graphs

Most of the time bar graphs seem to be superior to circle and line graphs for presenting information. However, divided-circle graphs (Fig. 3.4), also called pie charts, are well suited for showing the relationship of a number of parts to the whole.

Although divided-circle graphs make a striking visual display, they present a fundamental problem – the impossibility of comparing areas. They are generally used best as attention-getting devices, and even then, only when comparing five or

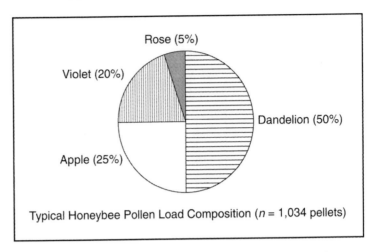

Fig. 3.4. This effective divided–circle graph shows flower contributions to a typical honeybee pollen load. To aid comparison, percentages are included.

fewer items. Pie charts are most effective when the segments are arranged by size, with the largest slice beginning at twelve o'clock. Continue placing progressively smaller segments clockwise. Note that some graphics software programs generate counterclockwise charts. Combine or exclude slices smaller than about 5% (18 degrees).

Let pictographs show numerical relationships in a visually symbolic manner

Pictographs are essentially bar graphs composed of pictures. They can be very visually effective. Pictographs are of two basic types. In one, each symbol corresponds to a specific quantity (Fig. 3.5). In the other, uniformly sized symbols each represent a given quantity with a key provided that explains their meaning (Fig. 3.6). Often the precise actual numbers are posted at the end of each row or column, since such graphs present an approximation.

Perhaps because their construction historically has fallen within the domain of graphic artists, pictographs rarely appear in scientific writing, though they might provide welcome variety. With the ease with which they can be constructed using computer graphics software and clip art, they deserve wider use. They are especially appropriate and effective for illustrating oral and poster presentations. If you choose to use this type of illustration, remember that pictographs are most effective when the symbols chosen represent the subject matter and are arranged in a way that presents an organized message.

Limit logarithmic and scatter graphs to professional audiences

A logarithmic graph has a series of open and grouped vertical lines in which the top and bottom of each group, called a cycle, is a decimal or multiple of ten. It is

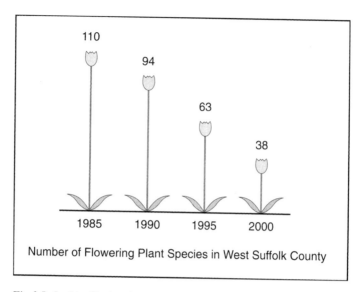

Fig. 3.5. In this effective pictograph, the length of the flower stems corresponds to the number of plant species.

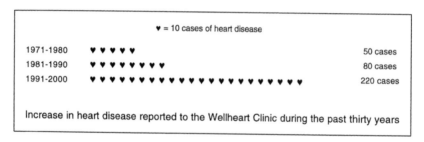

Fig. 3.6. A pictograph that uses heart symbols to show disease incidence effectively reflects the subject of the graph.

commonly but not exclusively used to compare data in which rate of change is more important than quantity of change. (An exception sometimes encountered in medical writing is the dose–response curve. Dose is logarithmically related to response in terms of number of receptors stimulated.) A logarithmic graph also is frequently used when the vertical range is so large that it is difficult to fit on a normal graph. However, because nonscientific readers may not be familiar with a logarithmic scale, they can find such graphs confusing.

Scatter graphs, which sometimes are charted logarithmically, use single unconnected dots to plot instances where two variables (one on each axis) meet (Fig. 3.7). The pattern of the dots expresses the relationship (a diagonal trend, which is sometimes approximated by a line on the chart) or lack of a relationship (random scatter) between the variables. Interpreting scatter graphs also can be difficult for nonscientific readers.

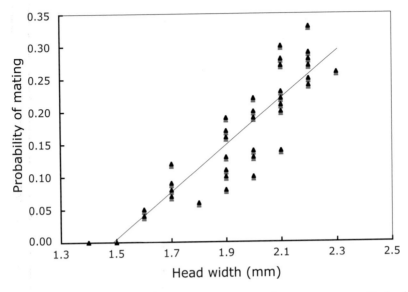

Fig. 3.7. This scattergraph shows that larger male wasps, as measured by head width, have greater mating success.

If you choose to use either of these graphing techniques, it is imperative that their significance be explained and discussed clearly in the text.

Keep graphs visually honest

Never finagle line fits, delete data points that do not fit the curve, or make data points so large that almost any curve would pass through them. Never distort the importance of a trend, tempting as this may be.

Begin at zero for the scales used for the axes of a graph whenever possible; choose these scales carefully and mark them clearly. Sometimes, a valid trend would disappear on a scale with a zero axis, and all the data points would bunch up at the top. In this case, signal readers that the graph's axis is not at zero, either with a statement in the text or with a break in the axis.

If a point represents the mean of a number of observations, indicate the magnitude of the variability by a vertical line centered at each point. State whether standard error (SE) or standard deviation (SD) is used and specify number of observations or sample sizes. Again, learning the capabilities of your graphing software ultimately will simplify the task. Most programs have the ability to insert such information automatically with a few keystrokes.

When two or more graphs or other figures are to be compared, draw them to the same scale. Then, if possible, group them into a single illustration. To minimize reduction during printing, place them one above the other rather than side by side.

Remember the limitations of your data. The extrapolation of a line or a curve beyond the points shown on a graph may mislead both the writer and the reader.

As Winston Churchill is said to have remarked in another context, "It is wise to look ahead but foolish to look further than you can see."

Photographs and other documentary illustrations

Image-based illustrations document discoveries. For most people, this is the first category that comes to mind when they hear that a paper has "figures." The photograph of a new organism, the print of gel banding patterns, the radiographic image of a patient's bone deformity . . . all would belong here, and in traditional publishing, all would be submitted as a photographic copy. Happily, electronic copy is now widely accepted, so all such illustrations usually can be scanned and submitted as digital files.

When it comes to showing exactly what something looks like, nothing beats the realism of a photograph. At the same time, the realism of a photograph can be disadvantageous. It may include clutter, extraneous information, or components you would rather not show. Happily, the ease by which digital images may be altered makes it possible to fix such distracting components (and almost inexcusable not to do so).

Photographs also will usually only show surfaces, not the components or interior parts that a line drawing or diagrammatic exploded view can provide. Sometimes a traditional drawing is still a better choice.

Obtain the best photographic documentation possible

Take a number of photographs. Focus sharply. Provide a plain, uncluttered background that does not draw attention away from the object you're depicting. Be alert to the distracting presence of miscellaneous items. Try a variety of angles.

Colored pictures usually are preferred for oral or poster presentations. However, most print journals still restrict photographs to black and white images unless color illustration is essential for reasons of evidence, efficiency, or emphasis. For example, color could be vital in illustrations of faint rashes, subtle histologic stain colors, or multicolor scan images. Note also that journals that still use nondigital images generally prefer color transparencies (slides) and color negatives (negatives for color prints) rather than color prints.

Compose the illustration to help the reader

After a photograph has passed the tests of quality and message, it should be tailored to give the reader as much help as possible. Crop the picture to a shape suitable for the journal's column dimensions without reduction in size while retaining the highest possible resolution. Select the center of the field to coincide with the center of interest. Affix letters and arrows identifying features of interest. Keep any lettering horizontal and consistent in size, font, and contrast for easy reading. In the legend, include a key to any symbols used. In the corner of the photograph, if appropriate, include a bar to represent a length suitable to the scale. Finally, consider grouping related figures into a single plate to fill an entire printed page, rather than scattering them throughout the publication.

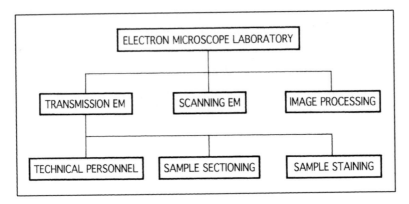

Fig. 3.8. A typical drawing tree gazinta describes a relatively stable situation.

Explanatory artwork

Explanatory figures are those produced to communicate organization, illustrate basic principles, or otherwise clarify text materials. This figure type includes both drawings and diagrams – all of those flowcharts, diagrams, maps, algorithms, and line art that some people characterize as "illustrations" as opposed to tables and photographs.

The effectiveness of explanatory artwork depends upon how well it focuses audience attention. This type of artwork must show the specific details of key features while omitting others to minimize the distraction caused by extraneous details. A common mistake in scientific writing is to present a figure that is much more complex than the accompanying prose. When this is done, illustrations confuse rather than inform readers.

What is a gazinta?

Bjelland (1990) uses the term *gazinta*, derived from the expression "goes into," to encompass those visuals that show the hierarchy and complexity of actions within an object, idea, or institution. A gazinta shows organization and interaction.

One type of gazinta, the drawing tree (Fig. 3.8), is essentially static. It shows the subassemblies that make up an assembly and the assemblies that make up an object or an organization. In a drawing tree, all subassemblies of the same relative importance or size appear on the same vertical level. As you progress from the bottom to the top of the tree, the subassemblies become larger, more complex, and fewer in number.

The other main type of gazinta, the block diagram (Fig. 3.9), depicts objects or materials in action. The block diagram is one of the most often used visuals in engineering and science to show how things interact with each other, be they electrical, mechanical, chemical, biological, or some combination of these.

Bjelland (1990) considers block diagrams to be the most useful of all visual aids for any type of technical writing, and recommends these guidelines. To reduce confusion, show only major actions and interactions, and limit the number of blocks to no more than 8 to 10. Use short functional names for each block, and

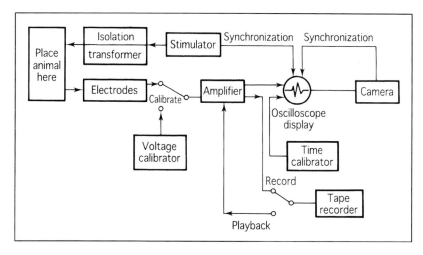

Fig. 3.9. A typical block diagram gazinta depicts a procedure. Redrawn after Rogoff, J. B. and S. Reiner, 1961.

use exactly the same name in the accompanying text. Keep the functional level the same within a specific block diagram. If abbreviations or specialized terms are used in the diagram, define them the first time they appear in the accompanying text or include them in the table legend.

Indicate each flow with a different type of coded line, reserving solid lines for the primary flow. Use arrowheads to indicate direction, which should flow the way one would read standard printed information. In the text, use an order of presentation that follows the direction of flow on the diagram and that carries the flow through the entire diagram.

Guide readers through sequential processes with algorithms

An algorithm, often written out as a flowchart, is a logical sequence of steps for solving a problem. Examples of algorithm use include such varied items as decision charts, taxonomic keys, income tax forms, and medical treatment guidelines (Fig. 3.10).

Algorithms have an important place in biological and medical communication, and deserve to be more widely used. Once people become familiar with their use, they generally find algorithms quicker and easier to follow than narrative instructions.

Study their use in your respective discipline, and follow style guidelines. For additional help, consult Wheatley and Unwin (1972). Remember that an algorithm's strength lies in its clarity, so it must be kept free of clutter and extraneous detail.

Use traditional drawings to focus on essentials

Not surprisingly, pen-and-ink artwork has long been an integral part of technical communication, particularly in the biological and medical sciences. Carefully

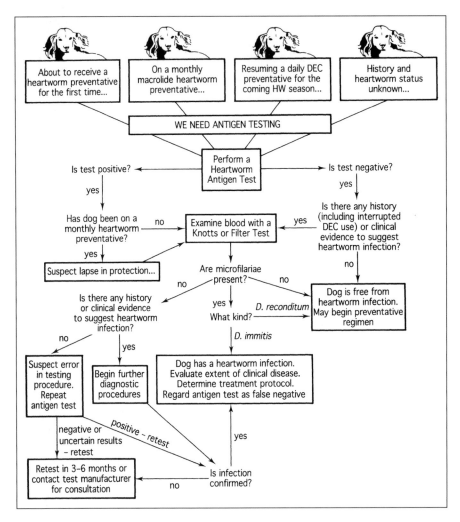

Fig. 3.10. This algorithm shows the steps involved in screening dogs for canine heartworm infection.

prepared two- or three-dimensional renderings of an object are often clearer than a photograph and thus preferable to it. The major advantage of drawings is that you can control the amount of precision while deleting extraneous details. Drawings also permit unique perspectives such as cutaway, blow-up, and exploded views.

Several computer graphics packages are on the market. Some are very good, but there is a vast difference between creating artwork on a computer and creating it with pen and ink on paper. For some people, producing their own drawings is exhilarating. If you are not one of them, employ a graphic designer or professional artist. For best results, communicate carefully and allow sufficient lead-time for the project. Remember that artists aren't technical experts. Sketch your ideas, explain your terms, provide correct spellings, and check everything carefully for errors during preparation of the artwork.

EXAMINING YOUR CHOICES

Visuals must mesh with your text, like two gears that drive a machine. They must work in concert, each dependent on the other, to describe an object, a process, or a concept.

– H. Bjelland (1990)

Now that you've considered your choices and prepared a number of possible visual aids, it is time to reflect on some questions that concern them all.

Is this illustration really necessary?

Any use of illustrations should begin with this question. Sometimes, scientists thoughtlessly include excessive illustrations, merely because they have them. Often a line or two of text would give the same information far more economically. Do readers really need to see a pie chart showing the same data that you've already presented in a table? Do they need to see a "typical" chicken afflicted with a well-known disease?

Am I pushing the limits?

Because illustrations cost more to reproduce than text, some publications strictly regulate their number, size, and type, and may even assess a surcharge for each figure or table. Knowing this at the outset can save time and money; check *Instructions to Authors* and format in the journal itself. Reduce the odds of editorial requests for last-minute revision by not pushing the limits unnecessarily.

An oft-stated general rule is that a scientific document should include no more than one table or illustration per 1,000 words of text. (Use the word count feature of a word processing program.) Another general guideline says to use no more than one table or illustration per four pages of double-spaced typescript text.

Some print journals accept only tables and line drawings (such as diagrams and graphs). Others also accept black-and-white photographs, which are then photographed again through a screen grid to produce dots that make up a printed image called a half-tone. Half-tones are usually of lesser quality than the originals because the printing process may transfer the image several times with some loss of clarity at each transfer.

If you feel a need to include colored pictures or graphics, be sure to investigate the journal's policy. Few print journals will publish color illustrations without passing at least part of the cost on to the author. On the other hand, electronic publications can easily include colored illustrations at no extra cost.

Exercise 3.1. Table and figure choices

The choice of a format in which to present data is a judgment call. What would you use for the examples below? Your choices need not match ours if you feel you have sound justification for them.

1. You've gathered a series of data concerning serum electrolyte values and acid–base variables for patients with Rocky Mountain spotted fever. How should you present this information?

2. You've examined mortality rates for male and female cats with thyroid disease in individual states of the United States. Should you use a table, graph, or figure?

3. You've measured maximum systolic blood pressure after giving white rats various doses of epinephrine, and have measured changes in their blood pressure throughout a two-week period. You also have a really nice photograph of one of your control rats. What should you publish, and in what form?

4. In a case series study, you have collected data from a physical examination of animals at admittance, from observations during the course of the illness, and from final autopsies. You've decided to present the data in a table; how should they be arranged?

5. You have written a paper about a new species of a bacterial pathogen implicated in a case of pneumonia. You have a chest roentgenogram showing typical findings of pneumonia, and an electronmicrograph of newly discovered structural details of the bacterium's flagellum. Should you include either or both in your paper?

6. You have identified a genetic syndrome that appears in members of a canine lineage as a Mendelian autosomal dominant trait. Should you present your evidence as a table, a graph, or text?

7. You have researched deaths from mycoplasmal diseases in turkeys and ducks, and found a significant difference in mortality rates. How should you show this difference?

Is each illustration independent but integral to the text?

Each table or figure should be a complete unit of communication, containing enough information so that a reader can grasp its essential message without referring to the text. For this, the title must be adequate, the headings complete and explanatory, and the data arranged logically. All symbols and images within the graphic aid should be explained. If necessary for understanding, experimental details should be given in the legend. If appropriate, matters such as degree of magnification and type of stain should be included.

Do not take chances on losing readers to frustration. During the editing stages, show your illustrations to someone who knows little or nothing about your research. Then listen, and be prepared to address the sometimes-surprising questions your illustrations may raise.

Paradoxically, while visual aids must be independent of the text, they also must be indispensable to its story. As mentioned before, readers almost always look at illustrative material first. Good visual materials should spark reader interest, and interested readers will have questions. To be effective, use the text to answer these questions. The text, in turn, must refer specifically to each table and figure by number and clarify why the information is needed. The statement that "Table 1 gives results" falls short in this regard, and simply wastes space. Instead, use the text to summarize or explain, as in "Affected animals had significantly lower weights (Table 1)."

Consider the set of tables and other illustrations in a document as a sequence. Together, they should tell a story – the message of the paper. However, avoid saying "as shown in the table above/below" because the position and page number of a table is not determined until typesetting by the printer.

Are figures labeled carefully and completely?

Scientific illustrations have two sorts of identifiers. One appears in public – the table titles and figure legends that identify them in the printed material and explain their importance. The other is their private label, a code assigned to travel with them to be sure they end up in the right place. Mistakes occur when the identifiers do not correspond well.

This can be a particular problem with conventional printed journals that require paper ("hard copy") submissions, because they tend to store and process illustrations separately from text. Tables and figures can be misplaced during handling and are particularly vulnerable to loss, a costly situation. As soon as an illustration is prepared, photograph or scan it, and identify both the original and the copy with your name, a short version of the article or report title, and a unique number. Check the *Instructions to Authors* for the mechanics involved; some journals require adhesive labels whereas others prohibit them, for example. To avoid the embarrassment of an incorrectly oriented figure, include the word *top*, accompanied by an arrow. Never write on the illustration itself; the writing can show through on the front. When it comes time to send your paper off to an editor or publisher, you will place hard copies of figures in a separate oversized envelope, and label the envelope with your name and a short title for the paper. These will be put into a larger envelope that also contains your typescript. You should plan to keep any original artwork and at least one duplicate set of all illustrations.

With digital submissions, it is easier to become complacent about these safeguards because the illustrations exist as electronic copy that can be included in the text file. However, in addition to the computer file that contains the illustrated text, it is still good form to include a separate file with a copy of each illustration.

Label each digital illustration with both its number and a short identifier, and append the file type. Unless the *Instructions to Authors* specify another format, here is an example to consider:

> *Figure legend:* Fig. 2. Outcomes of 158 courtship pairings of *Melittobia digitata* males with females of the long-winged form.
> *Hardcopy label*: Gonzalez, Courtship ms. Fig 2. Pairing flowchart.
> *Digital file label:* Gonzalez Courtship Fig2.jpg

4

Visual support for the spoken word

How can I know what I've said until I see what I'm saying?

Visual communication has both a verbal component – usually visual presentation of the written word – and an illustrative component such as drawings, diagrams, photos, and charts. Although both elements have long received attention in the context of the primary research article, scientific writing instruction has tended to treat other avenues of visual communication as a relatively minor afterthought. The implicit assumption has been that oral presentations and posters, for example, involve only minor repackaging of a written document and its supporting graphics. In recent years, however, this assumption has been challenged by new developments that have increased the status of visual communication and given it a surprisingly powerful role to play in modern scientific exchanges.

First, there is an increased understanding that when people look at a visual pattern, they process it differently than text (Gurak, 2000). Humans read each word of text and decipher it, but they quickly and efficiently perceive visual information as a unit. (How many times have you tried to assemble something and after puzzling over the written instructions, found yourself turning to the diagram?)

Second, communication has become increasingly international, with the outcome that science and technology must be accessible to people across a variety of languages. The use of symbols rather than written words can make concepts understandable around the world. At the same time, web publishing has given visual communication much greater force and international presence.

Last, but equally important, graphics are no longer the domain of paid specialists. Visual materials have become easy and inexpensive to produce, and in response, people tend to use them more. Presentation software makes it relatively straightforward to generate graphics that once took hours or days to create.

As a consequence, visual communication has become a basic part of almost all effective scientific presentations. With this widespread use, there has come the realization that while in some ways, the process of choosing and using visual aids is the same regardless of whether they will support a written or a spoken text, in other ways, it differs markedly.

79

ORAL PRESENTATIONS

PowerPoint is both the most professional and the most boring means of giving a presentation. (There is an interesting contradiction to be explored here.)
– *M. Alley and K. A. Neeley* (2005a)

From time to time you undoubtedly will be called upon to make an oral presentation to colleagues, administrators, or a general audience outside your special area of expertise. Nearly every such presentation uses some type of visual aid. Traditionally the most popular has been the 35-mm slide, followed by overhead transparencies, flipcharts, films, videotapes, and even filmstrips and the old schoolroom standard, the chalkboard or marker-board.

Increasingly, oral presentations are being accompanied by computer-based visuals, and several excellent supporting software programs now exist. By far the most popular of these at present is Microsoft PowerPoint®, which is estimated to have at least 250–400 million users around the globe (Alley and Neeley, 2005b).

It is difficult to overstate the impact that PowerPoint has had upon presentations in academia, business, and professional societies, where it now is being used to make an estimated 20 – 30 million presentations every day. Few scientists have escaped becoming familiar with the now nearly universal PowerPoint slide: a phrase headline supported by a bulleted list. In fact, the name PowerPoint is rapidly becoming a generic synonym for bulleted lists and "presentations." Part of the program's popularity is undoubtedly the ease with which the default templates allow a busy person to construct and deliver an outline-style talk.

In response to this popularity, we'll concentrate on electronic presentation software in this chapter. However, we'll also remind you of alternatives and present some background on a PowerPoint controversy that has arisen.

Media choices for oral presentations

Oral presentations come in many forms, from a simple classroom talk at the chalkboard to a glitzy multimedia computer-based presentation accompanied by abundant handouts and web-based video clips. The world's current fascination with technology has led presenters inexorably toward presentation software. However, it is important to realize that other options continue to be available, and for some situations may still be a better choice.

In fact, the very popularity of PowerPoint has raised problems. Presentations can be so predictable and generic that for the audience, all presentations begin to look and feel the same. Everyone present is lulled into complacency, including the speaker. When PowerPoint takes front-and-center stage in a presentation, a speaker easily can lose the opportunity to connect with his or her audience. At one time or another, probably all of us have had the sense that the text-dominated slides in such a presentation are serving more as notes for the speaker than as aids for our own understanding. When full sentences are projected on the screen (Fig. 4.1) while the speaker reads them verbatim, the results can be especially deadly.

Additional problems have arisen as speakers stretch the limits of this presentation software, trying to use a single set of slides not only as speaker's notes and

---

HONEY FACTS

- Honey is significantly sweeter than table sugar and has attractive chemical properties for baking.
- Liquid honey does not spoil. Because of its high sugar concentration, it kills bacteria by osmotic lysis.
- Natural airborne yeasts cannot become active in it because its moisture content is too low.
- Natural, raw honey varies from 14% to 18% moisture content. As long as the moisture content remains under 18%, virtually no organism can successfully multiply to significant amounts in honey.

Fig. 4.1. What not to do: full sentence points on a presentation slide. The only thing worse would be to subsequently read them verbatim to the audience.

slides the audience will see, but also as handouts to be studied after the talk and as a substitute for a written paper. Seldom can this all be done simultaneously and well.

Simple choices still work well

The simplest of visual aids for a spoken talk is a chalkboard, whiteboard, or large paper pad (flipchart). From the presenter's point of view, the downside of these simple aids is that they can be difficult to prepare in advance. However, from the audience perspective, this is an advantage because a live performance is always more interesting to observe than a prepackaged one. The most effective way to use these aids is selectively. Intersperse face-to-face commentary with written items.

Midway between a live and a packaged approach is the overhead projection transparency. Not too long ago, one of these projectors was in almost any workplace, conference room, or classroom. It will be a shame if they are totally eclipsed by laptop-based presentations. Overheads are easy to use, require few technical connections, and don't crash or suffer other computer hang-ups.

Even more important from a pedagogical standpoint, transparencies can be developed in advance, but easily and simply modified with a wipe-off marker during the talk. (One should note that there are ways for the manually dexterous user to do this with PowerPoint, too, but not as simply or intuitively.) By underlining, circling important points, or writing words in the margins, you can give your presentation extra life. If this is done in response to audience input, listeners will be drawn closely into your talk and feel a stronger connection with you than you would ever attain with a canned approach.

For some oral presentations, particularly those that require many photographs, 35 mm slides are still a good choice, either in a simple carousel projector or imported into a computerized presentation as digital copy. Audiences tend to enjoy the movie-like atmosphere. However, they may get drowsy sitting in darkness, and disconnect with you and your message. Avoid giving one long slide show. Instead, dim the room lights only enough so that slides can be seen while some light is still focused on you. Show slides in batches, with breaks in-between where you turn away from the projector and connect directly with your audience.

Teleconferencing and such: real-time but cyberspace

Teleconferencing (also known as interactive television or ITV) connects presenters and an audience in another location. Popular both as a way to save travel costs and as a way to provide distance education to students in different physical locations, it shares similarities with face-to-face oral presentations. However, a good teleconference is more than simply a camera aimed at a presenter. Ask for advice from professionals, and take it.

Close cousins to teleconferencing include multimedia modules and computer-based training (CBT), but these relatives are not live presentations, and thus they lack the real-life interactions that occur between a presenter and an audience. They are more akin to conventional writing, spiffed up with heavy use of graphic aids and specialized computer capabilities.

The choice to use computer-driven presentation software

Rather than automatically turning to PowerPoint or its kin when you are asked to speak before a group, begin by learning what is expected and customary for this particular presentation. Consider your audience and purpose. Perhaps you will even find that presentation software would be overkill. If so, choose one of the other presentation formats. A presentation doesn't have to be PowerPoint to be professional.

As we urged in the context of written works, with presentation software it's also important to know when to quit. Don't overdo the technical features. Audiences welcome a simple layout with well-planned color and graphics.

Developing a traditional text-based oral presentation

Though PowerPoint and its kin have eased the mechanics of preparing slides, they are but a tool, and in actuality the process of preparing an effective oral presentation hasn't changed all that much. First, a presentation must be designed according to sound communication principles and techniques. Then, slides are created to outline an introduction, main points, and a conclusion. Transitions, graphics, and other aids to understanding are inserted in appropriate places. The talk is given a trial run before a small group of interested individuals who (one hopes!) will give appropriate input to help the presenter polish any rough edges in the talk. Then the presentation is practiced, much as one always would have done in the past, but now it is accompanied by an electronic slide show.

First, organize your material

All the technical expertise in the world will not be enough if a talk is poorly organized. If you want an audience to follow along, you must provide a road map. This is as true for spoken exchanges as it is for written ones. When you are planning to use computer-based text-heavy graphics, it is doubly true.

Talks can be organized on a deductive or inductive pattern. With deductive organization, you present your bottom line (conclusion, solution) at the onset. Then, you provide the background and information that led you to this conclusion. Inductive organization is more or less the opposite of deductive. First, you give a general sense of the main topic, then present specific instances or examples as evidence, leading to the conclusion that you state at the end.

Deductive organization is probably the more common approach to scientific presentation, with good reason. This scheme helps audiences understand and follow a speaker, because they can see clearly how supporting material fits into a bigger picture. In contrast, even a well-done inductively organized presentation can be difficult to follow. For this reason, we recommend avoiding this approach unless you are sure it is the only possible alternative. For example, inductive presentations are sometimes useful if you know the audience might not readily agree with your conclusion unless they are led through the train of thought leading up to it.

Other organizational systems less commonly used in oral presentations also may be worth considering. Refer back to Table 2.1.

Pay special attention to transitions and your conclusions section

Transitions play a particularly important role in a well-done oral presentation. When people read information, they can always turn back a few pages if they forget something. As a speaker, you have to remind your audience where you are headed as you advance through the presentation.

Conclusions are also even more important than in paper copy, because they are the part of the talk that people remember best. To create a solid organization, construct the conclusion at the same time as you create the introduction. Conclude by succinctly reminding your audience about the points you have made and why you consider them to be important. (Do not introduce new ideas or new topics, however.) When appropriate, restate an appeal for action, and/or provide resources for further information. Don't just say, "well, that's all I have for you today."

Remember to use a transition to lead to your conclusion, just as you did for the rest of the talk. It can be simply the time-honored bridging phrase, "In conclusion . . ." Other possibilities include "Let me close with a few final ideas" or "Where does this leave us?"

Follow simple guidelines

The "how" of slide production is less important than the "what." The mechanics of using text-based presentation software are fairly straightforward, and rely heavily on default templates to guide you through the steps involved. Follow the suggestions in Table 4.1, and it will be hard to go wrong.

Table 4.1. *Creating an effective electronic presentation (based on material from University of Georgia Center for Teaching and Learning)*

Area of concern	Guidelines
Content	Include only one idea, point, or comparison per slide.
	Present concisely worded material in outline form.
	Include some interactive elements (e.g., questions, polls) to keep audience engaged.
Format	Limit slide titles to 2–5 words.
	Use horizontal orientation rather than vertical.
	Left-justify text and left-align bullet points.
	Use color with caution.
Graphic aids	Use charts or graphics rather than data tables.
	Place graphics off-center to the left (leaves more room for text and leads eye to text).
	Simplify graphics.
Things to avoid	Complex drawings lifted directly from paper publications.
	Extraneous or excessive information.
	Lengthy data tables.
	Gratuitous sound effects and slide transitions.
	Slides read directly to the audience.
Back up plan	Know at least two ways to advance the slides, in case one method doesn't work.
	Know how to black out the screen to draw audience attention back to you.
	Know how to get directly to any slide in the presentation.
	If technology fails, spend no more than 5 minutes maximum trying to fix it.
	Be prepared to speak directly to the audience without any aids.

Visual elements of text, tables, and figures

Simplicity is classy.
– R. R. H. Anholt (2006)

Appropriate typefaces, fonts, and other text features are all part of communicating visually, whether you create an overhead, a 35 mm slide, or a presentation software screen. Once, these decisions were the domain of graphic artists, printers, and typographers. Today, with personal computers, even children use fonts and typesetting. However, few people use them effectively.

Terminology

Mainstream type fonts are of two basic kinds, serif and sans serif. A serif is a "foot," one of the crosslines at the bottom or top of a letter such as I. Serif fonts have these crossbars; sans serif fonts do not. Helvetica and Arial are two common sans serif typefaces; the block strokes that form their letters are straight up and down.

Type also comes in two kinds of dimensional spacing: monospace and variable width (proportional). With monospace fonts such as Courier, every letter occupies the same amount of space, just as they did on an old typewriter. Proportional typefaces have letters of varying widths, more akin to traditional printing styles.

Most conventionally published journals use a proportional serif font style such as New York or Times for their basic text. (Electronic journals often use only sans serif fonts.) Serif fonts are often considered the most readable, because the serifs help guide the eye from letter to letter. Serif typefaces include the oldest type styles, and thus are the most familiar. They are also considered more formal.

Type size is based on points, an old system of measuring type that has carried over into the digital age. For most typefaces, the size in points approximates the distance between the tops of the tallest letters (which may be either the capitals or the lowercase letters with ascenders, like b and h) and the bottoms of the letters with descenders, like p and q. For this reason, a given point size may change in measurement when a different font is selected.

How to choose typefaces and fonts for oral presentations

Historically, with conventional printing, fonts were expensive. Each font was an actual physical device that the typographer purchased. For any given typeface, most typographers had four basic fonts (regular, bold, italic, bold italic). Today, with computerized printing, the choices are endless, and fonts and typefaces can be easily changed with a simple click. But such easy choices bring with them the temptation to mix and match so much that you end up with a mishmash that distracts the audience so that they miss your message.

Unless specified otherwise by the group sponsoring your presentation, the following conventions are generally accepted. (The same guidelines should follow for handouts, the printed materials you may wish to distribute as part of your message.)

Stay within one family of typefaces, or use one family for the body copy and another for the headings. For example, consider using Helvetica bold for headings, Times New Roman for body copy, and plain Helvetica for captions and labels on charts and graphs.

Use primarily plain text fonts. Avoid ALL CAPS and use *italic* and **bold** sparingly.

How big should my text be?

Type size should be appropriate for the room layout and audience, which means generally larger than you first think is right. Swinford (2006) suggests basing text size on the "8H rule"– the maximum viewing distance should be no more than eight times the height (H) of the screen. If you then keep your font size at least 1/50th the height of the screen, your text will be legible at the maximum viewing distance. (In PowerPoint, this translates to an absolute minimum font size of roughly 14 points in a font such as Arial or Helvetica. If the text seems too small, it should be increased to roughly 28 points.)

For large rooms, some experts suggest 30 point boldface sans serif type. Never use less than 14 points, even for a small conference room.

Make all headings at least 2 points larger than the body text.

Simplify tables and other numerically based visual aids

A table is a good visual device to show choices between categories of information. However, in print format, users can refer repeatedly to tables if they need to reference information; during an oral presentation, they can't.

Spreadsheets or tables containing too much information have the potential to become the worst type of visual aid possible. Audiences simply cannot assimilate all of those columns and rows. Furthermore, overloaded tables can be difficult to read on a screen. Never ever plan to include such material with the comment, "I know you can't read this, but . . ."!

If you must share complex information in table format, make a simpler version for the talk and bring along handouts of more complex or detailed tables for your audience to review later if they wish.

Bar charts, line graphs, and pie charts need similar simplification. Watch not to use too many different types of shading and screening to separate their components. When these visual aids are kept simple, clear, and easy to read, they can pack a lot of information into a concise format. Again, save complex details for handouts.

Include other illustrative materials

Well-chosen drawings, diagrams, photographs, and other illustrations capture audience interest and attention, and can help explain complex ideas. Adding them to your text message can enliven a presentation and make information more understandable. Unfortunately, illustrations drawn from material prepared for print publication can suffer from too much detail for effective use in an oral presentation. Simplify whenever possible. If the larger picture is necessary, briefly orient the audience to it. Then isolate the relevant portion, enlarge it, and present just that part.

Proportion and scale: the shape of graphics

In general, graphics should be greater in length than in height unless the nature of the data suggests otherwise. Tufte (2001) suggests that graphics be about 50% wider than tall. He uses the horizon as an analogy; our eye is naturally practiced in detecting deviations from the horizon, he says, and graphic design should take advantage of this fact. Furthermore, horizontal graphics can more easily be labeled. It is easier to write and read words that stretch horizontally from left to right, rather than vertically.

Give your graphics a test run

Before you spend a lot of time refining a particular visual aid, make sure it reproduces well in your visual medium. Sometimes a chart or table doesn't look the same when it is copied into presentation software.

At times a graphic may look good on a small computer screen, but be too detailed when projected. Remember, if you present too much information, people won't understand any of it. Ideally, test your visuals on a sample audience. What looks clear to you may be confusing to others.

Pay attention to details. Is your graphic of an appropriate size? Remember, it must be large enough for the room in which you'll be presenting. Are all the axes and parts labeled? Does the graphic itself have a short, clear informative title?

Don't expect the audience to know what to look for. Point out the important features with appropriate indicators such as type of a different color, use of bold type, highlighting, or arrows.

Finally, if the material is not wholly your own, include a reference stating where you obtained this information. A simple author and source citation will usually suffice. Use a smaller font size than other text.

Use color wisely

Like fonts, charts, and other visual communication, color was once a scarce commodity. Color printing was expensive, and color overheads required hand applications of color overlay material. New technologies have simplified the technical aspects of using color, but wise color use is still a complex issue. Judge each situation on its own merits; just because you can use color doesn't mean you necessarily need to.

Do your homework. If you will be speaking to an international audience, be sure to note that certain colors take on different meanings in different cultures. Red means prosperity in China but implies death in many African countries. An Internet search almost certainly will yield the background you need. If you will be speaking to an organization, company, or industry group, you may be required to use a specified color palette and/or format template. Check in advance.

Instead of relying solely on color to make your points evident, build in some redundancy. Remember that an estimated one of every 10–12 men has some type of color perception problem. (Blue–green and red–green combinations are particularly problematical.) If you are presenting a line graph, for example, define the lines both with color and with line thickness or pattern.

When using colors to differentiate text and backgrounds, note that despite the many instances of white text on blue you may have seen, audiences generally prefer dark text on a light background rather than the reverse. Avoid either white text on yellow fills or dark colors on dark backgrounds or fills. Aim for contrast, but avoid a stark white background because when projected, its brightness sometimes gives people headaches.

The PowerPoint controversy

As PowerPoint use has become ubiquitous, an acerbic backlash to its use has also gained momentum. Use of the program's default slide design, in particular, has been blamed for everything from the Space Shuttle Columbia disaster (Tufte, 2003) to economic losses in the business community (Simons, 2004). Editorials have asked "Is PowerPoint the Devil?" (Keller, 2004) and "Does PowerPoint

Make You Stupid?" (Simons, 2004). As outlined by a host of critics, Power-Point's short phrase headings and bulleted lists limit the amount of detail that can reasonably be presented. They create many layers of hierarchy, and these ultimately obscure logical connections (or the lack of them) between the facts used to make an argument. Their use oversimplifies and fragments the subject matter. Other criticisms include the fact that bullet points may leave critical assumptions unstated, and that the format gives an illusion of preparation, whether or not it is justified (Bell, 2004).

"Intelligent use"

Supporters who defend PowerPoint generally agree as to the validity of the criticisms. However, they endorse the program itself as an extremely efficient timesaving, enabling tool that can be used poorly or well. An intelligent approach, these advocates say, is to avoid simply slipping mindlessly into what everyone else is doing. Among the most vocal advocates of "intelligent use" is Cliff Atkinson (2005). He views PowerPoint not as a presentation method, but as a medium – an entirely new category of mass communication in which, almost like a second language, it takes a significant effort to become fluent.

These advocates urge presenters to learn how to override the program's defaults and start developing slides in styles that better address the needs of the audience and the specific nature of the material being presented. (This task may or may not become easier as newer, more sophisticated versions of presentation software arrive on the scene.) They also urge that a presentation be understood as a total experience of which slides are just one part, paying thoughtful attention to non-slide aspects of design, structure, and delivery.

Alternative Design

Michael Alley and various colleagues have been leaders in the search for a more effective slide format to substitute for PowerPoint's bulleted text approach. As part of this search, Alley and Neeley (2005b) undertook a four-year study that involved interactive critique sessions of more than 400 technical presentations. The result was an approach the two researchers call simply "Alternative Design." It includes the guidelines shown in Table 4.2.

The two most striking differences between traditional PowerPoint slides and Alternative Design are the use of a full sentence headline and the inclusion of supporting graphics in every slide. The contrast is striking when slides of both types are placed next to one another (Fig. 4.2). (Note also the difference between both of these slides and the same subject matter in Figure 4.1.)

When a speaker uses alternative design, it appears that the use of a sentence headline (rather than the traditional phrase) better directs the audience toward the slide's main point, both during the presentation and later when the slides are used as a set of notes. Furthermore, presenting details in a visual graphic (rather than with a bullet list) makes them more memorable. Although it sounds counterintuitive, this and other research shows that audiences actually pay more

Table 4.2. *Guidelines for alternative slide design (based on Alley and Neeley, 2005b; Atkinson, 2005)*

Style	State each slide's main assertion in a sentence headline. (If you can't phrase an assertion, omit the slide.)
	On every slide, include supporting evidence presented in a visual way (image, graph, table, etc.).
	Avoid bullet lists and merely decorative images, including PowerPoint background art.
	Include visually oriented "mapping slides" to keep audience oriented.
Layout	Limit blocks of text, including headlines, to one or two lines.
	Left-justify the headline in the slide's upper left corner.
	Limit lists to two, three, or (rarely) four items.
	Instead of bullets and sub-bullets, use vertical white space and indention to indicate separations and subordinate points.
	Present listed items in parallel grammatical construction.
	Avoid sub-lists, if possible.
	Be generous with white space.
Typography	Use the bold version of a sans serif typeface such as Arial, Helvetica, or Comic Sans MS.
	Choose an appropriate type size for the room, generally 32–44 points for slide title, 28–32 points for slide headlines, 18–28 points for body text, and 14 points for reference listings.
	Avoid any text in all capital letters.
Timing	Limit number of slides so that at least 1 minute can be spent on each.
	In a longer presentation (such as a 1-hour seminar) spend even more time per slide.

attention when less written information appears on a slide (Atkinson, 2005; Mayer, 2001).

If the alternative approach is better, why doesn't everyone use it?

Alley and Neeley (2005b) believe the answer lies in both practical reasons and emotional resistance. Practical hurdles include the challenges of writing a succinct sentence headline, finding or developing visual aids, and overcoming PowerPoint default settings. To overcome these hurdles, they suggest understanding one's subject more fully, employing digital and computer graphics programs, and using alternative slide design templates downloaded from the Web.

It may be harder to answer the challenge posed by resistance to trying some-thing that is out of the norm. In workshops given to faculty, graduate students, and professionals, only about half of the participants were willing even to try using the alternative design (Alley and Neeley, 2005b). The sentence headlines on the slides – the aspect that differs most between alternative and traditional design – were more apt to be a sticking point for participants than the visual evidence. Three months later, 45% of the survey respondents were still using

HONEY FACTS

- significantly sweeter than table sugar

- moisture content 14% – 18%

- bacteria and fungi killed by osmotic lysis

- fermentation at moisture >18.6%

(a)

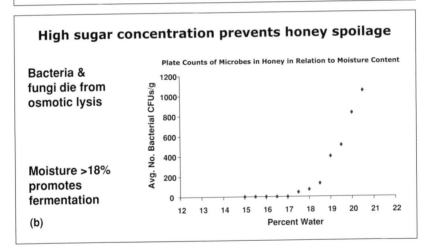

High sugar concentration prevents honey spoilage

Bacteria & fungi die from osmotic lysis

Plate Counts of Microbes in Honey in Relation to Moisture Content

Moisture >18% promotes fermentation

(b)

Fig. 4.2. The subject of Fig. 4.1 presented in two better ways: (a) As a traditional text-heavy presentation slide with illustrative graphics and a background template. (b) As an alternative design slide with full topic sentence headline and supporting graph.

visual aids for most of their slides, and 37% reported using them on all of their slides.

Sometimes presenters stick with the norm because they feel doing something different will risk their acceptance by listeners. However, Alley and Neeley (2005a) found that their audiences were quite amenable to the change. In their survey, 66% of audience members were somewhat or mostly receptive to the alternative design, and only 4% were somewhat or mostly adverse.

Base choices on effectiveness rather than mere convention

Even when a new idea has observable merit, its acceptance is enhanced by a "critical mass" of supporters who make the others feel willing and perhaps even slightly pressured to try the new idea. Alley and Neeley's (2005) solution is to teach the method explicitly in their own academic classes and require it for graded assignments. We hope you will be inspired to try this alternative approach as well. While it is probably not the ultimate best answer for presentations, it is a significant step forward. Compared to the default bullet-point presentation, this alternative approach better follows established principles of effective presentation, is more original, and when well done, is generally more responsive to the audience's needs.

SPEAKING IN PUBLIC: THE HUMAN FACTOR

When at a loss how to go on, cough.
  – *Greek proverb*

By now it should be clear that actually giving a talk is only part of an oral presentation, because every oral presentation has three major facets: content, design, and delivery. The quality of each of these aspects affects both the overall quality of the presentation and the extent to which the other aspects can be realized. For example, a confident delivery is much easier when you have good content and good organization. On the other hand, if the design of the talk is poor, even if the delivery is polished, it will be difficult for the audience to understand the content. We've presented guidelines for content and design. We've tried to help with the background work of researching, organizing, and preparing for your talk. In this section, attention turns to delivery – the human elements in the way a spoken presentation actually occurs.

Control nervousness

It is often said that people rank speaking before a group as one of their biggest fears, and this may well be true. Most of us have relatively little experience with it and the potential for embarrassment seems high because speaking occurs in real time, so mistakes can't be sucked back in for correction. The physical symptoms of nervousness – butterflies in one's stomach, pounding heart, squeaky voice – are familiar to most of us as well. They are a result of adrenaline released by the body to escape an uncomfortable or threatening situation. First let's consider ways to get this under control. Then we can turn our attention to other aspects of delivery.

Keep your composure

Thankfully, nervous reactions can be controlled or minimized in two powerful ways. The first is to change one's state of mind. The other is to prepare, organize, and deliver the presentation in ways that reduce anxiety.

Exercise 4.1. Slide presentation format

A. Organize this text in traditional slide format with a short-phrase title and bulleted sentence fragments.

"Carbon dioxide dissolves readily in water and forms small quantities of carbonic acid. The salts of carbonic acid and simple carbonates usually account for the largest part of the electrolytes in aquarium water. This means the absorption of carbon dioxide by plants is closely linked to the complex system of aqueous carbonic acid and carbonates."

B. Organize this text in Alternative Design format. Suggest a graphic aid that would be helpful.

"Twenty-one species in the order Crocodylia are known around the world. Of these, only the American Alligator and the American Crocodile are native to the United States. However, a third species, the Spectacled Caiman, has been introduced in extreme southern Florida."

C. Match the numbered and lettered items to identify optimal visual elements for an effective computer-generated slide.

1. Good font for body text	a.	All capital letters
2. Preferred typeface for headings	b.	Complex spreadsheet
	c.	14 point type
3. Minimum type size for body text	d.	San serif font such as Arial or Helvetica
4. Good type size for projection in large room	e.	Vertical
	f.	Serif font such as Times New Roman
5. Worst kind of slide graphic		
6. Preferred graphic orientation	g.	White letters on blue background
7. Preferred color combination	h.	Decorative image with sound effects
8. Alternative Design slide title	i.	28–30 point type
	j.	24 point type
9. Best kind of slide graphic	k.	Visually based support for the title's claim
10. Worst style for headings	l.	Horizontal
	m.	Dark letters on a light but not white background
	n.	Complete sentence

Although it may not feel like it, state of mind is a choice. You can dwell on personal shortcomings, or you can take an optimistic, enthusiastic view about the excitement of talking about something you enjoy to an audience that is on your side and wants you to succeed. As Gurak (2000) points out, your audience can't tell whether you are nervous inside, but only whether you show it outside. She notes that anxiety and confidence are a cycle. Feeling anxious causes you to lose confidence and losing confidence causes you to feel anxious. However, feeling confident lessens anxiety, and lowered anxiety increases confidence.

A speaker actually should feel some intensity in order to be alert and enthusiastic. This is far better than sounding tired and bored with the entire presentation! Don't let these feelings frighten you. Confidence will soon take over if you are well prepared.

Take concrete action to be well prepared

The decisions you make about content and design will help convert your high adrenaline level to enthusiasm. Whenever you have a choice, select a subject that you know well. Be extremely well prepared. Develop interesting, organized visual aids so that people's eyes will be on them, not just on you. (But don't plan on hiding behind them!)

Put together a particularly interesting introduction and conclusion. Rehearse them to the point of near memorization. A well-mastered introduction will provide your talk with a solid framework to get you beyond your initial nervousness; most people find that after the first few moments of speaking, their anxiety lowers significantly. The well-mastered conclusion will leave your audience with a good impression even if you should stumble somewhere in the body of the presentation.

Don't memorize anything word for word, however. For one thing, it can sound stuffy and insincere. For another, if you forget one word or phrase, you will lose your place – and probably your composure. Instead, memorize the outline's key points, along with key words you want to use. You will sound polished and professional, yet natural.

Expect the best but prepare for the worst

Have a backup plan for any technology you plan to use. No matter what tool you choose to use, it can fail you at some time in some way. Even the simple chalkboard can turn out to be missing its chalk. Decide what you will do if the computer fails to work. Bring an extra bulb for the overhead projector. Check the batteries for the projector's remote control. Become so familiar with your handouts that you can speak solely from them if all else fails. As the old saying goes, "you're only paranoid if you're actually wrong."

Whether you have written notes, a set of transparency sheets, or a tray of 35 mm slides – any time your talk depends on more than one of something, number them! Accidents happen; things get dropped. You know the rest.

Practice with the equipment as well as with the talk itself. If your choice involves a projector, know where the on/off switch is, and where a spare bulb is located (often in a small compartment on the side or bottom). Figure out how to focus the equipment and zoom to fit screen size. Check the range of the remote control. Try out the microphone in advance, so you won't need the famous "testing-testing-one-two-three" drill once the audience is seated and ready to begin.

Before your talk is scheduled to start, familiarize yourself with the room and the equipment. (If talks are back to back, perhaps you can get into the room over the lunch hour, during a break, or on the previous day.) Pay attention to such aspects as room size, how the lights and projector are controlled, and where you will be expected to stand relative to the audience. If possible, try out the pointer, the remote control for slide advance, and the microphone. The equipment may not be identical to that you practiced with.

Finally, as your ultimate backup plan, be prepared to give your presentation on your own, with no technology or visual aids. Knowing you are able to do so brings a measure of confidence and security that is hard to match.

Delivering the speech or presentation

At this point, you have constructed a slide set you are proud of, organized your material carefully, psyched yourself into a positive frame of mind, and practiced your talk before a small but helpful audience. Now it's time to consider the mechanics of actually giving the presentation.

Several general tips can improve presentations with any visual medium. For starters, look at the audience. Don't talk to the projector, the screen, or the board on the wall. Casually move around the room, if possible; don't pace, but don't stand in the same location for the entire talk. Remember, your primary role is not to be a robot imparting information, but a human being making a connection with the audience.

Use your visual aids effectively. Whenever possible, reveal information sequentially. With PowerPoint, design slides so that bulleted points appear as you talk about them. If you must put material on a chalkboard or whiteboard in advance, see if there is a pull-down projection screen mounted above it. If so, consider writing the points in reverse order; by raising the screen gradually, you can reveal points as needed. With transparencies, place the entire sheet on the platform and then cover it with paper, sliding the paper down line by line to reveal each new point; switch to a new transparency only when you are ready to have the audience look at it.

If you are using a remote and it won't move the slides forward, first check to be sure you're pointing it at the remote receiver, not at the screen! Then try moving forward; you may be too far away from the receiver for the remote to pick up the signal. If this fails and you're using a computer, note that keyboard keys (usually the right and up arrow keys and several others) can be used to advance the slides.

During the talk, if your mind momentarily goes blank, don't panic. As Swinford (2006) reminds us, silence is golden – it is all right to look at your slides and

Table 4.3. *Suggestions for ways to handle questions*

Situation	Possible responses
You don't know the answer.	Say simply that your research has not supplied an answer to that question. Suggest how you would investigate the question. Offer an educated speculation on the topic. Offer information on a closely related area. Ask the questioner his or her thoughts.
Question is too complicated.	Acknowledge that it is a difficult question. Give the beginning part of an answer, and suggest more discussion afterwards.
Questioner seems hostile.	Stay cool. Accept the question with a smile, followed by a serious, professional reply that is related to the subject.
Questioner asks repeated questions or wants extended discussion.	Make a positive comment about the complexity of the subject, and suggest you meet to discuss the matter further after the session.
Questioner interrupts during your talk.	Respond courteously, answer as briefly as you can, and return to the prepared speech.

collect your thoughts. Don't keep talking when you're doing it. Although the silent moment will seem long and awkward to you, the audience will find it to be natural.

Handling questions

Always plan to end your formal presentation with some time left for questions. Be patient – they may take a moment or two to begin. It is all right to fill the awkward-feeling pause by saying in a relaxed manner something like, "While you are collecting your thoughts, I'd like to just elaborate on one of the points I made earlier." However, if you do this, be extremely brief!

Sometimes, there truly may be no questions. That's all right, too. It's not a sign you failed somewhere. Thank the audience and the moderator, and sit down.

Some speakers approach the question-and-answer phase of the presentation with trepidation. What if someone asks a question that you can't answer? Or one that seems to negate the whole study? Or is openly hostile? There are ways to handle all these situations (Table 4.3). Be prepared, then relax. It's important to realize that, whatever happens, you are still in charge.

Be sure you understand the question

When someone asks a question, listen closely. Make sure the questioner is asking what you think he or she is. Don't interrupt before the question is complete, even

"Did you skip over the interesting parts of your talk on purpose?"

Ted Goff. © 2002 Reprinted with permission.

if you think you know what is being asked. Ask for clarification if necessary. As a courtesy to your audience, if necessary repeat, rephrase, or recast the question.

Then pause to think for 2 or 3 seconds before answering. Your answer will probably be better for having done so.

Answer briefly and directly

Never dismiss a question without a response; any question is important even if it sounds trivial. If one listener has missed a basic detail, others may have also. However, don't belabor any point either. This is not the time or place to start a new speech.

Always remain professional

Maintain your dignity. Many speakers tend to shed their professional demeanor at the conclusion of their formal presentation. Don't loosen a tie, lean on the podium, or relax your diction. As Davis (2005) notes, "Yeah" is not a good way to begin the answer to a question.

Never answer sarcastically or with anger. If you feel someone is asking a "loaded" question only for purposes of impressing others, remain courteous and patient. Even if a question or comment was not asked with dignity, you can dignify it by supplying a serious, professional reply.

Remember the whole audience

Maintain eye contact with all the audience most of the time, not just the individual who has asked a question. Although one person is asking, you should be answering to them all.

Make a conscious effort to take questions from various parts of the room. If one person seems to want to monopolize the floor, suggest that you meet to discuss the matter further after the session.

Never bluff, but you can steer

When you don't know an answer, honestly say so. Don't just guess. Suggest ways that an answer might be found. Alternatively, remember the old dictum attributed to politicians: "The question they ask doesn't have to be the question you answer." It is perfectly acceptable to steer your answers in directions you'd like to discuss as long as you don't appear devious or deceitful while doing so.

Stay within your allotted time limit

If questions continue and the moderator doesn't end them, do so yourself. Make a final summarizing statement if possible, and thank the audience one more time. You're finished, and you survived!

POSTER PRESENTATIONS: A HAPPY HYBRID

> A drug is a substance that when injected into a white rat produces a scientific poster.
>
> – *Graffito*

Poster presentations were almost unknown before being introduced into scientific meetings in the United States in the mid-1970s. Since then, however, they have rapidly become a major format for scientific communication at conferences and other scientific meetings. In general, a given poster will be displayed (as one of a dozen to hundreds) during a given time frame; for at least part of this time, the author will be on hand to discuss the subject with a relatively small number of interested viewers who stop wandering among the poster displays long enough to listen and converse.

Conference organizers tend to love poster sessions, because posters offer advantages both for meeting arrangements and for communication efficiency. Compared to oral presentations, more posters can be scheduled in less space, and more research can be presented in the same amount of time. In addition, posters do not require numerous meeting rooms and visual projection equipment.

Presenters find posters appealing, too. They are generally less stressful than a standard scientific presentation. Instead of imparting information to a room full of strangers, one generally converses more informally with a small group of truly interested people. Both the presenter and the audience derive mutual benefit from the discussion, and following up on ideas is easier because contact information can easily be exchanged.

Exercise 4.2. Answering questions

Discuss how you would handle these imaginary scenarios. More than one correct answer is, of course, possible.

1. You've just finished a talk in which you presented evidence that bacteria can break down a commonly used flame retardant into more toxic forms. An industry representative in the audience challenges your findings, on the basis that no one has found massive amounts of the breakdown products in the environment. How might you respond?

2. The same industry representative gains the floor again, and launches into a long speech on the lives saved by these chemicals. How might you respond?

3. You've presented research showing that children with bipolar disorder are more likely than other children to read hostility in bland facial expressions. A teacher in the audience interrupts during your talk to note that she sees classroom evidence that these children miss facial cues altogether. She wonders if your work could be developed into a test to help therapists better diagnose and treat bipolar disorder. How do you handle this interruption?

4. Scrub jays will steal food from one another. You've done some clever experiments to show that these birds get sneakier about hiding food if they know another jay is watching them. A questioner in the audience asks whether parrots might show the same behavior. You don't know. How might you respond?

5. In a stunning presentation, you've revealed the isolation of a protein from white blood cells that could offer a new way to repair damaged nerve cells. A graduate student excitedly asks how long it will be until you can completely regenerate injured nerves and restore full function to paraplegics. How do you handle his question?

Preparing a poster

Perhaps more than any other form of scientific communication, a successful poster combines visual, oral, and written elements. Because poster sessions have evolved so rapidly, their format is still more flexible than better-established forms of scientific communication. Despite this leeway, posters still require paying attention to elements of text, type size and style, color and texture, shape and arrangement, and the ways in which data are presented and illustrated. If you feel

Podiatry 101

© Mark Anderson. Reprinted with permission.

you need guidance beyond the points briefly mentioned here, good information is available from Woolsey (1989), Briscoe (1996), and Davis (2005).

A poster is a synopsis, not a paper

A scientific poster should follow the same organizational conventions used for other scientific writing, with an Introduction, Objectives, Materials and Methods, and Results. The Discussion should be limited, and can be included under the single heading of Results and Discussion. If literature is cited, a References section must be included; however, it can be in smaller type and in a less prominent position than other sections. Include Acknowledgments to recognize contributions to the research or poster construction.

Despite following the same general organization, however, a poster differs in many ways from a paper written for publication. Poster format demands concise presentation of information, clearly coordinated with visuals. Many people find it helpful to view the poster-writing process not as trying to condense a paper but rather as expanding and enriching the abstract. The most common problem with poster presentations is the attempt to present too much text and too many data. As Davis (2005) recommends, be willing to make one or two points and leave your other information for future papers. In comparison to a written paper, add more photographs, graphics, and color. Omit the separate abstract unless the sponsoring society requires it.

Make sure the text of the poster can stand on its own merits. Part of the time you will be present to answer questions, but some viewers will peruse the display when you are gone. Note that even then, most will not read the poster from beginning to end. Most commonly, viewers start by viewing data in tables and figures, or by reading the conclusions or objectives. Try reading these independently yourself, and see if they carry your central point of emphasis.

Consider readability and style

Readability (see also Chapter 5) is of primary importance with a poster. The title needs to be legible from a distance of 5 to 10 meters if it is to catch people's attention; then, because viewers generally stand 1 to 2 meters away as they read a poster (Davis, 2005), it must be clearly legible at that distance to keep their attention.

Readability depends on the size and style of type. Common typefaces generally recommended for titles include Helvetica, Tahoma, and similar block sans serif styles. A mix of capital letters and lowercase is easier to read than all capitals. These same typefaces may be used for text, or choose a conservative serif type such as Times New Roman, Bookman Old Style, or Palatino Linotype. Use italics only where scientifically required.

Text readability also depends on line length. (With current software and a wide sheet of paper, you could actually produce a one-page poster containing a single line of type two meters long – imagine the nightmare of trying to read it!) Use short expanses of text and short paragraphs. Good limits would be fewer than 65 characters and spaces per line and no more than 20 lines of text in a section. Whenever possible, present material in lists rather than sentences. Sections such as Objectives and Conclusions especially benefit from this.

To be viewed to best advantage, graphics also must be large and may need to be simplified. Davis (2005) provides a number of useful guidelines. For photographs to show at their best, they should be at least 5 inches by 8 inches (12×20 cm). Table entries should be limited to 20 items or fewer. Graphs should include no more than three or four lines or six to eight bars.

Spacing, arrangement, and poster size

At different meetings, poster display boards may be as small as 3 ft × 3 ft (1 m × 1 m) or as large or larger than 4 ft × 8 ft (1.3 m × 2.6 m). Sometimes they must be mounted horizontally on a stand or table, whereas others must stand vertically on the floor. Before attempting any layout, check written materials from the conference organizers to find out the exact dimensions that will be allowed for the display board. Section the poster into modules based on the organization of the material. Then construct the poster in such a way that sizes and shapes are roughly balanced, with no more than four or five blocks or columns on the board.

Blank space is important, too. It gives the eye a place to rest. As much as 50% of the poster should be blank, including space used to separate parts of the poster.

Table 4.4. *The two most common ways of constructing scientific posters*

Method	Advantages	Disadvantages
Separate sections, each mounted on mat board or poster paper.	Durable and attractive. Easy to modify. Pieces can be carried in a small portfolio and assembled on site.	Can be time-consuming to prepare. Use of too many small pieces can be distracting.
Single page developed with computer software (usually PowerPoint) and printed on oversized glossy paper.	Relatively easy to prepare. Poster can be rolled carefully and packed in a tube for transport.	Any modifications require reprinting entire poster. Poor or inappropriate use of color or full-page graphic backgrounds distracts from the scientific communication, and can render parts of the text illegible.

Poster construction: the unit method and the computer-printed single sheet

Increasingly, posters are being printed as a single large page after developing them with PowerPoint templates. It can seem strange at first to think of using a slide format for such a large item, but many people find it works well. At some meetings, this is already the predominant construction mode.

Various poster sizes can be constructed by combining slide size and printing size options. Currently, the largest slide size available in PowerPoint is 56×56 inches (142×142 cm). Posters are often sized 60×48 inches (152×122 cm); set the slide size to 30×24 inches (76×61 cm), and print the slide at 200%.

Sometimes posters need to be printed as separate "tiles" for an even larger presentation. Although PowerPoint doesn't currently have the option to tile printing, recent versions of Adobe Acrobat® do. One can create a PDF of the poster from PowerPoint using a downloaded PDF print driver, then print it from Acrobat (Swinford, 2006).

Before these options came along, the favored approach for poster construction was to print logical sections of the text separately, frame each on a stiff colored backing, and assemble them together on a larger background. The resultant posters were time-consuming to prepare, but when carefully done they were very attractive. This look can also be achieved now by printing each of a series of PowerPoint slides individually, then mounting them on foam core or similar material using spray adhesive.

Unless the conference presenters specify otherwise, feel free to choose between these construction methods according to your own preferences. Each has advantages and disadvantages (Table 4.4).

Presenting a poster

Despite the relative informality of the poster situation, it is still your responsibility to maintain a professional attitude. Be at your poster when you are scheduled to be; some people will make a point of being there to talk with you. If friends stop by for unrelated small talk, be sure any poster audience takes precedence over the social one.

Finally, resist the temptation to do competitive head-counts. Your success does not depend on the number of people who stop by your poster versus someone else's display. As you stand by your poster watching people pass in the aisles, it can feel disheartening. Most will walk on by. If they stop, they will generally look at only your main points, usually for less than 90 seconds.

Remind yourself that your audience is not all these people, but a small subgroup of people who are already interested in your general subject, but are not familiar with your data. If you design your poster in such a way that you attract and keep their interest, and as a result have the opportunity for clear communication conveyed with knowledge and sincerity, the experience will be worth their time and yours.

5

Revising to increase coherence

Put it before them briefly so they will read it, clearly so they will appreciate it, picturesquely so they will remember it and, above all, accurately so they will be guided by its light.

— *Joseph Pulitzer*

Almost every writer needs to correct and improve his first drafts. Those who can write a finished document and first draft at the same time are few, and might be compared to the rare musical prodigy who can play symphonies without ever taking a music lesson. Revision most often is the step in scientific writing that separates the beginner from the master craftsman. It's the reason why professional writers have such big wastebaskets! They keep working on a piece until it is right.

Two processes are involved in written communication. The first, in your mind, is the selection of words to express your thoughts. The second, in the mind of the reader, is the conversion of the written words into thoughts. The essential difficulty is in trying to ensure that the thoughts created in the mind of the reader are the same thoughts that were in your mind. Revisions are just a way to fine-tune this transfer. Coherence – the quality of being logically and aesthetically consistent – is the desired result.

WORK EFFICIENTLY

Do you remember the Process Approach that was presented in Chapter 1? It counseled breaking the writing task into discrete stages, each to be approached by the most systematic, efficient, and effective means that could be determined. You have already undertaken the initial steps in the process – planning, gathering, and organizing information, then writing a first draft and setting it aside long enough to view it with a fresh eye. Now comes revision, another essential part of the process. That step is the focus of this chapter and the two that follow.

Start with organization and logic

During the process of writing a first draft, most of us include things in one place that should be in another location. This is not a failing, but simply a reflection of the way that human beings process information. Thinking, planning, writing, and revision are interwoven processes. Even after careful planning, we think of additional things as we write. We use words as they come to mind, but our first thoughts are not necessarily the best and they may not be arranged in the most effective order. However, because thinking and writing interact, when the writing task is complete, our understanding of the subject will have been improved.

Revising by the Process Approach entails a series of nested steps, each concentrating on successively finer points. The first and broadest step concentrates on the document's structure and basic style. It includes matters such as organization, logic, accuracy, brevity, and clarity.

As you read the first draft, examine the order of presentation. Check whether all of your lines of reasoning hold up. Correct any misquotations. Evaluate your inclusion of literature citations. Watch for padding – a common temptation is to include references that merely relate to the same complex of ideas rather than having a true bearing on the argument. Combine or simplify tables where necessary. In short, do any and all of your major cut-and-paste work.

Use the power at your command

Less than a generation ago, major revisions required literal cutting and pasting of paper copy, then tedious retyping. Today, thanks to computers and word processing software, major revisions in organization and logic are more easily accomplished than they have ever been.

Always work on a copy

Never make changes directly on the original document, either on the screen or on paper. As you move things about, change wording, or add and delete paragraphs, there is always the chance that you might decide you liked the original or an earlier version of the document better. Save a copy of your paper with a new name and date (such as 4/08revisedthesis.doc) and revise this copy instead.

If you are working on a really involved project, you may find yourself needing to work with fresh copy several times. To save your sanity, be twice as careful as usual about labeling each version. Place previous versions in separate electronic or paper folders and archive them in a location where you won't be able to work on the wrong one accidentally.

Use the computer first

Word processing tools can be your most powerful comrade in the document revision battle. Commands such as "track changes" and "compare documents" make it easy to keep a record of your changes. Later, you can either reevaluate each one or choose to accept them all at once. You can flag material for follow-up. When you are happy with your revised version, you can protect the document from various types of further changes or accidental deletions.

A potential problem with such technology, however, is that the clutter of marked-up pages can become confusing. If you find yourself losing a sense of the big picture, try updating a working outline as you go. Keep this outline open in a narrow window on the screen alongside the pages you are revising.

Switch to paper, sooner or later

No matter how many changes you make to the screen copy, plan to edit a printed typescript at some point. You will almost always see different things when shuffling papers and making handwritten corrections than you do when scrolling through screen copy. The computer screen shows only a small part of the typescript at a time. Some problems – such as scrambled organization, or redundancy – simply aren't very noticeable unless several pages of the typescript are spread out in front of you.

Whatever the eventual format of your typescript will be, save a copy with double-spaced lines and wide margins for paper-based revision. An inch of margin on each side, with at least an inch on the top and bottom, is not excessive. Use a standard font in a reasonable size, such as 12-point Arial, Helvetica, Times New Roman, or New York. Number the pages automatically in a header or footer (a separate text block that contains information repeated at each page top or bottom, respectively). Include a brief identifying title for the typescript and (especially in collaborative writing situations) your own last name or initials. To visually distinguish the header or footer from the text, format this material in a different font and smaller point size and include extra space around it.

Command the program to insert a date and/or time into the header or footer, as well. These fields also are particularly useful when more than one person is working on a document, or when a document goes through several revisions. Dates and times can either be frozen, or can reflect the current date and time each time a document is opened or printed.

Note that although it may seem old-fashioned and is admittedly slower, some people still find it most effective to use paper copy to examine overall organization, as well. If you are one of them, begin by making two or more paper copies of the document. Read one copy. Write notes in its margins such as "delete," "move to discussion," or "combine Tables 1 and 2." Follow the notes on the first print as you physically cut up the second copy and tape parts together in the new order. Save the annotated reading version as a safeguard against accidentally losing one or more paragraphs of text during your cut-and-paste work.

IMPROVE THE BIG PICTURE

The word "revise" comes from the Latin, *revidere* – to see again. It means a willingness to make changes, often big changes. It's no accident that a synonym for "first draft" is "rough draft." Most are disjointed and overwritten. They contain grammatical errors, jargon, contractions, wordiness, repetition . . . and this is fine! We write as we speak. However, there are many differences between spoken language and written language. In spoken language, phrases and ideas are often repeated, in order to give the listener time to absorb them, and to provide clues to meaning. Inflection and timing – including the use of silence – give a listener additional clues to the message. In written language, a reader can, if necessary, reread a passage but the inflection and timing clues are absent. Meaning depends entirely on word choice. Revision of the conversational-style

Understanding scientific writing: A tongue-in-cheek key

What the scientists said	What they meant
It has long been known that ...	We haven't bothered to look up the reference, but ...
Of great theoretical and practical importance...	Interesting to me ...
Typical results are shown ...	The best results are shown ...
It is suggested that; It is believed that; It may be that	We think ...
It is generally believed that ...	A couple of other folks think so, too.
It is clear that much additional work will be required before a complete understanding ...	We don't understand it.
Unfortunately, a quantitative theory to account for these results has not been formulated.	We can't think of one, and neither can anyone else.
Correct within an order of magnitude ...	Wrong.
Thanks are due to Joe Clotz for assistance with the experiments and to Boyton Fird for valuable discussion.	Clotz did the work, and Fird interpreted the data.

— Author unknown

first draft, therefore, is essential if you want to come up with a well-written scientific paper.

Rework for clarity

A scientific article should hold the attention of its readers by the importance of its content, not by its literary presentation. For this reason, the simplest writing style is usually best. This does not mean that one should avoid technical words. Often they are not only necessary, but the very best way to express a thought. What it does mean is that verbose words and phrases should not be included in a vain attempt to impress the reader with the writer's intellect and scientific status. Sentence structure should not have to be puzzled over. Paragraphs should not ramble on and on.

Clarity includes what some call "grace of expression." People have grace when they go beyond politeness and act with an eye to the needs and comfort of others. Graceful prose is much the same. It does not offend readers or divert their minds from the message. It does not try to impress readers with its erudition, or force them into side issues. It serves readers without imposing upon them. "Good prose is like a window pane," wrote George Orwell, the English essayist – it is transparent in the sense that it puts no visible obstacle between the reader and the message.

Although the content of a document is more likely to determine whether it is accepted for publication than is its prose style, gracefully written text gives readers a sense that the author has mastered his or her subject. The first of those readers will be the editor and the document reviewers.

Consider person and point of view

As a writer, you can choose to present a subject in a personal or impersonal manner. In a personal point of view, you play the role of writer and reporter openly, using *I*, *me*, and *my*, or *we*, *us*, and *our*. The impersonal point of view, on the other hand, requires avoiding all explicit reference to yourself.

As a writer, you also choose the level of formality of the writing, a closely related but independent factor. The decision is not solely between personal informality and impersonal formality; a personal point of view can accompany a very formal writing style.

On many occasions one point of view or the other is preferable. This book includes both. When we have offered you tips and suggestions, we've taken an openly personal point of view, feeling that it is a friendly approach to a very personal subject – your efforts at scientific writing. When we have had to present stern pronouncements or inflexible dictums, a more impersonal and formal style has often been used.

In their professional publications, scientists almost always maintain an impersonal writing style, which the scientific culture generally views as somehow having more prestige and objectivity. Usually, it is coupled with passive constructions and avoidance of the first person.

Speed Bump. By permission of Dave Coverly and Creators Syndicate, Inc.

Total avoidance of the first person in scientific text is neither necessary nor desirable, however, as increasing numbers of journal editors are realizing. It has been rumored that some journals do not allow the use of personal pronouns, but our informal survey of over 200 of them located none that formally specified this in their *Instructions to Authors*. We suspect that scientific writing's heavy reliance on the passive voice is more a matter of tradition than a formal requirement.

Using the first person is often shorter, simpler, and less pompous than avoiding it. For example, "the authors are prepared to argue" can be shortened to "we contend." "The authors wish to thank" can be shortened to "we thank." An added benefit is that active verb forms can replace passive ones, making it difficult to construct dangling participles.

When referring to published results and then giving one's own, directly claim the latter. A common source of confusion is narratives such as the one below. Whose results are whose? And who found which inconsistencies? Phrases such as "it was found that" leave readers wondering who made the discovery. They are best avoided.

> *Confusing:* This result was elucidated by Smith (1990) and Jones (1991). In these studies the authors found inconsistencies in the results. It was found that the data differed slightly.
> *Better:* Smith (1990) was first to explain this result; Jones (1991) expanded upon the idea. Our research uncovered minor inconsistencies in the data given in both of their studies.

Exercise 5.1. Person and point of view

Change the use of third and first person in the following sentences. Many variations are possible.

1. The laboratory technician will find that the new procedure is an improvement; you will not need to sterilize the skin.

2. Kristen Preston and colleagues showed that some bacteria do not give off molecular oxygen but the authors herein contend that they still photosynthesize.

3. The authors wish to gratefully acknowledge and thank Dr. C. F. Snow for technical assistance and expertise.

4. It was found that the disease is contagious and that you should avoid contamination (van der Veen, 1850); the author concurs that cleanliness is essential.

5. It is postulated by the author, working alone and writing herein, that we have discovered a new species of *Australopithecus*.

When using the first person, employ it consistently and correctly. Sudden and illogical shifts in point of view make a document difficult to read.

> *Inconsistent:* We have reached the point where one should do further experiments. *[Does this mean we intend to do them? Or are we suggesting someone else should do it?]*
>
> *Better:* We have reached the point where we should do further experiments.
>
> *Unclear:* The authors established the gene-splicing service in 1976, and we have expanded it ever since. *[Are we and the authors one and the same?]*
>
> *Better:* We established the gene-splicing service in 1976 and have expanded it ever since.

One further point on correct use of the first person: When you are the sole author, do not refer to yourself as *we*. You must use *I* – unless you are a monarch or pregnant!

Rewrite for readability

A common complaint about scientific documents is that they are difficult to read because of the complexity and length of their words, sentences, and paragraphs. To present ideas effectively, minimize the combined weight of these factors. As

DILBERT © Scott Adams/Dist. By United Feature Syndicate, Inc.

the complexity and length of words increase, reduce the complexity and length of sentences and paragraphs to compensate.

To reading experts, "readability" refers to aspects that can be measured and subjected to a formula. Systems such as FOG, SMOG, Fry, Flesch, and many others are widely available on computer software and online. They are generally based on relationships between average word length (or number of syllables) and average sentence length, and rank readability by difficulty or by grade level.

To scientists writing for other scientists, these scores can be helpful in tailoring material to a particular audience or in maintaining uniformity in multi-authored compilations. However, they generally do not adequately address three important elements of scientific writing: content difficulty, the recognition factor, and document design. Even general readers easily recognize some multi-syllable biomedical terms. Conversely, highly technical material may use short words, but still be difficult for any but specialists to comprehend. Finally, design aspects such as column width and font size also affect readability.

Strive for sentences that average about 20 words

For maximal readability, most sentences should be between 15 and 20 words. More than 40 words generally are too many. If your sentences consistently include fewer than 12 words – rare in scientific writing – consider linking and expanding some. As a bonus, a set of sentences 15–20 words long often will express an idea in somewhat fewer words overall than a set of overly long or short sentences does.

> *Too long:* Two canine cadavers with orthopedic abnormalities were identified which included a first dog that had an unusual deformity secondary to premature closure of the distal ulnar physis and a second dog that had a hypertrophic nonunion of the femur, and the radius and femur of both dogs were harvested and cleaned of soft tissues. *[54 words in 1 sentence]*
>
> *Too short*: Two canine cadavers with orthopedic abnormalities were identified. The first dog had an unusual deformity. It was secondary to premature closure of the distal ulnar physis. The second dog had a hypertrophic nonunion of the femur. The radius

and femur of both dogs were harvested. They were cleaned of soft tissues. *[51 words in 6 sentences; average, 8.5 words per sentence]*

A readable balance: Two canine cadavers with orthopedic abnormalities were identified. The first dog had an unusual deformity secondary to premature closure of the distal ulnar physis; the second, a hypertrophic nonunion of the femur. The radius and femur of both dogs were harvested and cleaned of soft tissues. *[46 words in 3 sentences; average, 15.3 words per sentence]*

Guidelines refer to averages, however. Variation in sentence length and complexity helps sustain reader interest. A publication crammed with overly long sentences is difficult to follow, but a sustained string of extremely short sentences can be choppy and annoying.

Children commonly string together a web of sentences connected by *and* or *but*, hardly stopping to draw a breath lest they lose their audience. Writers often unconsciously practice a similar approach, unnecessarily linking loosely related thoughts with conjunctions, semicolons, or commas – and lose their audience as a result. When faced with overly long sentences in your own writing, locate the connecting words and punctuation. Separate the thoughts into independent sentences.

An overly long sentence with weak connections: Exposed poults developed enteric disease and exhibited 21% mortality during the first 3 weeks but controls had no enteric disease and exhibited no mortality; 20-week-old exposed turkeys weighed 0.6 kg less than controls and had a higher incidence of angular limb deformities and also had a greater incidence of rotated tibias and showed bowed tibias, while controls had a significantly higher measurement for tibial shear strength. *[69 words in 1 sentence]*

Separated at weak connections, then edited for wordiness: Exposed poults developed enteric disease with 21% mortality during the first 3 weeks. Controls exhibited neither enteric disease nor mortality. When compared to controls at 20 weeks, exposed turkeys weighed 0.6 kg less, had more rotated and bowed tibias and angular limb deformities, and showed significantly less tibial shear strength. *[49 words in 3 sentences; average, 16.3 words per sentence]*

Limit average paragraph length

Paragraph length and complexity also influence readability. A paragraph length of about 150 words has been judged to be optimal for a scientific article. A paragraph that covers more than two-thirds of a page when typed double-spaced usually should be shortened. Select a few representative paragraphs, and use the word processing program to check their word count.

A paragraph that is too long and complicated is tedious to read. Reexamine the paragraph to see whether it includes more than one idea; often it will. Divide the paragraph between ideas. If paragraphs in a scientific publication consistently

---

Exercise 5.2. Readability

Improve the readability of these sample paragraphs by changing the sentence lengths and word order as needed.

1. The Haversian system consists of a canal in the center containing blood vessels and a nerve surrounded by concentric rings of bony matrix and between them scattered tiny spaces called lacunae filled with bone cells connected by canaliculi to one another and the central canal. Through this canal the cells are nourished and kept alive.

2. The kidney is a very important organ. It has the ability to secrete substances selectively. This makes it able to maintain proper composition of the blood and other body fluids. The various end products of metabolism are injurious if allowed to accumulate.

3. Sex-linked genes explain red-green color blindness in man, and if a woman heterozygous for color blindness marries a normal-visioned man, all of the daughters of this combination will have normal vision, but half of the sons will be color blind; however, half of the daughters will be heterozygous for the defect but the normal sons will show no trace of the anomaly and will never transmit it to their children; while the heterozygous daughters can have color blind sons, the homozygous daughters will never pass the trait on to their sons or daughters.

---

include fewer than 50 words (five average typewritten lines), they may seem scrappy and annoying to readers. Reexamine the text to see which paragraphs could be combined.

Present ideas in expected word order

In the English language, changing the word order clearly changes the meaning:

> Hunter kills bear.
> Bear kills hunter.

Proper word order is obviously needed to provide the intended meaning. In addition, studies have shown that people's ease in reading and understanding sentences depends to a surprising degree upon the grammatical order in which words appear.

The use of standard and expected word order – in English, this is subject, verb, object, or SVO – makes ideas easy to follow because the words appear in the sequence in which things happen. When one writes "The cow swallowed a magnet," the reader mentally follows the action, seeing the cow, then the swallowing motion, and then the magnet, the object being swallowed. If instead, one writes

Table 5.1. *Some of the hedging words commonly used by biologists and medical researchers*

Nouns	Adverbs	Verbs
supposition	presumably	appear
idea	probably	postulate
speculation	possibly	suggest
conjecture	apparently	seem
possibility	not unlikely	may be
inference	seemingly	speculate

"A magnet was swallowed by the cow," the reader unconsciously unscrambles the backward construction, converting it back into SVO order before grasping it fully. This takes extra mental energy and always interferes to some degree with effective communication.

This is one of the reasons why overuse of the passive tense makes scientific documents difficult to read. Studying the works of 20 top writers (10 fiction and 10 nonfiction), Bjelland (1990) found that over 75% of their sentences used standard SVO order. However, in scientific writing, heavy reliance upon passive constructions results in an overwhelming number of inverted sentences. Change sentences back to SVO order whenever possible, while simultaneously keeping other aspects of readability under control.

Remove unnecessary hedging

To "hedge" is to protect one's arguments or statements with qualifications that allow for unknown contingencies or withdrawal from commitment. It also means to allow for escape or retreat. Whether from timidity, awe at the complexity of natural phenomena, or a misunderstanding of scientific "objectivity," scientists love to hedge (Table 5.1).

In fact, double and triple hedges are common. However, each additional qualifier drains more force from the sentence. Sometimes the result is a sentence that says nothing at all.

> The cause of the degenerative changes is unknown but *possibly* one cause *may* be infection by a *presumed* parasite.

One way of saying "I'm not sure" is usually enough in a sentence. When one hedging word is already in a sentence, prune away all the rest. However, if qualifying clauses must be used in a statement for accuracy, by all means include them. If there are many, consider itemizing them.

Condense for brevity

Editing for conciseness is both a matter of choosing the shorter, simpler alternative to express each word, phrase, and idea and a matter of eliminating redundancy. Wordiness is a common problem both within and outside the scientific community. Manuscripts are regularly returned to authors with the instructions, "Shorten this considerably before resubmitting it." Do not despair if this happens. A wide range of methods is available to edit for conciseness without having to remove significant material from the text. However, by attending to these matters before submitting the typescript, you may avoid that dreaded editorial directive entirely.

Beware of verbiage

Verbiage, which coincidentally rhymes with garbage, means the use of many unnecessary words. Often it leads to a sort of ritualistic, pompous writing style like this:

> Following termination of avian exposure, there was a substantial incrementation in lung volume and at this moment in time, it would appear that there has been a marginal degree of improvement in diffusing capacity. [*34 words*]

Even the most diehard among us would welcome with relief a shorter and more specific rewrite such as:

> After the man stopped keeping birds, his lung volume increased and diffusing capacity apparently improved slightly. [*16 words*]

There are no shortcuts around a fundamental step: Line by line and word by word, check through the first draft of the text. Ask "Is this word necessary? How can this be shortened? Does this say what I really mean?" Work on this point is not just an altruistic act directed toward readers. Practice directed toward simplifying expressions sharpens a writer's vocabulary and thinking skills.

Remove empty fillers

In spoken English, many words and phrases act as "fillers." They have little more meaning than *and-um* or clearing one's throat. Unless they are used to excess, neither the speaker nor his audience is even aware of them. In the lecture hall, a case for their utility can even be made – they pace a lecturer's talk to the slower pace of note-taking by listeners.

In scientific writing, where each word should count, empty fillers have no place. Yet they sneak in, persistently and repeatedly. Certain of them are so common as to require special attention (Table 5.2). Most "it . . . that" phrases, such as "it is interesting to note that," are pointless fillers. Strike such phrases entirely. Particularly avoid those that contain thinly disguised double negatives.

When equivalent alternatives exist, choose the one that takes the least space. This rule is, after all, the single idea behind all the more specific hints. A corollary, however, is that when clarity and brevity conflict, clarity is more important than brevity.

The editor's creed

If you've got a thought that's happy—
 Boil it down.
Make it short and crisp and snappy—
 Boil it down.

When your brain its coin has minted,
Down the page your pen has sprinted,
If you want your effort printed,
 Boil it down.

Take out every surplus letter—
 Boil it down.
Fewer syllables the better—
 Boil it down.

Make your meaning plain, express it,
So we'll know, not have to guess it,
Then, my friend, 'ere you address it,
 Boil it down.

Skim it well, then skim the skimmings,
 Boil it down.
Trim it well, then trim the trimmings,
 Boil it down.

When you're sure 'twould be a sin to
Cut another sentence in two,
Send it in, and we'll begin to
 Boil it down.

— *Author unknown*

Table 5.2. *Examples of "it . . . that" phrases that can be removed or replaced*

Phrase with empty fillers	Shorter equivalent
It would thus appear that	Apparently
It is considered that	We think
It is this that	This
It is possible that the cause is	The cause may be
In light of the fact that	Because
It is often the case that	Often
It is interesting to note that	*omit*
It is not impossible that	*omit*
A not unlikely cause could be that	*omit*
It seems that there can be little doubt that	*omit*

Table 5.3. *Examples of tautology and hiccups; omit the italicized words*

Hiccups		Tautology	
continue *on*	1 a.m. *in the morning*	*positive* benefits
refer *back*	at this point *in time*	*true* facts
check *up on*	collaborate *together*	large *in size*
all *of*	circulate *around*	many *in number*
true facts	*end* result	red *in color*
enter *into*	*mandatory* requirement	repeat *again*
face *up to*	*new* beginning	*past* history
	optional choice	*complete* stop
	five *in number*	prioritize *in order of importance*

Omit "hiccups" and other needless repetition

Short words (often prepositions) that unnecessarily accompany verbs or other parts of speech are sometimes termed "hiccups." Omitting the italicized words in Table 5.3 column 1 does not change the meaning, a sure sign that the hiccup is unnecessary. A longer sort of hiccup occurs with roundabout, indirect constructions such as "There is a cure available. It consists of . . ." This can be rewritten simply as "The available cure consists of . . ."

Tautology, a closely related problem, is defined as needless repetition of an idea in a different word, phrase, or sentence. Poor scientific writing often includes many phrases in which one of the terms implies the other or in which one term in a phrase is in the general category to which the other term belongs (Table 5.3, columns 2 and 3). For example, a *consensus* is defined as an agreement in opinion, so *consensus of opinion* is redundant.

A similar sort of wordiness occurs when words that are absolute are mistakenly modified. There is no difference between *absolutely complete* and *complete*, for example. Other absolute words that resist modifiers include *dead, extinct, fatal, final, honest, horizontal, impossible, inferior, libelous, lifeless, matchless, moral, mortal, obvious, peerless, perfect, permanent, rare, safe, straight, unique, universal* and *vertical.*

Some writers attempt to give their prose an air of elegance by using terms that contain two words which both mean the same thing. Common examples include *basic and fundamental; final and conclusive; null and void; each and every; first and foremost;* and *visible and observable.* Omit one word in each pair; the meaning is unchanged.

Shorten modifying phrases and clauses

Restrictive ("that") and nonrestrictive ("which") clauses have a valuable place in scientific writing, but they are often overused. These types of phrases have shorter equivalents. Replace "that" and "which" phrases with participles or other verb forms:

> *Wordy:* The organism that Chu (1993) found was a guppy that laid eggs.
> *Better:* The organism Chu (1993) found was an egg-laying guppy.

Prepositional phrases are also often overused. Scrutinize all prepositional constructions, especially those introduced by *of.* To reduce the length of wordy passages, substitute the adjective form of the nouns that are the object of these prepositional phrases. Alternatively, place nouns or noun substitutes in apposition.

> *Unnecessary prepositional phrases:* The dog with dyspnea was referred to a clinic in the neighborhood.
> *Better:* The dyspneic dog was referred to a neighborhood clinic.
> *Wordy prepositional phrase:* Group One includes a number of plants of the genus *Coleus.*
> *Nouns placed in apposition:* Group One includes *Coleus* plants.

Redundancy and verbosity are often coupled with jargon (see Chapter 6) and worn phrases which are so familiar that they pass unnoticed.

> *Verbose:* Due to the fact that breeder flocks in most cases are being subjected to periodical vaccination programs . . .
> *Better:* Because breeder flocks usually are vaccinated periodically . . .

When all these various kinds of changes are taken together, substantially shorter text can result:

> *Wordy:* The genera of the group of fungi that was studied by Fitzpatrick at this time are placed in the group of genera that are called the order Hypocreales because of the work of Miller (1941). [35 words]
> *Shorter:* The fungal genera studied by Fitzpatrick are now placed in the order Hypocreales because of Miller's (1941) work. [17 words]
> *Wordy:* The kitten which was the sole offspring of the calico was devoid of hair that was orange in color. [19 words]
> *Shorter:* The calico's sole offspring was a kitten without orange hair. [10 words]

Condense figure legends

Many journals prefer a clipped, sentence-fragment style of writing in figure captions; examine recent issues. Usually, articles (*a, an, the*) can be omitted and prepositional phrases can be treated as above, shortened, or omitted.

> *Full sentences:* Fig. 1. The chromosome characteristics of the unknown strain of *Tetrahymena* are illustrated; notice the large and heavily stained object in the center of the photograph, which is the macronucleus. [*28 words*]
>
> *Clipped form:* Fig. 1. Chromosome characteristics of unknown *Tetrahymena* strain; note large, heavily stained macronucleus (center). [*12 words*]

WHEN SHORT MIGHT BE TOO SHORT

In scientific and technical writing, abbreviations, initialisms, acronyms, and symbols are on the increase. You undoubtedly are already well steeped in their use in your own research field. Here we offer some brief guidelines and a plea for restraint. If they are not sufficient, entire chapters in various other scientific writing manuals are devoted to stylistic conventions for the many types of shortened word forms.

Abbreviations, acronyms, and other shortened forms

As a general rule, use abbreviations and acronyms sparingly and with discretion. They should be an aid to readers, not simply a convenience to the author. In particular, avoid using a string of either. This sort of shorthand is fine in a researcher's notebook, but not in a publication.

> Use of IV 2-PAM and ATR lessened 1.5 LD_{50} OP toxicity at 3 h PO.

Some authorities decree that one should eliminate any abbreviation that is not used at least eight times in the text (including tables and figure legends). When a cumbersome name or phrase must be used frequently in the body of the typescript, first try replacing it with a pronoun or shortened version ("the drug," "the substrate"). Then go back and substitute abbreviations only where the text seems really to require it. Whatever abbreviations you use, make sure they remain uniform throughout your paper. Inconsistent abbreviations, more common than one would assume, are exceedingly annoying to readers.

An abbreviation is the shortened version of a word *(temp., cm, avg.)*. Acronyms and initialisms are both formed from the initial letters or syllables of two or more consecutive words or each part of a compound term. An acronym is pronounced verbally as a single word *(NASA, ELISA)*. Each letter in an initialism is pronounced individually *(NSF, ATP)*. Theoretically, these distinctions should make it easier to apply rules of punctuation and capitalization to these forms, but sometimes they only add to the confusion because some authorities call initialisms a type of acronym, and others call acronyms a type of initialism.

The British distinguish further between true abbreviations (such as *diam.*, formed from the front part of a word, and requiring a period) and suspensions (such as *Mr* or *dept*, formed by removing the interior of the word, and in Great Britain used without periods). This British distinction has not caught on in the United States, but the general move to omit periods is becoming increasingly widespread. Periods are disappearing throughout the English language as it evolves. The best all-purpose rule is "be consistent."

> Doctor of Philosophy . . . Ph.D. or PhD
> United States . . . U.S. or US
> National Institutes of Health . . . N.I.H. or NIH
> amount . . . amt. or amt
> average . . . avg. or avg (preferred over ave.)

Shortened forms of capitalized words, and acronyms formed from them, generally should be capitalized and shortened forms of common nouns generally should not. Thus it is no surprise to find *SI* for *Système Internationale* or *sp. gr.* for *specific gravity*. Exceptions include certain acronyms that have become accepted as common nouns *(laser, quasar, radar, scuba)*.

Initialisms take many forms. They may be written lower case (when generally they require periods) or upper case (when generally they do not require periods). Thus we have *c.o.d.* for *collect* (or *cash*) *on delivery*, but *TA* for *teaching assistant*. Many initialisms are written in all capitals without periods, even when the word itself is not capitalized. Thus we write *deoxyribonucleic acid*, but *DNA*. Internationally accepted biochemical abbreviations (*DNA, ADP, NADH*) do not need to be defined.

To decide whether to use *a* or *an* before a shortened form, decide on a pronunciation rationale. Do not use an abbreviation or its plural form to denote a person by title or status. To do so is slang.

> *Incorrect:* Two MDs were consulted.
> *Correct:* Two physicians were consulted.

Use approved forms

Some technical, scientific, and industrial groups have adopted specific forms of abbreviations. Internal and terminal punctuation marks are often omitted. Carefully note such matters as punctuation, spacing, capitalization, and spelling. Many journals include a list of permitted abbreviations under *Instructions to Authors*. Commonly accepted lists appear in many places, including the *Handbook of Current Medical Abbreviations* (1998) and *Medical Terms and Abbreviations* (2002). See also Baron (1994), Campbell and Campbell (1995), Jablonsky (2004), and Leigh (1998).

The form and acceptability of abbreviations for dimensions, distances, time, degree, measures, and weights are particularly apt to vary somewhat from one publisher to another. Abbreviate these terms only when they follow numerals. (Note that SI metric measures are nearly always preferred, and usually required.)

In the reference list, abbreviate the journal names by the system used by your intended publisher. Examine recent issues, and check the journal's *Instructions to Authors*. Most biological and medical journals follow the abbreviations in the BIOSIS List of Serials (*Biological Abstracts*) or PubMed/MEDLINE (*Index Medicus*). These generally are available in the reference section of science libraries and online. The systems differ slightly from one another in both spelling and capitalization, but single-word titles (*Science*) are always spelled out in full.

Define shortened forms at first mention

The first time it appears, spell out any term you want to shorten, then give its abbreviation, acronym, or initialism in parentheses. Thereafter use the shortened form. If the abbreviation appears in the abstract (not generally recommended), define it again, since this may be published separately.

> The whooping crane (WC) differs from a lattice boom crane. Observers of the WC must watch that they don't become confused.
>
> For a partial list, consult the International Union of Pure and Applied Chemistry (IUPAC). The IUPAC list includes only those . . .
>
> Cultures were grown in trypticase soy broth (TSB). After TSB was added to the flask, the cultures . . .

Even if a word or phrase is defined at first mention, readers who consult only part of a chapter or journal article may have difficulty deciphering the abbreviation. Many conservative authors spell terms out at their first appearance in each major section of the typescript.

Pluralize correctly

When dealing with units of measure, use the same abbreviations for singular and plural forms *(50 mg, 25 IU, 100 ml)*. For all-capital abbreviations, form the plural by adding *s* without punctuation *(EKGs, IQs)*.

An apostrophe normally indicates the possessive case *(the animal's bones)*. It may also be used correctly to indicate the plural of words or lower case letters when adding an *s* alone would be confusing ("mind your *p*'s and *q*'s"). Omit the apostrophe when pluralizing all-capital abbreviations and numerals, including years.

> *Incorrect:* In the early 1960's, RCB's . . .
> *Correct:* In the early 1960s, RCBs . . .

The words *page* and *species* have special plural forms when abbreviated that sometimes cause confusion in scientific writing. One page is "p." (not "pg.") and many are "pp." (not "pgs.").

> One species is "sp." and many are "spp."

> To determine the identity of *Xanthoxylon* spp. consult Smith (1999, pp. 10–48).

> As the author states, "Infection by *Amblyomma* sp. is a serious matter" (Jones, 1998, p. 5).

Table 5.4. *Standard abbreviations for U.S. states, territories, and possessions*

Ala. (AL)	Ga. (GA)	Md. (MD)	N. Mex. (NM)	S.D./S. Dak. (SD)
Alaska (AK)	Guam (GU)	Mass. (MA)	N.Y. (NY)	Tenn. (TN)
Amer. Samoa (AS)	Hawaii (HI)	Mich. (MI)	N.C. (NC)	Tex. (TX)
Ariz. (AZ)	Idaho (ID)	Minn. (MN)	N.D./N. Dak. (ND)	Utah (UT)
Ark. (AR)	Ill. (IL)	Miss. (MS)	Ohio (OH)	Vt. (VT)
Calif. (CA)	Ind. (IN)	Mo. (MO)	Okla. (OK)	Va. (VA)
Colo. (CO)	Iowa (IA)	Mont. (MT)	Ore./Oreg. (OR)	Wash. (WA)
Conn. (CT)	Kans. (KS)	Nebr. (NE)	Pa. (PA)	W. Va. (WV)
Del. (DE)	Ky. (KY)	Nev. (NV)	Puerto Rico (PR)	Wis./Wisc. (WI)
D.C. (DC)	La. (LA)	N.H. (NH)	R.I. (RI)	Wyo. (WY)
Fla. (FL)	Maine (ME)	N.J. (NJ)	S.C. (SC)	

Watch the names of geopolitical entities

When they stand alone, names of geopolitical entities should be spelled in full. The abbreviation U.S. (which sometimes appears without spaces or periods) is an adjective, as in U.S. Fish and Wildlife Service. As a noun, spell it out ("wildlife conservation in the United States").

In lists, tables, and when combined in an address, the names of U.S. states, territories, and possessions may be abbreviated in standard ways (Table 5.4). The preferred form still is the conventional system. However, it is rapidly giving way to the two-letter postal code system specified by the U.S. government for use with zip-code addresses and shown here in parentheses. Whichever system you use, be consistent. Do not switch from one system to the other.

When in doubt, spell it out

Here is a quick summary of some places not to abbreviate. Unless an abbreviation is internationally accepted *(DNA, RNA)*, avoid using it in the title or abstract. Titles and abstracts are often translated into foreign languages, where readers may find the abbreviations perplexing.

Do not begin a sentence with an abbreviation. Do not abbreviate generic names when they are used alone. (*Drosophila melanogaster* or *D. melanogaster* is acceptable, but never simply *D.* or *D. m.*) Do not abbreviate units of measurement when they are used without numerals. (Never write "Several ml. were added.")

Finally, do not abbreviate when confusion might result from doing so. If two words have the same abbreviation, both should be spelled out.

Noun clusters and strings of pearls

In English, a noun can be used to modify or describe another noun. Such noun clusters are common in our language, adding variety and flexibility to writing.

Exercise 5.3. Shortened forms

The following abbreviations are used incorrectly. Why?

1. *A title:* Assay for TCGF Activity in SPAFAS Chickens in the U.S.

2. *An abstract:* The present study provides first evidence for the presence of TCGF in supernatants of Con A stimulated chicken spleen cells incubated for several hrs.

3. *A text sentence:* Con A stimulated BALB/C spleen cells were used to prepare TCGF preparations by the MF I and MF II methods.

4. *A table title:* Distribution of ATPase in El treated membranes expressed as μ/mg of protein and total U.

5. *A footnote:* Pheasants were obtained from hatcheries in Ala., TN, and S. Carolina.

For example, *liver disease* (a two-noun cluster) and *hepatic disease* (an adjective and a noun) have the same meaning, and may be used interchangeably.

Two-noun clusters are acceptable, even desirable, and usually cause no problems. However, scientists have a tendency to take this ability to extremes, running together whole series of nouns (and adjectives) that modify one another and the final noun in the chain, until the reader becomes lost. This construction – several modifiers stacked up in front of a noun – has been dubbed a "string of pearls" (Table 5.5). Consider this excellent example that was actually published:

> Five two week old single comb white leghorn specific pathogen free chickens were inoculated with approximately 105 tissue culture infected doses of duck adenovirus. *[Which nouns are substantive and which are modifiers?]*

Uncouple long strings of nouns and adjectives

Strings of pearls often arise from an overly zealous attempt to be brief. However, lucidity is too important to sacrifice on the altar of brevity. Additional words and punctuation are preferable to barely comprehensible meanings. Suppose you encounter the phrase *aged dog meat samples*. It might have at least five meanings: samples of aged meat used for dogs, samples of aged meat from dogs, aged samples of meat from dogs, aged samples of meat used for dogs, and samples of meat from aged dogs. While this example may seem silly and extreme, similar examples are common in scientific writing. How would you interpret *brown egg laying flocks*? (It turned out that the eggs, not the flocks, were brown.)

Table 5.5. *Strings of pearls: revising noun phrases that have too many modifiers*

Sentence fragment containing a string of pearls	How it might be revised for clarity
A system necessitated automated motor starting circuit	An automated motor-starting circuit required by the system
A 4 month secretory cell produced mucosal accumulation history	A 4-month history of accumulation of mucosa produced by secretory cells
The negative penicillin skin test result group	The group with negative results on the penicillin skin test
Blue absorbing pigment spectral curve	Spectral curve for blue-absorbing pigment
Climate controlled gene cluster phenotype variation	Climatically controlled variation in gene-cluster phenotype
Two dimensional real time ultrasonographic blood flow detection techniques	Ultrasonography techniques that detect blood flow in two-dimensional real time
A calibrated transit time ultrasonic blood flow probe cable end	The cable end from an ultrasonic blood-flow probe calibrated to measure transit time ultrasonically

Disconnecting strings of pearls is tedious but straightforward. Working methodically through the typescript, circle every batch of more than two nouns. The goal should be to reduce these strings to simple pairs. As a memory trick, recall that "two is company, but three's a crowd." Because hyphenation links two words to reduce a three-word cluster to two, it often bends this rule a bit. However, any cluster beyond two or three words usually spells trouble.

Strings of pearls can be revised in many ways. Decide the precise relationship of one word to another, and express this relationship by inserting necessary words. Start with prepositions, commas, and hyphens. Watch for unintentional changes in meaning. Noun and adjectival forms often have subtly different definitions (as in *paramedic training* versus *paramedical training*). Do not add an adjectival ending if the noun more correctly expresses the thought.

Exercise 5.4. Clarity and brevity

A. Rewrite each of these at least twice to express different meanings clearly.

1. mature muscle iron

2. chronic depression symptoms

3. renal lithium excretion

4. The three cases all had histologically confirmed metastatic malignant intraabdominal tumors.

5. The present study examines various immunospecific drug sample combinations and their inhibition producing effects upon human peripheral blood leukocytes.

B. Reduce the following examples to a single hedge word apiece. Your interpretation may influence which hedge word is kept.

1. These observations serve to suggest the probable existence of a possible female sex pheromone.

2. It seems that it might possibly be very wise to follow the outlined procedure.

3. Our belief is that the study may show an apparent link between cigarette smoking and lung cancer.

4. A possible cause-and-effect relationship is not unlikely.

5. The results appear to indicate that the mixture may have been more or less saturated with oil.

C. Identify and remove redundancy.

1. It is interesting to note that the new organism is green in color, round in shape, 5 × 10 mm in size, and active with respect to motility.

2. The authors envision that approximately 20–30 steps that are collectively referred to as electrophoresis will be necessary in the majority of cases.

3. In the event that we hold a meeting at this point in time with reference to the data, consensus should not be difficult to attain.

4. It is not irrelevant to mention here that the case load included 15 young juveniles and 10 mature adults.

5. Fig. 1. The lateral white cells as they have been shown to appear in a living abdominal ganglion of a cockroach. The ventral view has the anterior at top. The scale bar is 0.1 mm.

6. The total absence of visible color was absolutely unique.

7. To determine the mobility activity of the organism, new state-of-the-art equipment was used.

8. For a full and complete understanding of the impacts and ramifications of the hot temperature upon the organism, it is our personal opinion that future plans should include a chilling procedure.

6

Improving word choice, style, and syntax

On the whole, I think the pain which my father took over the literary part of the work was very remarkable. He often laughed or grumbled at himself for the difficulty which he found in writing English, saying, for instance, that if a bad arrangement of a sentence was possible, he would be sure to adopt it . . . When a sentence got hopelessly involved, he would ask himself "now what do you want to say?" and his answer written down, would often disentangle the confusion.

– Charles Darwin's son, Francis (Darwin, 1897)

Like Charles Darwin, most of us need to go over our writing to disentangle confusion, particularly in word choice, syntax, and style. Syntax refers to the relationships between the words and other elements in a sentence. Style means the way something is done, or its basic "personality." Thus we speak of a scientific writing style characterized by clarity and organization, an editorial style that presents written material in a certain way, or a typographic style with various artistic elements.

The importance of these three aspects of scientific writing springs from the precision which science requires. More than one interpretation of a sentence or phrase is unacceptable, so careful attention must be paid to both word choice and word arrangement.

This step may have been what you have been expecting – and dreading – from the start. Admittedly, it can be hard work, but stick with us. Mastering the fundamentals of scientific style demands no special inspiration or genius that stamps a person as different from all others. It is simply a skill akin to doing crossword puzzles or solving logic puzzles. It is a word game in which the winning combination is a sort of functional beauty that arises from barrier-free communication.

Don't get so close to the supposed difficulties that you lose sight of the pleasure in it . . . for there is pleasure to be derived from any effort of creative activity, including this one. Like the hand-turned table you might build or the picture you might paint, each article you write is an original vehicle of self-expression. The material you choose to include, the arrangement of your arguments, the criticisms you raise, and the conclusions you reach, all reflect your own personality and intellect.

Calvin and Hobbes   by Bill Watterson

CALVIN AND HOBBES © 1993 Watterson. Dist. By UNIVERSAL PRESS
SYNDICATE. Reprinted with permission. All rights reserved.

Calvin and Hobbes © 1993 Watterson. Reprinted with permission of Universal
Press Syndicate. All rights reserved.

CHOOSE A BETTER WORD

"When I use a word," said Humpty Dumpty, in rather a scornful tone, "it means
just what I choose it to mean – neither more nor less."

– Lewis Carroll

How nice it would be if word choice were as simple in our own world. Instead, like
the bugs that plague computer programs, these flaws creep into scientific writing
unnoticed (Weiss, 1990; Dupré, 1998). Almost always, there is more than one
way to get rid of them. Like programmers, writers and editors may do anything
to eliminate a bug – except add a new bug.

Recognize and minimize jargon

Jargon is a term derived from a medieval French word for the chattering and
twittering of birds. It consists of highly specialized technical slang arising from

Table 6.1. *Types of scientific jargon*

Origin	Examples
Careless extension of language rules	The kidneys were ground and the grindate was chilled.
	The material was rechromatographed.
	The mass was biopsied.
Acceptable words used in grammatically unacceptable ways	The substance was reacted with acetic acid. (An intransitive verb such as "react" does not take an object, and has no passive voice.)
	The feline developed leukopenia. (Words like feline, canine, or bovine are adjectives; when you mean cat, dog, or cow, say so.)
	No histology was found in the liver. (Histology is a medical discipline; it is jargon to use it as a synonym for abnormality.)
Spoken fads	Inoculize, prioritize, verbalize, visualize, or any such attempt to make a verb by adding "-ize." (We have even encountered "formalinized samples" as a description of samples placed in formalin.)
	Reactionwise, stepwise, or any such "-wise" except likewise.
	Phrases with "experience" tacked on the end, as in "a learning experience."
Words or phrases formed by dropping parts of a word or phrase	Prepped (prepared)
	Jugular ligation (jugular vein ligation)
	Osteopath (osteopathic physician)
	Vet (veterinarian)

the overuse and misuse of obscure, pretentious, or technical words or phrases. Eventually, the changing English language may even fully embrace it. Until that time, however, a jargon word or phrase can pose an insidious trap for a scientific writer because its familiarity makes it seem acceptable before conservative usage embraces it as being correct.

Like other slang, jargon follows cycles of popularity, and fads are common. With a little reflection, you can probably add new examples to the ones we've listed in Table 6.1. Many of these arise by back formation, with a legitimate word or grammatical construction that gives rise to illegitimate offspring. Modern dictionaries describe many of these words and phrases as "variants." This just means that many people are prone to the error.

When conventional words or phrases within a discipline are overused, the result is also jargon (Table 6.2). A list of these terms could go on and on. The basic idea is to substitute shorter, everyday terms for polysyllabic synonyms of Greek, Latin, or Romance language derivation.

Table 6.2. *Suggestions to replace common overused words and phrases*

Instead of	Use
at this point in time	now
dorsal or lateral recumbency	on its back or side
due to the fact that	because
employ, utilize	use
high degree of accuracy	accurate
implement	do
in the event that	if
method	way
neonate	newborn
oftentimes	often
plethora	excess
postoperatively	after surgery
prior to	before
retard	slow
sacrifice, euthanatize	humanely kill or destroy
subsequent to	after

Eliminating jargon does not mean removing all technical terms, however. Technical terms are often polysyllabic, yet also concise because to convey their precise meaning in any other way would require many more words. When technical terms are used, be sure they are used correctly. Avoid using scholarly words or phrases in a pseudo-scholarly way. Such jargon results in statements that are inaccurate as well as verbose. Words such as *spectrum, strategy, parameter*, and *approximated* have a meaning in the disciplines in which they arose. Used in a pseudo-scholarly way in other disciplines, they can be misleading.

Watch out for spoken biomedical jargon

Biomedical terms can pose a special hazard because some are used incorrectly so often in speech that the misleading ring of familiarity can lend them false authenticity. Some examples follow.

biopsy – This is not a verb. (The mass was not "biopsied," but a biopsy of the mass was performed.) Observations are made on a biopsy specimen, not on the biopsy itself.

die of, die from – Persons and animals die *of*, not from specific diseases.

euthanatized, euthanized – Which of these words, if either one, should be used is a debated but unresolved matter; neither term even appears in some unabridged dictionaries. Use *humanely killed*, if possible. Avoid the term *sacrificed*, which has witch-doctor overtones.

parameter – Reserve this word for its specific statistical meaning of a potential variable to which a particular value can be assigned to determine the value of other variables. Do not use *parameter* to mean measurement, value, indicator, or number.

significant(ly) – Use only when statistical significance is meant, and include a probability (*P*) value. For other uses, change to *important, substantial, meaningful,* or *notable.*

Watch -ology *word endings*

The suffix *-ology* on words means the study of something. Words with this ending become jargon when used in sentences such as these.

Jargon: No pathology was found.
Correct: No pathologic condition was found.

Jargon: Cytology was normal.
Correct: Cytological findings were normal.

Jargon: Serology was negative.
Correct: Serologic findings were negative.

For example, "the only pathology found" translates into "the only study of pathogens found." It does not mean what scientists intend, "the only pathogens found" or "the only tissue damage by a pathogen." Likewise, "etiology" is not a pompous synonym of "cause" to be used in phrases like "the etiology of the disease"; it is the study and description of causes.

Note that words ending in *-ical* need an editorial check. Some editors drop the *al*, but others don't, as in *pathologic* vs. *pathological*. Be consistent.

Avoid coining new words, phrases, or usage

Rarely, a new scientific discovery truly justifies adding a new word to the language; if this happens, define the word carefully at its first mention in the document. Usually a little thought and dictionary work will produce an equivalent word that already exists in the English language. The work of translating a scientific paper is difficult enough without putting these additional stumbling blocks in the path of the foreign reader.

New grammatical constructions that arise by back formation are particularly dubious. These include such "counterfeit coins" (Weiss, 1990) as *administrate* for *administer, preventative* for *preventive, remediate* for *remedy*, and *deselect* for *reject*. Sometimes they become slightly silly, as when the legitimate word *attend* gives rise to *attendee* rather than *attender*.

Minimize computer jargon

Jargon, acronyms, and abbreviations are proliferating with the digital age of electronic communication. Language is always changing, and we anticipate that with time many of these terms will become widely accepted. For now, be conservative. Used excessively with an audience that is unfamiliar with it, computer jargon can easily come across as pretentious.

Many new compound words pertaining to technology have not yet found their way into standard dictionaries. How should they be punctuated? The iconoclastic approach of computer manual writers seems to be "when in doubt, close it up," and they are the ones introducing new terminology and coining new meanings. Thus these new compound words commonly appear without hyphenation. Examples include desktop, download, email, keyword, online, toolbar, website, wildcard, and workstation.

Exercise 6.1. Jargon

A. Find a substitute for the following pretentious words and phrases.

1. a sufficient number of

2. has the capability of

3. produced an inhibitory effect

4. on a theoretical level

5. on a regular basis

B. What do the following sentences literally mean? What did the author intend?

1. The etiology of this disease is puzzling.

2. Histopathology stages were based on 10 dogs.

3. The necrology confirmed the intestinal occlusions.

C. Reword these sentences to remove jargon and extra words.

1. The bovine was postoperatively traumatized by a defective electrified fencing enclosure, necessitating euthanatization.

2. Positionize the slide carefully to visualize the quite unique spatial configurations with a high degree of accuracy.

3. It is the author's opinion that it is not an unjustifiable assumption that this chemotherapeutic agent has the capability of significantly ameliorating and attenuating the symptomology of the disease process.

Use bias-free, inclusive language

Words, like Nature, half reveal
And half conceal the Soul within.

– Alfred, Lord Tennyson
("In memoriam A.H.H.," 1850)

Nowadays, people have become much more aware of the ways in which language shapes our thinking. Many thoughtful discussions of the topic have appeared, and many guidelines have been developed; for examples, see Schwartz *et al.* (1995), Schaie (1993), and Maggio (1991, 1997).

To avoid charges of prejudice and insensitivity, language and visual aids must be accurate, clear, and free from bias. Just as you have learned to check what you write for spelling and grammar, practice reading over your work for bias. Cultivate at least three kinds of awareness: (1) noting potential bias in the kinds of observations and characterization being made; (2) recognizing the impact of various value-laden terms; and (3) being sensitive to certain biases that are inherent in the structure of the English language.

It is a writer's job to maintain the audience's willingness to go on reading the document. Readers who are offended are likely to stop reading. Test your writing for implied or irrelevant evaluations on the basis of gender, sexual orientation, racial or ethnic group, disability, or age. Try substituting your own group for the one being discussed or imagining you are a member of the group you are discussing. If you feel excluded or offended, the material needs revision. Another suggestion is to ask people from that group to read your material and give you candid feedback.

Use language inclusively, specifying only those differences that are relevant

Precision is a necessity in scientific writing. When you refer to a person or persons, choose words that are accurate, clear, and free from bias. For example, some writers use the generic masculine exclusively. This offends many readers, because it seems to be based on the presumption that all people are male unless proven female. Using *man* to refer to all human beings carries the same implication, and is simply less accurate than the phrase *men and women*.

Another part of writing without bias is recognizing that differences should be mentioned only when relevant. Marital status, sexual orientation, racial and ethnic identity, or the fact that a person has a disability should not be mentioned gratuitously.

Beware of group labels

Sometimes in scientific writing, participants in a study seem to lose their individuality. They are either categorized as objects (*the elderly*) or equated with their conditions (*the demented*). (Matters are not improved by changing this to *the demented group*!) Do not label people by their disabilities. Broad clinical terms such as *borderline* are loaded with innuendo unless properly explained. Calling one group *normal* may prompt the reader to make comparison to *abnormal*, stigmatizing individuals with differences (*the lesbian group* vs. *normal women*). Likewise, do not use emotionally loaded adjectives, such as "stroke *victims confined* to wheelchairs." Substitute neutral wording such as "individuals who had a stroke and use a wheelchair."

Labels such as *Group A* are not offensive, but they are not particularly descriptive either. The solution that is currently preferred places the people first, followed by a descriptive phrase (such as *people diagnosed with schizophrenia*).

Guard against the perception of bias or prejudice

Any verbal or visual reference that presents racial or ethnic groups as unequal or excludes one group in favor of another implies prejudice. Most of us are probably most sensitized to racism and sexism. However, many other *-isms* have been defined by groups and committees that are working to reduce perceived bias in language. Extensive discussion of this topic is beyond the scope of this book; for helpful overviews and inroads to the literature, consult the Internet and see works by groups such as the American Psychological Association (*Publication Manual*, 2001).

Although racist language in scientific documents is rare, visual aids often do not show the same sensitivity. Sexism includes any verbal or visual reference that presents men and women as unequal or excludes one group in favor of another; it can take many forms, some of them subtle.

Find alternatives to sexist language

Though it may be unconscious and unintentional, sexism is common in scientific writing. Consider these examples.

> Hard-driving veterinarians in private practice should take more time for their wives and children.
> Fuch's endothelial dystrophy in man occurs with a predilection for aged females.
> The client's behavior was typically male.

Some people are also quite sensitive to nonparallel usage that seems to suggest an inequality.

> The study included 10 men and 16 females.
> The researchers were surprised to find so many cautious men and timid women.

Avoiding sexist language isn't always easy, because the English language lacks a gender-neutral singular pronoun. A writer always has options, however; listed below are six of them.

1. Use a gender-neutral term when speaking generically of your fellow creatures

> *Instead of:* man; mankind; manpower; man on the street
> *Use:* the human race; humankind, people; work force, personnel; average person

2. Be sensitive to alternatives in titles and salutations. When a good gender-neutral term is available, use it in place of a clearly gender-oriented title.

> *Instead of:* spokesman; policeman; stewardess
> *Use:* speaker, representative; police officer; flight attendant

3. Use plural constructions when you can. Often, it is possible to recast a statement in the plural, thus circumventing the need to use the third person singular pronoun. Avoid breaking the rules of English grammar, however.

Sexist: A doctor should advise his patients.
Grammatically incorrect: Every doctor should advise their patients.
Better: Doctors should advise their patients.

4. Replace the third person singular possessive with articles. Avoid s/he, he/she, and his/her. These constructions look awkward and interfere with reading.

In some disciplines, it is popular at the moment to alternate the use of "he" and "she" in text and oral presentations, supposedly to show sensitivity. This has the potential to be seriously distracting, however; rather than paying attention to content, people begin playing silent games about which form will be used next.

If none of the other guidelines has been helpful, one can use the slightly less awkward forms "he or she" and "his or hers." However, a more graceful alternative simply omits the possessive form in favor of neutral wording.

Instead of: Have the scientist send his manuscript to Dr. Blow.
Better: Have the scientist send the manuscript to Dr. Blow.
Instead of: Each technician must be sure that s/he signs his/her time card.
Better but awkward: Each technician must be sure to sign his or her time card.
Better yet: Each technician must be sure to sign a time card.

5. Address readers directly. If you can do so appropriately, substitute "you" for the third person singular pronoun. A direct instruction or command also works in many cases.

Instead of: If the veterinary researcher cannot mail in his samples, he should ask his assistant if she can do it.
Better: If you cannot mail in your samples, ask your assistant to do it.
Instead of: A nurse must be sure that she uses disposable syringes.
Better: Nurses must use disposable syringes.

6. Use the passive voice. (Notice that this option is at the bottom of our list!)

Instead of: Each conference participant should have received his schedule.
Better (but only marginally): Schedules should have been received by conference participants.

Avoid awkward coinage

Some people feel strongly that a writer should avoid using words that are gender-specific when the roles that they denote are not gender-related. These purists have gone so far as to coin new words for any term that is gender-specific, as in substituting *parentboard* for the computer's *motherboard*. In the words of Dupré (1998), "even if the word is awkward, it shows your reader you are sensitive."

Or does it simply make you look silly? Experimental ways of making English more neutral have not caught on very well. Many commentators vehemently argue against artificial tampering with words. So-called political correctness, an attitude that carries language sensitivity to an extreme, has come under a great deal of public ridicule. Our advice is to take the middle ground. Use gender-neutral words when they are appropriate, be aware of nuances in our changing language, and avoid awkwardly coining new words.

Exercise 6.2. Handling language sensitively

Improve the word choice in these examples.

1. A researcher must be sure that he double-checks all his references.

2. The sample consisted of 200 Orientals.

3. The depressives and the epileptics reacted differently to the drug.

4. The chairman confronted the female for plagiarizing.

5. The ten ladies in the study included one who was afflicted with cerebral palsy.

6. Breast cancer is one of the oldest diseases known to man.

7. We need 14 females willing to man the project.

8. A scientific writer's point of view must be clearly stated by him at the beginning.

Choose the right word

> The difference between the almost-right word and the right word is really a large matter – it's the difference between the lightning bug and the lightning.
> – *Mark Twain, in an October 15, 1888 letter to George Bainton*

The list of almost-right words is endless, and computer spell checkers and grammar programs are little help with this problem. To rid your own writing of such mistakes, there is no easy alternative to learning what the right word is.

Some would like to believe that any widespread practice of writing or speech will become acceptable in time, and thus conclude that there is no cause for criticizing anything if it occurs regularly in the writing of educated people. If everyone confuses *affect* and *effect*, won't the dictionary eventually allow them as synonyms? And if so, can't we use them now? In a word, no. Good scientific writing is conservative.

Remember, the function of writing is to permit communication across time and space. Most of us would have trouble speaking Shakespearean English today, but we can understand the King James edition of the Bible, even though the English was written 400 years ago. Americans, Jamaicans, and Australians may have difficulty with each other's speech, but they have almost no problem with each other's writing.

Watch out for commonly misused and confused word pairs

Words are not always what they seem. Use a dictionary when you write so that people don't need to have one on hand when they read what you've written. Be especially careful about words that look similar but mean different things. The English language contains a great number of words that are commonly misused or mistaken for each other. Some commonly encountered "devil pairs" are given below. This list is only a beginning, and no substitute for a good dictionary.

accuracy/precision – *Accuracy* is the degree of correctness of a measurement or statement. *Precision* is the degree of refinement with which a measurement is made or stated, and implies qualities of definiteness and specificity.

acute/chronic – Reserve these terms for descriptions of symptoms, conditions, or diseases.

affect/effect – *Affect* is a verb that means to act upon. The noun *effect* means outcome. (As a verb, effect means to bring about, as in "it will effect a change," an awkward phrase worth replacing.)

aggravate/irritate – When an existing condition is made worse, it is aggravated. When tissue is caused to be inflamed or sore, it is irritated.

as/like – Rather than "like we just mentioned," say "as we just mentioned." *Like* can mean many things, but *as* is the conjunction for all but the most colloquial use.

case/patient – A *case* is a particular instance. It can be evaluated, followed, and reported. A *patient* is a person who is under medical care. (Avoid calling an animal a patient.) A sick person not receiving treatment is not a patient, so one cannot speak of untreated or normal patients.

compliment/complement – *Compliment* means praise, but *complement* means to mutually complete each other.

continual/continuous – *Continual* means happening over and over. *Continuous* means occurring without interruption.

dose/dosage – A *dose* is the quantity to be administered at one time, or the total quantity administered. *Dosage*, the regulated administration of doses, is usually expressed in terms of a quantity per unit of time. (Give a dosage of 0.25 mg every 4 hours until the dose has been ingested.)

examine/evaluate – Patients, animals, and microscope slides are examined; conditions and diseases are evaluated.

follow/observe – A case is followed; a patient is observed. To *follow up* on either approaches jargon, as does *follow-up study*. However, in medical writing the use of both terms is increasing.

gender/sex – *Gender* is cultural, and is the term to use when referring to men and women as social groups. *Sex* is biological; use it when the biological distinction is predominant.

imply/infer – To *imply* is to suggest, indicate, or express indirectly. To *infer* is to conclude.

infect/infest – Endoparasites such as intestinal worms *infect* to produce an infection; ectoparasites such as fleas *infest* and produce an infestation.

infectious/contagious – *Infectious* means harboring an agent that can cause infection, or having been caused by an infecting agent. *Contagious* is the adjective that means the agent in an infectious disease has a high probability of being transmitted. Under some conditions, an infectious disease is not contagious.

necessitate/require – *Necessitate* means to make necessary. *Require* means to have a need for. A patient requires treatment. The treatment may necessitate certain procedures.

negative/normal – Cultures, tests for microorganisms, tests for specific reactions, and reactions to tests may be *negative* or *positive*. Observations, results, or findings from examinations and tests are *normal* or *abnormal*.

over/more than – *Over* can be ambiguous. (The cases were followed up over two years.) Instead, say *more than*. (The cases were followed for more than two years.)

prevalence/incidence – *Prevalence* is the quality or state of being widespread or common. *Incidence* is the rate of occurrence.

principal/principle – A *principal* is a leader; used as an adjective, it means highest rank. A *principle* is a fundamental truth or law. Dr. Jones was the principal investigator on a grant to study biological principles.

regime/regimen – A *regime* is a system of management of government. When a system of therapy is meant, *regimen* is the correct term.

symptoms/signs – A conservative rule states that *symptoms* apply to people, *signs* apply to animals.

toxicity/toxic – *Toxicity* is the quality, state, or degree of being poisonous. A patient does not have toxicity. *Toxic* means poisonous; a patient is not toxic.

use/utilize/employ – Generally, *use* is the intended term; *utilize* suggests the discovery of a new, profitable, or practical use for something. The word *employ* is best reserved for putting a person to work.

vaccinate/immunize – Although these words are sometimes used as synonyms, they carry different implications. To *vaccinate* means to expose a person or animal to an antigen purposively in hopes of eliciting protective antibody. To *immunize* implies that exposure successfully elicited protective antibody. Not all vaccinated organisms are immunized.

varying/various – *Varying* means changing, but *various* means of several kinds.

while/whereas – *While* indicates time and a temporal relationship. *Whereas*, often the word the writer intended, has such meanings as "when in fact," "that being so," and "in view of the fact that."

Exercise 6.3. Devil pairs

Place each member of the devil pair in the proper place in the sentences below.

Like/As:

1. The results of our study were _____ those of McGowen (1967). A significant number of study animals staggered _____ drunks do.

While/Whereas:

2. Young dogs are very susceptible to distemper, _____ older dogs are often immune. Cattle often develop respiratory disease _____ being shipped to market.

Varying/Various:

3. Clients often have ponds which may be of _____ sizes. Each group received _____ combinations of antibiotics over the study period.

Effect/Affect:

4. Although we gave penicillin and terramycin, the drugs had little _____. The _____ of the treatment was minimal.

5. Trypsin-catalyzed digestion has the _____ of converting the substrate to short-chained peptides. Giving erythromycin _____ a change in the nuclear shape. In double-blind experiments, researcher bias does not _____ experimental results.

Principal/Principle:

6. He resigned as a matter of _____. The _____ effect of centrifugation was to separate cell types. The _____ of independent segregation is fundamental to genetics.

Complement/Compliment:

7. To determine the appropriate value, one must find the _____ of the angle. The authors would like to _____ Ms. Jones on her diligent effort. In the replication process, DNA and RNA _____ each other.

Beware of "which" and "that"

Your manuscript is both good and original; but the part that is good is not original, and the part that is original is not good.

– Samuel Johnson

Exercise 6.4. Which and that

Improve the following sentences in whatever ways seem sensible and correct, paying particular attention to "which" and "that."

1. It is relevant to mention here that novel paleontological findings have uncovered the strong probability that the genus *Cantius*, an early genus of primates of a primitive nature, had a large pedal digit that could grasp and which possibly may have figured in the evolutionary scenario of all of today's more modern primates.

2. It should be noted that the use of low molecular weight dextrans should be avoided in these patients which appear to pass through the damaged endothelium of pulmonary vessels.

3. Occasionally a parasite will be noted by the client on a fish which is more worrisome to the owner than to the fish.

4. According to this interpretation it is then concluded by the authors of this present study that ten thousand five hundred tons of lead, that are in addition to the ninety thousand tons which are presently being emitted, will be emitted into the atmospheric envelope during the course of the next calendar year.

5. Our efforts did not result in the location of the proposal which was missing.

This pair of words causes much confusion. Sometimes the words can be used interchangeably; more often, they cannot. A phrase or clause introduced by *that* is restrictive; it cannot be omitted without changing the meaning of the sentence. Such essential material must not be set off with commas.

A nonrestrictive clause adds information, but does not limit what it modifies. Because it can be omitted without changing the meaning, a nonrestrictive clause is separated from the rest of the sentence by commas. Technically, the word *which* can be either restrictive or nonrestrictive. One could write "dogs which were treated recovered" or "dogs, which were treated, recovered," depending upon the sense of the sentence.

Many scientists overuse *which* as a connective, perhaps in a misguided attempt to make their writing more formal. As a result, correct comma use suffers. This simple rule of thumb is almost always correct: use *that* without commas with all restrictive clauses and *which* with commas with all nonrestrictive clauses.

Restrictive that *clause:* Dogs that were treated with antibiotics recovered.

Nonrestrictive which *clause:* The researcher's decision, which did not come easily, was final.

When we read the words *which* or *that*, we interpret such words to refer to whatever went immediately before them in the sentence. If either word becomes separated from its true subject, confusion results. To cure the confusion, move the *which* or *that* next to the word to which it refers. Alternatively, rewrite the sentence to avoid using *which* or *that*. (This is an especially desirable route if the sentence is very long and/or complex.) Consider breaking the sentence into smaller ones.

Potentially confusing: Tumors were palpable in the animals that remained. *[Which remained, the animals or the tumors?]*

Ways to clarify the meaning: In the animals that remained, tumors were palpable. Tumors that remained were palpable in the animals.

Focus fuzzy nouns and qualifiers

Sometimes, words like those listed below have a definite meaning. More often, they indicate that the thought needs to be sharpened. Think carefully about what is really meant, and substitute a more precise word.

area	character	conditions	field
level	nature	problem	process
situation	structure	system	

Likewise, vague qualifiers (such as *fairly, few, minimal, much, quite, rather, several, slight, very*) usually can and should be omitted, since they add nothing.

CHECK THE VERBS

Hardly anyone will say that your writing has improved. Rather, they'll remark on how much smarter you seem lately.

— *E. H. Weiss* (1990)

Scientists are infamous for their plodding writing style. Frequently, their problem arises from poor verb use. Most of the time, they have chosen weak and overused verbs, or hidden perfectly good verbs in noun form. In other cases, they have overused the passive voice, and/or lost track of subject-verb agreement.

Choose livelier verbs

Scientists often write as though only seven verbs exist: *demonstrate, exhibit, present, observe, occur, report,* and *show*. Certainly most scientific papers would be seriously crippled if these verbs were removed from the language. Consider this example:

> The mean hepatic weights observed to occur in normal and thyroidec-
> tomized rats were 154 and 27 mg, respectively. The kidney was
> also observed to exhibit a four-fold difference in the two groups,
> but as we have shown, no significant difference was demonstrated
> in the spleen.

All of these verbs are overused, hackneyed, and trite. Whenever possible, substitute more vigorous verbs.

Furthermore, to be technically accurate, these lazy verbs should not be coupled with nonhuman subjects. For example, a scientist will write "the results demonstrate," an action that results, being inanimate, cannot do. Likewise, a researcher may say, "The tissue exhibited necrotic foci." A tissue cannot present anything for inspection, as the sentence literally implies. This misuse is so widespread that most readers have come to accept it. Nonetheless, this problem should provide additional incentive to substitute alternate wording whenever it can be done gracefully. The substitution will usually improve the writing in other ways as well.

> *Inaccurate:* Results show dog weight increased and reduced angulation
> occurred.
> *Better:* Dogs weighed more and angulation decreased.
> *Inaccurate:* As Figure 1 indicates, disease was seen to occur in 72 of the
> demented group.
> *Better:* Disease developed (Fig. 1) in 72 patients with dementia.

As a supplement to any other grammar-checking programs you may have – or as a fairly powerful checker on its own – consider using your computer's "search" or "find" command to flag the warning words and lazy verbs that appear in this section (or at least those you recognize as potential problems in your own writing). Each time that one is highlighted, examine the sentence in which it appears. You will soon become sufficiently sensitized that you no longer need the mechanical help to alert you to their presence so that you can avoid or fix them.

Unmask disguised verbs

Habitual use of nouns and pronouns is a common cause of monotonous, verbose science writing. Abstract nouns formed from verbs and ending in "-ion" are a particularly common offender. Such words are really verbs in disguise, richer and more concise than the lazy verbs they are capable of replacing. Consider using them directly as verbs or in their infinitive form. (For more help with this, see "Active and passive voice".) Experiment with their use as adjectives, adverbs, and participles, as well.

> *Overuse of abstract nouns:* Following activity termination, the patient
> experienced an amelioration of his condition.
> *More forceful equivalent:* After the patient stopped moving, his condi-
> tion improved.

Exercise 6.5. Fuzzy words and disguised verbs

A. Improve the following sentences in whatever ways seem correct and appropriate. Be alert for lazy verbs.

 1. By early adulthood, more of the males than females were observed to exhibit severe symptoms characteristic of the occurrence of copper deficiency.

 2. Under standard conditions, diazepam was chosen for inhibition of the initial rate of protein phosphorylation, as Figure 1 demonstrates.

 3. The site of action of soap is observed to be at the cell surface.

 4. Stanozolol caused prolongation of appetite, as the results demonstrate.

 5. Isolation of *A. hydrophila* occurred.

B. Use infinitives to replace verbal nouns, and improve the wording of the following sentences.

 1. The physicists' hope is for the solution of the question of whether science can harness alternative energy sources.

 2. Transformation of the data was necessary for the statistical analyses relevant to resolution of the hypotheses.

> *Buried verbal nouns:* Results showed protection by the vaccine, but degeneration of lymphocytes occurred.
> *Resurrected verb:* The vaccine protected the patients, but their lymphocytes degenerated.

Sometimes, words that are perfectly good on their own still can indicate the potential for trouble. For decades, the following "warning words" (adapted from Woodford, 1968) have remained relevant as indicators that unclear, ambiguous, or prosaic prose lurks nearby.

accomplished	achieved	attained	carried out
conducted	done	effected	experienced
facilitated	given	implemented	indicated
involved	made	obtained	required
performed	proceeded	produced	

These overused, colorless verbs occur most commonly as the past participle. They usually should be eliminated in favor of a more vital verb hidden (often in *-ion* form) in the sentence.

Colorless: The provision of assistance implemented in 2007 resulted in the production of a viable method for establishment of a basis for long-term improvement.

Better: Assistance begun in 2007 led to a method that produced long-term improvement.

Active and passive voice

"Voice" is the form of transitive verbs that shows whether the subject acts or is acted upon. When the subject of a sentence performs the action expressed by the verb, the voice is said to be active. When the subject undergoes the action of the verb, the voice is passive. The phrase *it was carried* is passive; *we carried it* is active.

The passive voice usually consists of some form of the verb *to be* plus the past particle of an action verb. (Forms of *to be* include *is/are, was/were, has/have been, had been, may be*, and *will be*. The past participle often but not invariably ends in *-ed* or *-en*.) Passive phrases include *were studied, is being considered*, and *will be examined*.

Who or what did the studying, considering, or examining? In the passive voice, the agent can be left unnamed. (It can, however, still be expressed with *by* if desired.) When the agent performing the action is unknown or irrelevant in the context, the passive voice is appropriate.

Darwin's most influential work *was published* in 1859.
Twenty-five genera of Capnodiaceae *are recognized* in the tropics.

The passive voice can also be used to emphasize something or someone other than the agent that performed the action. You might write *Johnson caught a fresh specimen* to emphasize Johnson or *a fresh specimen was caught by Johnson* to emphasize the specimen.

Use the active voice unless you have good reason to use the passive

Many scientists overuse the passive voice. They write as though it were somehow impolite or unscientific to name the agent of action in a sentence. They seem to feel that every sentence must be written in passive terms, and they undergo elaborate contortions to do so. However, in any type of writing, the active voice is more precise and less wordy than the passive voice. It is the natural voice in which most people speak and write. The active voice also adds energy to your writing, and forces you to decide *what* you want to say. The passive often obscures your true meaning and compounds your chances of producing pompous prose. Compare the alternatives in Table 6.3.

To convert a sentence that is in the passive voice to one in the active voice, search for the true subject, and name it. Then find the verb, and mentally drop the form of *to be*. Convert what is left of the verb to the active voice.

Passive: The genetic relationship was studied by Berger and Shanks (1981).
Active: Berger and Shanks (1981) studied the genetic relationship.

Table 6.3. *Active and passive voice*

Vague passive phrasing	Active, precise wording
It is recommended by the authors of the present study that . . .	We recommend . . .
The animal was observed to be situated in dorsal recumbence which had the effect of rendering its legs useless.	Lying on its back, the animal could not use its legs.
The data which were obtained by Johnson were probably indicative of . . .	Johnson's data probably indicate . . .
The following results were obtained . . .	We obtained these results . . .
It was discovered that a sustained coordinated effort will be required . . .	We need a sustained coordinated effort.

Exercise 6.6. Active and passive voice

Rewrite these passive sentences in the active voice. Condense and clarify the wording if you can.

1. It might be expected that this treatment would be effective.

2. No feed was available to the pathologist to analyze.

3. Inoculation was performed on 25 chickens by Jones and colleagues.

4. A collecting trip was made by this writer to Georgia for the purpose of collecting Lepidoptera.

5. Passages A and B should be marked for revision.

6. If certain words are discovered to be missing from this medical dictionary, it must be remembered that no equivalents for modern technical words were to be had by ancient speakers of Greek and Latin.

7. Three incineration systems are being studied for the university president by administrative personnel at the Biology Building.

A more vigorous active verb also may be hidden in a noun ending in *-ion*. You can often exhume these buried verbs to convert the sentence into the active voice.

> *Buried verb hidden in "-ion" noun:* Antibody detection was accomplished by Team A.
> *Resurrected verb:* Team A detected antibodies.

Exercise 6.7. Subject–verb agreement

Correct the following sentences if needed. Explain your reasoning.

1. The remaining fluid was drawn off and the kidneys washed.

2. Due to the small number of test animals used, that data was not significant.

3. Karyorrhexis, karyolysis, and cellular degeneration of hepatocytes was evident within the centrilobular regions.

4. The data indicates that Jones together with his wife and children was the first to discover the phenomenon.

5. None of the animals was harmed in the course of this study.

6. A sample was assessed by radiocarbon dating and sections analyzed by potassium–argon methods.

7. Neither the rats nor the chimpanzee were kept in the laboratory.

Subject–verb agreement

Because of the writing style that they have adopted, scientists find it surprisingly difficult to use correct verb forms. The two most common grammatical errors in scientific writing are errors in verb use: subject–verb disagreement and dangling participles.

Attention to subject–verb agreement is especially crucial because of the confusion that results from this sort of error:

> The effect of feeding rations containing concentrations of aflatoxin on the immune systems of young swine with lesions and enzymes were studied.

Were the effect and the enzymes studied? Or did the swine have both lesions and enzymes? Is *effect* the subject, in which case the *were* is incorrect? Because of lack of subject–verb agreement, the reader cannot be sure. The writers knew that the subjects and verbs must agree in number, but they allowed the two to become separated so widely that they lost track of them.

To check a sentence, temporarily omit all phrases that separate the subject and verb, including those that begin with such words as *together with, including, plus,* and *as well as.* This will give a sentence in which subject and verb are readily apparent. Both should be singular, or both should be plural. Correct the grammar, and move the subject and verb closer to one another to improve the sentence. For good measure, whenever possible also tighten the wording and recast the sentence in the active voice.

Incorrect grammar with separated subject and verb: A high concentration of sialic acids which are a group of substances principally composed of amino sugars attached to polysaccharides, lipids, or proteins are found in the mammalian epididymis.

Omit intervening phrases: A high concentration . . . are found in the mammalian epididymis.

Improved, grammatically correct sentence: The mammalian epididymis contains a high concentration of sialic acids, principally composed of amino sugars attached to polysaccharides, lipids, or proteins.

BEWARE OF STRANGE LINKS

Flitting from flower to flower, the entomologist observed the bees.

Sometimes, you may find that your words and phrases become linked together in strange and unanticipated ways. Confusion, ambiguity, or downright humor can result.

Usually, the problem lies in unclear antecedents or poorly placed modifiers. An antecedent is a word or phrase that a subsequent word refers back to. Modifiers are words, phrases, or clauses that expand, limit, or make more precise the meaning of other elements in a sentence. Because both antecedents and modifiers must be linked to another word or phrase in the sentence, they cause problems when they appear in the wrong location.

Ambiguous antecedents and misplaced modifiers

A word or passage is ambiguous when it can be interpreted in two or more ways. Common causes of ambiguity include ambiguous pronoun references, misplaced modifiers, and incomplete comparisons (see the last section in this chapter).

Pronouns often cause ambiguity because – since they serve as stand-ins for another word or group of words – pronouns always have antecedents. Ambiguous pronoun reference often takes the form of two-sentence clusters, in which the first sentence has two possible antecedents for the pronoun in the second sentence.

Ambiguous: Inadequate training in PCR techniques resulted in incomplete data. This has been our most pervasive problem. [*Does this refer to poor training or incomplete data?*]

Specific: Inadequate training in PCR techniques resulted in incomplete data. Training inadequacies have been our most pervasive problem.

Check such words as *all, it, its, this, that, their,* and other pronouns. Clarify their antecedents.

Misplaced modifiers

Because modifiers provide detail and clarification, they are the darlings of the scientific writing world. We've already noted how scientists stack them and fill them with jargon. Scientists also place them in strange locations that cause ambiguity and unintentionally shift their meaning. Whether they are single words or entire phrases, most modifiers function as adjectives or adverbs. To correct a misplaced modifier, simply move it as close as possible to the word it modifies.

> *Unclear:* The researcher tested the women observing this schedule.
> *[Who observed the schedule, the researcher or the women?]*
> *Better:* Observing this schedule, the researcher tested the women.

Dangling participles

Phrases that do not clearly and logically refer to the correct noun or pronoun are called dangling modifiers. A modifier is said to "dangle" when its implied subject is not the subject of the main clause of the sentence.

Though various parts of speech can dangle, participles are the undisputed champions. Many dangling participles are misleading, confusing, or unintentionally ludicrous.

> Being in poor condition, we were unable to save the animals.
> Lying over the heart, you will discern a large growth.

Most participles end in *-ing, -en*, or *-ed*. Examine the text for words with these endings. Those most apt to cause problems usually appear at the beginning (less commonly, the end) of the sentence as an introductory phrase. To correct a dangling participle, either rewrite the sentence so that the subjects agree or turn the phrase into a dependent clause with an explicit subject.

> *Dangling:* While having the committee meeting next door, the spectrophotometer exploded.
> *Subjects agree:* While having the committee meeting next door, we heard the spectrophotometer explode.
> *Dependent clause:* While we were having the committee meeting next door, the spectrophotometer exploded.

Following and using

Two common "-ing" words are especially troublesome. One is *following*. Often it is used incorrectly to mean *after*. Following is a noun or adjective meaning that which comes next, as in "check the *following* reference" or "animals were examined the *following* day." It causes problems because it sounds like a participle to the reader. "*Following* a fat meal, the animal collapsed" sounds as though the animal was trailing the meal when this happened. Substitute the word *after*, which is clearly a preposition.

The other "-ing" word to distrust is *using*. It often dangles. Even when correct, *using* is a dull word that appears too commonly in scientific writing. Substitute a richer, more interesting word whenever you can. If you cannot think of one, at least substitute the safer word *with*.

Exercise 6.8. Dangling participles and other misplaced modifiers

---

Untangle the sentences below. Transform the sentences into the active voice when you can.

1. Progressing toward the anterior chamber a lamination was evident.

2. No bacteria were observed using dimethyl sulfoxide.

3. Following experimentation, bacteria multiplied.

4. Using this method the result demonstrated a correlation between the variables.

5. Intestinal sections can be examined for metazoan parasites using an inverted ocular.

6. Two stopwatches belonging to researchers that had been left leaning against cabinets were badly damaged.

7. For sale: Laboratory table suitable for researcher with thick legs and large drawers.

8. Two microscopes were reported stolen by the campus police last night.

9. Commercials have been prepared by the French government encouraging the use of condoms that are thought to be blunt enough to shock even liberal Americans.

Dangling participle: No mosquitoes were found using the standard bait traps.

Better: No mosquitoes were caught with standard bait traps.

Three ways to fix a dangling participle

Reliance upon the passive voice is a major reason why participles so often dangle. This is because the true subject is usually hidden in passive voice. Therefore, one straightforward way to correct a dangling participle is to rewrite the phrase to include the true subject of the verb that was turned into a participle.

Dangling participle: Using our inoculation procedures, infected hamsters developed granulomata.

True subject included, but wordy: When we used our inoculation procedures, infected hamsters developed granulomata.

Alternatively, omit the verb of the participle entirely.

Verb of the participle omitted: Our inoculation procedures produced granulomata in infected hamsters.

Table 6.4. *Examples of verb use with collective nouns and the pronoun "none"*

Singular in context	Plural in context
A pair of animals was housed in each cage.	A pair of animals were watching.
All of the protocol was carefully followed.	All of the data were incorrect.
Statistics is a difficult subject.	The statistics are easily gathered.
The number of people in the study is dwindling.	A number of people have dropped out.
None of the information was used.	None of the trials were finished *OR* Not one of the trials was finished.

A third way to correct dangling participles is to switch to gerund phrases. A gerund looks superficially like a participle, because it also ends in *-ing*. However, a participle functions as an adjective, and a gerund functions as a noun.

A gerund often can be used as the subject of a sentence. When you say, "Writing is easy," the gerund is *writing*. (Sometimes gerunds also appear in the predicate part of a sentence, as in, "He explained the Kreb's cycle by *drawing* a diagram.")

> *Dangling participle:* Flushing the flask, the impurities were removed.
> *Participle changed to gerund:* Flushing the flask removed impurities.

THE MISCHIEF OF MULTIPLES

Hungry Joe collected lists of fatal diseases and arranged them in alphabetical order so that he could put his finger without delay on any one he wanted to worry about.

> – *Joseph Heller*

Whether compiling disease lists or parenting twins – more than one of anything takes extra care. In scientific writing, collective nouns, comparisons, and lists require special attention.

Collective nouns and noun phrases

Most nouns are clearly either singular or plural in both sense and form. However, whether collective nouns are singular or plural depends on context and your emphasis as the writer. You must decide whether the action of the verb is on the group as a whole (and treat the noun as singular) or the action is on group members as individuals (and treat the noun as plural).

The pronoun *none* can also be singular or plural. When the noun that follows is singular, use a singular verb; when the noun is plural, use a plural verb. If you mean *not one*, use that phrase with a singular verb instead of *none*. Some examples appear in Table 6.4; consult a good dictionary if in doubt about the form of others.

Collective terms denoting quantity are particularly tricky to handle. When regarded as a unit, these nouns take singular verbs, but when considered individually they take plural verbs. We say "ten liters *is* a good yield" but "ten liters *were* poured into carboys." The problem is that, even with careful attention and the help of a good stylebook, such sentences often sound illogical or clumsy. Many writers simply prefer to redo such sentences. Write the sentence in the active voice and/or reorder it so the collective noun or quality is no longer the subject. Alternatively, use parentheses for the quantity.

> *Instead of:* Five milliliters of serum was added to the mixture.
> *Write:* We added 5 ml of serum to the mixture.
> *Instead of:* Two-tenths of a milligram per liter of mebendazole and 0.9 mg/L of trichlorfon effectively control freshwater *Gyrodactylus.*
> *Write:* A combination of mebendazole (0.2 mg/L) and trichlorfon (0.9 mg/L) effectively controls freshwater *Gyrodactylus.*

Phrases like *a total of* can be particularly troublesome. *Total* is singular, and should take a singular verb. Do not say "a total of 35 animals *were* examined." Even the correct phrasing, "a total of 35 animals *was* examined," will cause many readers to stumble. It just sounds wrong! Usually the phrase *a total of* should simply be omitted.

Remember that although the word *data* is sometimes used as a singular noun (particularly in nonscientific journalism), it is still correctly considered to be plural. (A *datum* is one of the single facts or pieces of information which collectively constitute the data.) Thus, in a scientific publication write, "Additional data *are* available."

Strings of subjects or verbs require special care

When the subject is composed of a singular and a plural noun joined by *or* or *nor*, the verb agrees with the noun that is closer.

> *Incorrect:* Neither the dogs nor the cat *were* in the cage when the assistant returned.
> *Correct:* Neither the dogs nor the cat *was* in the cage when the assistant returned. *OR* Neither the cat nor the dogs *were* in the cage when the assistant returned.

When a single subject is coupled with more than one verb, auxiliaries such as *was* and *were* can safely be omitted with verbs after the first. Many writers shorten sentences by doing so. However, a problem can easily arise when this condensing technique is used for a sentence with more than one subject.

> *Single subject, auxiliary verbs omitted:* Tissues were fixed in 10% buffered formalin, embedded in paraffin, cut, and stained with hematoxylin and eosin.

Two subjects, both plural, correct but confusing: Samples were obtained from kidneys and sections cut and stained with lead citrate. *[Were samples taken from kidneys and sections?]*

Improved by removing one subject: Kidney sections were cut, then stained with lead citrate.

If the number of the subject in the sentence changes, one must retain the verb in each clause. When two or more verbs are used with two subjects, one singular and one plural, keep the auxiliary words such as *was* and *were* with their verbs.

Incorrect: The positions of the tubes were reversed and the test repeated.

Correct: The positions of the tubes were reversed and the test was repeated.

The grammar of comparisons and lists

Most grammatical problems that occur with comparisons and lists arise from the omission of important words. When words are missing, the reader intuitively finds a parallelism among the words that are present. Strange, illogical comparisons sometimes result.

Nonparallel construction: These results were in general agreement with others who found increased mortality. *[The Results and "others" cannot logically agree with one another.]*

Parallel construction: These data and others' results generally agreed.

The need for clarity always outranks the need for brevity. When comparing two agents under two conditions, fully specify which items are being compared. In the second part of a parallel construction, include all the words necessary to complete the comparison.

When comparing one person or thing with the rest of its class, use a word such as *other* with the comparative. Do not compare one with *all*, for it could be misinterpreted as the sum of the others.

Incomplete comparisons: Solution A yielded more amino acids than protein. The trial was significantly longer. The animal's weight was greater than all the others.

Completed comparisons: Solution A produced a greater yield of amino acids than of protein. The trial was significantly longer than the other trials were. The animal weighed more than any of the other animals did.

When comparing only two things, use the comparative term *(better, poorer, lesser, more)* rather than the superlative *(best, poorest, least, most)*.

Of the two medications, this is the *less* (not *least*) effective.

The brown dog was the *sicker* (not *sickest*) of the two.

DILBERT © Scott Adams/Dist. By United Feature Syndicate, Inc.

Some words are not comparable because they already represent the ultimate state – for example, *full, impossible, correct*, and *unique*.

> *Incorrect:* A more correct evaluation would say that our study was the most unique of its kind.
> *Correct:* A more nearly correct evaluation would say that our study was unique.

Check to ensure that the word *as* or *than* is next to the comparing word. Look carefully when you have a phrase set off by commas or parentheses in the middle of the comparison. Check your grammar by omitting the phrase. Does it still make sense? Moving *than* and adding another *as* will correct the problem.

> *Incorrect:* Group A was as large, if not larger, than Group B. *[Does "Group A was as large . . . than Group B" still make sense?]*
> *Correct:* Group A was as large as, if not larger than, Group B.

The grammar of lists

Lists carry their own sets of grammatical pitfalls. If there is an introductory preposition or article, either use it with only the first item or phrase in your list, or include it with every one. When some items take *a* and others take *an*, you must repeat the article with each item.

> Group 1 included a salamander, an alligator, and a skink.
> Do not categorize clients by sex, by age, or by birthplace on these forms.
> The patient's skin exhibited a red rash, an itchy lump, and a scar.

If a list is not inclusive, introduce the series of words or phrases with *such as*. Alternatives *like* and *e.g.* are less desirable. *Et cetera (etc.)* is rapidly falling out of favor, and at any rate, should never be used with these phrases.

> *Incorrect:* Laboratory animals, like rats, mice, gerbils, etc., were evaluated.
> *Correct:* Laboratory animals such as rats, mice, and gerbils were evaluated.

For guidelines on punctuating lists, see Chapter 7.

Exercise 6.9. Collective nouns, comparisons, and lists

A. Write these sentences so that the collective noun or quantity is no longer the subject.

   1. Ten to 50 parts per million of chloramphenicol is an appropriate dose.

   2. A committee of scientists was convened by the university president.

   3. A total of 12 liters of serum were infused into the elephant by the veterinarian.

B. Rewrite the following sentences to correct their comparisons and lists.

   1. The authors' mild pulmonary hypertensive stage was similar to our present study.

   2. In comparison to Group B, Group A was more unique.

   3. The cat had a recovery that was better than the other cats.

   4. The emergency medical kit contained a bandage, applicator, towel, brush, and a rubber sponge.

   5. The fox was heavier than all the other animals in the study group.

   6. Of the two alternatives, this is the most interesting.

7

Attending to grammar, numbers, and other mechanics

Sticklers unite, you have nothing to lose but your sense of proportion, and arguably you didn't have a lot of that to begin with. Maybe we won't change the world, but at least we'll feel better.

– Lynne Truss (2003)

Proper grammar, formatting, and citations are essential to effective written and oral communication. These fundamentals help avoid misunderstandings and reduce the chances of error in fact or interpretation.

Attention to detail is a little like housekeeping. When it is done well, no one is aware of it. When it is not, everyone can tell. If you skip this step, readers will notice. They may be willing to overlook small inconsistencies, but major blunders will distract their attention away from the primary purpose of the writing. No longer concentrating on the technical content, they start searching for more errors instead.

TWEAK THE TEXT

The difficulty is not to write, but to write what you mean.

– Robert Louis Stevenson

If effective scientific communication is like a well designed and smoothly operating machine, then grammar – the accepted system of rules by which words are formed and put together to make sentences – forms the nuts and bolts that hold it all together. The individual fasteners of punctuation, capitalization, and such may seem simple and unexciting to look at, but they are undeniably important if the machine is to hold together and function properly.

In this section, we suggest ways of avoiding and correcting some common mechanical mistakes that scientific writers tend to make. For further advice, style manuals of special utility for biomedical writers include *Science and Technical Writing* (Rubens, 2002), *Publication Manual of the American Psychological Association* (2001), *American Medical Association Manual of Style* (Iverson, 1997), and *Scientific Style and Format* (Council of Science Editors, 2006).

153

A dozen fumblegrammar rules
for scientists

1. It is recommended by the authors that the passive voice be avoided.
2. Subjects and verbs even when separated by a word string has to agree.
3. Writing science carefully, dangling participles must not appear.
4. If you reread your writing, you will find that a great many very repetitious statements can be identified by rereading and identifying them.
5. Avoid using "quotation" marks "incorrectly" and where they serve no "useful" purpose.
6. The naked truth is that editors will read the riot act to any Tom, Dick, and Harry that uses clichés; avoid them like the plague.
7. In formal scientific writing, don't use contractions or exclamation points!!
8. If we've told you once, we've told you a thousand times, a writer who uses hyperbole will come to grief.
9. In science writing, and otherwise, avoid commas, that are, really, unnecessary.
10. Subjects and their verbs whenever you notice and can do so should be placed close.
11. Remember it is better not to, if you can avoid it, split an infinitive.
12. Proofread your manuscript carefully to be sure you didn't any words out.

— Adapted from Safire (1990)

Punctuate for clarity

Writing the words "a woman without her man is nothing" on the chalk-
board, the professor directed the students to punctuate it correctly.
The men wrote "A woman, without her man, is nothing."
The women wrote "A woman: without her, man is nothing."
Punctuation is everything.

– Unknown

Punctuation has one purpose – to help the reader understand the structural
relationship within (and thus the intention of) a sentence. For this reason, the
best approach to punctuation is almost always the simplest. Punctuation should be
almost automatic. If you are puzzled over how to punctuate a particular sentence,
you probably have created a sentence that will puzzle readers too, no matter
how you punctuate it. Rewrite the sentence in a form that requires only simple
punctuation.

Prefer the period

Semicolons, colons, and dashes indicate that two statements are closely related.
Their use sometimes also helps condense material. However, sentences separated
in this way are usually more difficult to read. The trend in scientific writing is to
eliminate semicolons, substituting separate sentences with periods.

> *Older style:* A mutant strain might be designated "red"; its genetic
> symbol, *r*.
> *Newer style:* A mutant strain might be designated "red." Its genetic
> symbol would be *r*.

Semicolons are still appropriately used to separate items in a series with internal
commas.

> Larval feeding habits of flies include: parasitizing beetles, moths, and
> other insects; mining in fern leaves, stems, and other plant tissue;
> burrowing in carrion, offal, and dung; and scavenging decaying
> vegetation.

Prevent false joining

Anytime a phrase would be nonsense without one or more commas, a dash, or
parentheses, use them. This rule is the rationale behind all the more specific
ones. When you have finished writing, check each sentence for reading errors
associated with incorrect punctuation or lack of punctuation. If two parts might
be joined erroneously, they should be separated by punctuation.

   Pay particular attention to sentences that vary from the usual "subject–verb–
object" word order (see SVO). The possibility of erroneous joining is nearly
always present when the introductory phrase contains a verb of some form, such
as an infinitive or a participle.

Reading error possible: Although additions of monensin were discontinued after 9 days the fermentors did not resume gas production.

Alternative interpretations clarified by punctuation: Although   additions
of monensin were discontinued, after 9 days the fermentors did
not resume gas production. *OR* Although additions of monensin
were discontinued after 9 days, the fermentors did not resume gas
production.

Insert commas for clarity and emphasis

The comma has a wide variety of uses, but its overall role is to add clarity or
emphasis to a sentence. Remember this fact, and the comma's many specific
applications begin to fit into a pattern.

Whenever a dependent clause or a long adverbial phrase comes before the
main statement of the sentence, it needs a comma. As an example, consider the
previous sentence.

To determine whether to use commas with a clause that is within a sentence,
read the sentence without the clause. Proper punctuation of a clause within
a sentence hinges upon whether the clause is essential (restrictive) or not. If
omitting the clause does not change the meaning of the main statement of the
sentence, separate the clause from the main statement with commas. If the clause
is essential to the meaning, do not use commas. This rule generally means commas
are used with the word "which," but not with "that." See Chapter 6 for more
information on "which" and "that."

The horses, which came from 6 farms, were dead.
Six horses lived and 28 died. The horses that died were buried.

Punctuate the elements of series clearly

Series range from straightforward lists of like items to extremely convoluted
sentences with all manner of nested phrases. For maximal clarity, they require
different sorts of punctuation.

With a simple series, place a comma before *and, or,* and between the items.
Your composition teacher may have instructed you otherwise – in literary writing,
and in United Kingdom scientific writing, this comma is often omitted on the
grounds that it interrupts the flow of words. However, American scientific writing
includes the comma, feeling it maximizes precision. Although the comma before
and is usually merely a nicety, sometimes it can be important to the meaning of
the sentence.

Complex series need something more. When the individual elements in a
series contain their own punctuation, separating the elements with commas may
confuse readers. Use semicolons, numerals within the sentence, or both.

Confusing: The criteria included that patients with unilateral dislocation
were included but those with bilateral dislocation were not, as
treatment of one hip may affect the untreated, and the child had

to be less than 36 months old when treatment was begun and that no child with other anomalies such as scoliosis, arthrogryposis, or trisomy 21 was included.

Better: All patients (1) exhibited unilateral, but not bilateral dislocation; (2) were younger than 36 months when treatment began; and (3) exhibited no other anomalies such as scoliosis, arthrogryposis, or trisomy 21.

Compound sentences can also be thought of as a type of series. Scientists are extraordinarily fond of coupling sentences, particularly when discussing their methodology. They also rely heavily on a single subject joined to pairs of verbs or adjectives. The words *and, but, for, or,* or *nor* are weak ways to join independent statements. Most critics of style shun them. Used to excess, such construction weakens the writing and creates a singsong cadence.

For stronger writing, examine each pair of sentences or compound predicates. First, consider dividing each statement into separate sentences, particularly if the statements are complex and/or long. Condense and tighten the wording. Then, if a weak connector still must be used, put a comma before it.

Weak writing, poorly punctuated: Experimental subjects were kept in a climate-controlled room, and were provided with food. Artificial light was provided, and dogs were acclimated to handling. In the study described herein, the investigators found that *L. pneumophila* cannot multiply under these conditions but they do survive for they remain viable and this indicates that a great range of habitats is capable of harboring this bacterium.

Better: Dogs were housed in a climate-controlled room with artificial lighting, provided with food, and handled. Under these conditions, *L. pneumophila* did not multiply, but they did survive, indicating that a range of habitats may harbor this bacterium.

Identify quoted passages from other texts

Any time you copy another writer's or speaker's exact words directly in the text, it must be set off in a way that shows it to be a quote. How this is done is determined by such factors as the quote's length (40 words or less is a common dividing point), the nature of the material being quoted, the country in which the document is being published, and both editorial and personal preferences.

Short quotes (called run-in quotations) are usually placed directly in the text, with quotation marks at their beginning and end. American and British styles for run-in quotations differ in their punctuation (Table 7.1). In general, U.S. and Canadian publications follow the American style, but U.K. and Australian publications follow the British style (Council of Science Editors, 2006).

The American style is to use single quotation marks only for a quote within a quote. The names of articles or book chapters are treated the same way. If a run-in quotation is more than a single paragraph, begin each paragraph with a quotation mark but close only the end of the last paragraph with a quotation mark.

Table 7.1. *Use of quotation marks in run-on quotations that appear within the text*

Context	American system	British system
To set off the primary quotation	double quotation marks at the beginning and end	single quotation marks at the beginning and end
To set off a quotation that appears within another quotation	single quotation marks at the beginning and end	double quotation marks at the beginning and end
Position of closing quotation mark in relationship to punctuation of the sentence	after a comma, period, exclamation mark, or question mark; before a semicolon or colon	"according to the sense" – before the punctuation except when the quotation is a complete sentence

> Matthews states that "In his 1997 book, *Digital Literacy*, Paul Gilster quotes Vannevar Bush's seminal 1945 article, 'As We May Think,' and calls it 'the first visualization of hypertext in the modern sense.'"

> According to the CDC director, recurrent polycystic kidney disease is "unparalleled in this population.

> "If the hospitalization rate for this disease continues to climb as it has done this year, we are facing a problem of enormous proportions."

Longer direct quotes (called block quotations, excerpts, or extracts) may be set off as a separate block of type by indenting each line on the left side (in the same position as a new paragraph), and single spacing without quotation marks. The right margin stays the same as for the regular text. Sometimes the excerpt is set in a smaller font size than the main text. If the text that introduces the excerpt does not make its source clear, the excerpt should end with a parenthetical indication of the source, placed after the closing punctuation mark of the excerpt.

> The problem of gobbledygook is especially prevalent in science, politics, and law. Alred *et al.* (2003) offer this example:

> > I hereby authorize the above repair work to be done along with the necessary material and hereby grant you and/or your employees permission to operate the car or truck herein described on streets, highways, or elsewhere for the purpose of testing and/or inspection. An express mechanic's lien is hereby acknowledged on above car or truck to secure the amount of repairs thereto.   (p. 243)

> These authors suggest direct rewording:

> > You have my permission to do the repair work listed on this work order and to use the necessary material. You may drive my vehicle to test its performance. I understand that you will keep my vehicle until I have paid for all repairs.   (Alred *et al.*, 2003, pp. 243–44.)

With any direct quotation, be careful to enclose only the actual words used, not your restatement or interpretation. Follow the wording, spelling, and punctuation exactly. Whenever possible, verify the quotation from the original. To indicate an omission in quoted material, use three spaced periods (ellipses).

> Employees of the U.S. government may file a statement attesting that a typescript was prepared "as part of their official duties."

> Pauling stated that "Vitamin C . . . appears to be of value . . ."

Place other punctuation marks in proper relation to quotation marks. In American usage, the comma and period always appear inside quotation marks. The colon and semicolon are placed outside the quotation marks. Question marks and dashes go inside the closing quotation mark when they belong to the quotation, but outside when they do not.

> What did the author mean by "anti-rotaviral"?
> The term "pyrexia" is replacing the word "fever."
> Both the subjects and the researchers in the test were "blind," but the observers knew.
> We studied "mating readiness"; the other research team studied "recalcitrance."

Know when not to use quotation marks

Quotation marks are used in two different ways – to draw attention to words or phrases, or to attribute them to some other speaker or author. Do not overuse quotation marks for emphasis. Instead of using slang and colloquialisms within quotation marks, search for more exact terms and use more formal English.

In journals, quotation marks are often used around new technical terms, old terms used in an unusual way, or simply to draw attention to a word. (In books, italics are often preferred.) Used sparingly, these are acceptable when used to point out that the term is used in context for a unique or special purpose; in this way, they substitute for *so-called*.

Indirect quotations are paraphrases of a speaker's words or ideas. Do not enclose indirect quotations (usually introduced by *that*) in quotation marks.

> *Direct quotation:* Albert Einstein said, "Technological progress is like an axe in the hands of a pathological criminal."
> *Indirect quotation:* Jim Samuels said that he saw the sequel to the movie *Clones*, and it was the same movie!

Common nicknames, bits of humor, technical terms, and trite or well-known expressions (if they must appear) can stand on their own without quotation marks. Proverbial, biblical, and well-known literary expressions do not need quotation marks. Commonly known facts available in numerous sources need neither a source citation nor quotation marks unless the material is taken word-for-word from one particular source.

Hyphenation rules are complex and changing

Hyphens have two general purposes, dividing and compounding. They function primarily as spelling devices, but also can link or separate words or replace

Table 7.2. *Ten hyphenation rules that generally apply*

Guideline	Examples
1. Use a hyphen to create compound modifiers that precede a noun	pollen-bearing hairs; three-pronged structure
2. Use a hyphen to avoid ambiguity	The food co-op bought a chicken coop; re-cover the cage so the birds can recover.
3. Use hyphens in compound numbers from 21 to 99	twenty-one, ninety-nine
4. Use hyphens in fractions and ratios that function as adjectives	a four-to-one vote; three-quarters gone
5. Use a hyphen to reduce redundancy in series	The first-, second-, and third-born offspring were larger.
6. Use a hyphen with letter or number modifiers	5-week-old chick, H-bomb
7. Use hyphens with strings of modifiers that express a single thought when the string comes before the noun, does not have an adverb as its first word, and would not make sense if each word modified the noun without the aid of the others	green-algae-covered ponds, scale-infested trees BUT NOT freshly collected samples, a new digital analyzer, or equipment that is out of date
8. Use a hyphen with a prefix when the root word is a proper noun	pre-Darwinian
9. Use a hyphen when the same vowel ends the prefix and begins the root word (especially if *i* is the repeated vowel)	anti-inflammatory; pre-existing
10. Do not use a hyphen when it isn't needed	Unless misleading or awkward letter combinations result, the following prefixes may be used without hyphenation: pre, post, re, sub, super, micro, mini, multi, non.

prepositions. Their most common use is to join compound words (such as *cost–benefit* analysis). They also form the compound numbers from *twenty-one* through *ninety-nine*, and fractions (such as *three-quarters*) when they are written out.

The decision whether to use hyphens with compound words – or omit them – often requires the aid of a good unabridged dictionary. The classical rules governing this set of uses are complex, covering such topics as whether the compound word is permanent or temporary and whether the words are so closely associated that they constitute a single concept.

As a spelling device, the hyphen is supposed to make life easier, but attempts to detail all its various uses tend to only increase the hyphenation confusion that many writers feel. In addition, the rules are changing, and even the authorities do not always agree. The use of hyphens in scientific writing clearly is declining. Although some rules still seem to generally apply (Table 7.2), there is a strong tendency either to form new single-word terms or to use strings of modifiers without hyphenation. Consult your intended publication for evidence of any strong prejudices, consult a standard dictionary for specific guidance, and then above all, be consistent.

Hyphens are also used to divide words at the ends of lines. Such divisions are made between syllables, but not all syllable breaks are acceptable end-of-line breaks. (Consult a dictionary.) Automatic hyphenation done by some word processing programs can produce some unusual word divisions. In general, it is best to turn off the automatic hyphenation option on such programs.

The main context in which this hyphenation role occurs is in the production of camera-ready copy. Much typesetting today is done in "ragged-right" style, with lines left unjustified so that the right-hand margin of the type column is irregular, but occasionally you may be asked to produce text that is "justified" (aligned to both margins). If justification is done with no hyphenation, the spacing between words is adjusted, sometimes to the extent of looking very strange.

When type is set in justified lines with hyphenation, it is inevitable that some words will be broken. Such text looks attractive, but it can be difficult to read. Furthermore, if a typescript is submitted in this style, there is a good chance that at least a few line-end hyphens may be carried over mistakenly as obligatory hyphens in the typeset copy. Unless your intended journal specifies otherwise, don't justify the text. By submitting ragged-right copy, you will minimize the chances of accidental erroneous hyphenation in the typeset copy.

Exercise 7.1. Punctuation

Correct the punctuation in these sentences.

1. Indicate optimum instrument settings for temperature humidity rainfall and performance.

2. When examined closely, the skeleton bears many bumpy spines, that project from the surface of the animal

3. Class Echinoidea which includes sea urchins sand dollars and heart urchins is not closely related to class "Ascomyceteae."

4. The adults are radially symmetrical but the larvae are bilateral and it is generally held that this phylum evolved from bilateral ancestors and that radial symmetry arose as an adaptation to a sessile way of life.

5. The clinician asked, How did the patient die?; the answer was not obvious.

6. The essay, The Future of Veterinary Medicine, appeared in the early 1960's.

Table 7.3. *Capitalization of proper and common nouns*

Proper noun	Common noun
Appalachian Mountains	the mountains
Eastern Hemisphere	the eastern world
Mesozoic era	an ancient era
Celsius (scientist's name)	centigrade
Chemistry 605	chemistry class

Capitalize consistently

In general, all books and journals are using fewer capital letters than they once did. Still, to state all the rules for employing capitals would be nearly impossible here. (Capitalization rules in the 1984 *U.S. Government Printing Office Style Manual* cover 36 pages!)

Usage varies, and almost every rule has exceptions and variations. This confusion is more apparent than real, however. Most capitalized words are proper nouns, major words in titles, or first words of sentences. However, a few problematic situations recur commonly enough in biomedical and biological writing to be worth special note. If you still have questions on capitalization of specific words after reviewing the guidelines below, consult a standard dictionary and follow its lead.

Remember proper and common nouns

You may not have consciously thought about this point of grammar for years, but when you were younger, language teachers almost certainly drilled you on it. A noun that designates a specific person, place, or thing is called a proper noun. A noun that designates any and all of a class of persons, places, or things is a common noun. These two noun types differ in their capitalization requirements (Table 7.3). All proper nouns begin with capitals. Common names generally do not (except in special situations such as titles, see below).

Common nouns include chemicals, generic names of medicines, diseases, anatomical parts, or common names derived from the scientific names of plants and animals. When such names include modifiers derived from proper nouns, however, these modifiers are usually capitalized *(German measles, Darwinian finches)*. In the same way, capitalize the significant parts of the name of a manufactured product *(Pyrex glass)* and the vernacular names of plant varieties *(Yellow Dent corn)*. Capitalize the full names of government agencies, departments, divisions, organizations, and companies *(Department of Agriculture, Warner Communications Inc.)*.

Animal breeds are common nouns. As such, their names should be lower case. However, in a paper mentioning several breeds of animals, capitalizing only modifiers derived from proper nouns gives the page a very uneven appearance. Some writers and editors feel this lack of uniformity in capitalization is undesirable. They capitalize the full names of all breeds as a matter of equality. Be sure to examine a copy of your intended journal choice for examples of their policy.

Uneven capitalization: The affected animals included Virginia deer, golden hamsters, and miniature Irish wolfhounds.

All breeds and species capitalized: The second trial used French Poodles, Maine Coon Cats, and Parakeets.

Capitalize significant words in titles

Whether the title appears at the beginning of a work or is mentioned within running text, the role of capitalization is to help readers more readily distinguish a title from the adjacent text. There are various systems for doing this. Note that some reference systems for scientific and technical publications do not follow the usual guidelines, but have their own systems.

The classic system is to capitalize the initial letters of the first and last words of a title or subtitle, as well as all major (or "significant") words. Do not capitalize articles *(a, an, the)*, conjunctions *(and, but, if)* or short prepositions *(at, in, on, of)* unless they begin the title.

> For the test, be sure to read the book, *How to Write and Publish a Scientific Paper*, but for now you can ignore *The 1984 Summary of Wildlife Disease Reports*.

Some systems capitalize prepositions if they contain more than four letters *(between, because, until, after)* and use lower case for shorter ones.

> She suggested that the participants should read the new book, *Weight Loss by Dieting Without Exercise*. I prefer *Lose Ten Pounds in Ten Days*.
>
> See Turton's 1802 classic, *System of Nature After the Three Grand Kingdoms of Animals, Vegetables, and Minerals*.

Others maintain that only a word's function, not its length, should determine whether to capitalize it. They feel that even long prepositions such as *between* nearly always are most properly put in lower case.

> His career really began with the publication of his insightful work, *Behavioral Interactions of Hospitalized Patients before and since the Arrival of Viagra*.

The first word of hyphenated compounds in titles is nearly always capitalized; the second word often is not, although either of these styles is correct. Some authorities capitalize the word following the hyphen only if it is a noun or a proper adjective, or if it is equal in importance to the first word. The word after such prefixes as *anti-, ex-, re-,* and *self-* may or may not be capitalized.

> *Aspirin and Anti-Heartworm Therapy*
> *The Role of Cancer-Inducing Agents*
> *Observations on a Hand-reared Baboon*
> *Short-term Goals and Long-term Management*
> *Self-measurements of Femoral Neck-shaft Angle*

All this seeming complexity and competition between systems may change with the popularity of word processing. Most word processing software programs include a case command with the option "sentence case" which capitalizes all words in the title automatically. Authors are certainly ready to make the switch as soon as editors are ready to embrace it.

Check journal requirements

Some journals, publishers, and graduate schools specify a capitalization style; others don't. Make every effort to mimic the style of the journal in which you intend to publish. Examine recent issues. Note the figure legends, table captions, reference lists, and typescript headings and subheadings. You will probably find a definite capitalization style, even if one has not been spelled out formally in the publication's *Instructions to Authors*.

Capitalization is particularly variable in reference citations. Sometimes, article titles have the significant words capitalized. However, many journals prefer that article or chapter titles be treated as though they were sentences.

> *Capitalized article title:* Yalow, R. S. and S. A. Bernson. 1959. Assay of Plasma Insulin in Human Subjects by Immunological Methods. *Nature* 184: 1648–1649.
>
> *Sentence-style article title:* Guhl, A. M. 1968. Social inertia and social stability in chickens. *Animal Behaviour* 16: 219–232.

Exercise 7.2. Capitalization

Indicate accepted capitalization in the following sentences and titles.

1. The afghan hound ate plaster of paris.

2. The Study Sample included 15 greyhounds, 14 malamutes, and 10 spanish terriers.

3. adenine and guanine are nucleotides called purines.

4. A person can live normally without the Adrenal Medullae, but not without the Cortices.

5. these bacteria inhabit all Biomes of the northern hemisphere.

6. *A book title:* what's so funny about science? by sidney harris

7. *The title of a scientific research paper capitalized by the "significant word" system:* assessment of the role of alcohol in the human stress response

8. *A research paper title capitalized by the sentence system:* A Synopsis Of The Taxonomy Of North American And West Indian Birds

---

Treat scientific names properly

The scientific names of all animals, plants, and microorganisms are based on the rules set forth in the most recent edition of one of four codes, which authors and editors are obligated to accept:

> *International Code of Nomenclature of Bacteria*. 1992. Washington, DC: American Society for Microbiology.
>
> *Virus Taxonomy: Classification and Nomenclature of Viruses. Seventh Report of the International Committee on Taxonomy of Viruses*. 2000. New York: Academic Press.
>
> *International Code of Zoological Nomenclature*. 4th ed. 1999. London: International Trust for Zoological Nomenclature.
>
> *International Code of Botanical Nomenclature (St. Louis Code), adopted by the Sixteenth International Botanical Congress, St. Louis, 1999, 2000*. Konigstein: Koeltz Scientific Books.

Because of differences in usage and in the nature of the organisms themselves, the four major codes differ in some aspects of terminology. For example, in botany a scientific name such as *Acer rubrum* is a "binomial" composed of a generic name and "specific epithet." In bacteriology, a name such as *Staphylococcus aureus* is a "binary combination." In zoology, *Homo sapiens* is a "binomen," and the specific epithet *sapiens* is a "specific name."

The codes also differ somewhat in practice. For example, the botanical code recognizes both subspecies and varieties. The zoological code also recognizes subspecies, but only those varieties named before 1961. The bacteriological code considers subspecies and varieties to be synonymous.

Additional useful references on bacterial nomenclature include *Approved Lists of Bacterial Names* (Skerman, 1989) and *Bergey's Manual of Determinative Bacteriology* (Holt *et al.*, 1994). Other helpful resources on biological nomenclature include Calisher and Fauquet (1992) and Jeffrey (1992).

Capitalize everything but species and variety

The basic systematic categories (*taxa*, singular *taxon*) in all of biology are, in descending order: kingdom, phylum or division, class, order, family, genus, and species. ("King Phillip came over from Germany soused" is one of many easy, if irreverent, mnemonic aids.) The scientific names of all of these taxa and any sub- and supra-divisions are Latin or Latinized forms. All these scientific names but the species name are considered to be proper nouns.

Do not capitalize the name of the species (except for the very rare journal which requires it). Technically, the species name is an adjective or similar modifier of the generic name, rather than a full name in its own right.

For this reason, the species name is never used alone. The same is true of varietal names. For example, you might write of the common house cat as *Felis domestica*, family Felidae, but would never refer to it as simply *domestica*. However, after first mentioning the name in full, you can shorten it to *F. domestica* if the context makes the meaning clear. Note that the shortened form should never be used to begin a sentence.

Underline or italicize names of the genus, species, and below

Word-processing programs commonly include italics. However, underlining (which cues the typesetter to use italics) is often preferred in a typescript because it is easier to read.

The genus and species names are italicized because historically italics were always used to indicate foreign words. Because they are in Latin form like the genus and species, infraspecific taxa such as subspecies or varieties are italicized as well. Names of cultivated varieties (cultivars) are not italicized when they are not Latin or Latinized, but are set off with single quotes.

> *Canis familiaris*, family Canidae
> *Tris tricolor* var. *hirta*
> *Lilium superbum* 'Calico'
> *Melittobia* wasps belong to the order Hymenoptera.

Note that one does not underline or italicize the names of higher taxa such as family or order. (This is one of the more common mistakes in popularized science writing.)

Make the first taxonomic mention a comprehensive one

Genus and species (and variety, if relevant) should be spelled out in full when an organism is first mentioned in a paper. Thereafter, a shortened form or use of the common name is acceptable.

> The pine siskin, *Carduelis pinus*, is common here. This gregarious siskin eats seeds.

The most conservative usage also adds the name of the scientist who first officially described and named the organism in print. This author citation need appear only once in the text, and usually does not appear in the title. Some publications take this concept to the extreme, and also include parts of the higher taxonomic classification of the organism.

> For an attractive ornamental plant, consider *Prunus australis* Beadle.
> *Spathius impus* Matthews (Hymenoptera: Braconidae) is parasitic upon bark beetles.
> *Musca domestica* L. is the common housefly. *[The L. is for Linnaeus, one of the scientists so widely recognized that a standard abbreviation for his name is allowed.]*

Note that the word *species* retains the *s* in both singular and plural, and that the plural of *genus* is *genera*.

> *Ixodes scapularis* is a species of tick known to transmit Lyme disease; other species of *Ixodes* may too. This genus is only one of several genera known to be involved.

When an organism has been identified only to the generic level, the abbreviation "sp." is sometimes used as a shorthand for "some unidentified species of." The abbreviation "spp." signifies "several species of." Neither should be underlined or italicized.

> *Zanthoxylum* spp. were abundant, but *Drypetes* sp. was apparently rare.

After this first mention, the organism may be referred to by its common (vernacular) name if you wish. Unless writing for a publication that prefers otherwise, do not capitalize this common name.

> *Solenopsis invicta* Buren . . . *S. invicta* . . . the red imported fire ant.
> The oak, *Quercus velutina* Lamarck, is found in North America. A relatively large tree, *Q. velutina* is prized for its wood. Its common name, yellow oak, alludes to the inner bark color.

Any family name can be transformed to a vernacular name by dropping the initial capitalization and the terminal *-ae*. Any generic name may be used as a vernacular name as well; this practice is common in bacteriology. Generic names are neither italicized nor capitalized when used in the vernacular sense.

> The family Chironomidae includes biting chironomids.
> *Salmonella typhosa* is a deadly salmonella.

Use foreign words and phrases to inform, not impress

Many words from other languages have been incorporated into the English language. In many cases, this happened so long ago that we no longer even recognize their foreign origin. These words seldom are an issue. The problem comes when words and phrases that are recognizably foreign are used primarily as affectation,

Table 7.4. *Examples of changing acceptance of foreign words and phrases*

Still considered "foreign" enough to take italicizing and/or original pluralization	Becoming "assimilated" enough to drop the italics and change its pluralization	
	Singular	Plural
sine qua non	formula	formulae has become formulas
coup de grâce	memorandum	memoranda and memorandums are both acceptable
per se	a priori	none
coup d'état (coups d'état)	milieu	milieux is becoming milieus
Nonitalicized scientific words from Latin such as mitochondrion (mitochondria), bacillus (bacilli)	serum	sera is becoming serums
Nonitalicized words from Greek such as analysis (analyses)	appendix, index	appendices is becoming appendixes, indices is becoming indexes

to impress readers rather than to make an idea clearer than its English language equivalent would.

Consider degree of assimilation

Words and phrases that have been full assimilated into the English language do not need any sort of special treatment, although for a while they may retain their original accent marks (especially if they are of French origin).

Foreign words and expressions that have not been assimilated fully (Table 7.4) should be italicized if printed, or underlined if typewritten. This rule is often bent, however. Scientific writing is clearly moving away from the use of italicized words and phrases. Find an example in the journal if you can. Better yet, reword the sentence to use a plainly English equivalent for the word or phrase.

Watch plurals, because their form also depends upon degree of assimilation. Latin words that end in *-a* are made plural by adding *-e*. Those that end in *-um* are made plural by changing the *-um* to *-a*. This can be confusing. Many scientists fail to pronounce and spell these words correctly, speaking of "one media" or "a single larvae."

These data are consistent because each datum is independent of the others.

Wasp larvae in general are common, but the larva of *Eumenes* is not.

A microfilaria is a worm-like creature; heartworm microfilariae sometimes invade a dog's heart.

Exercise 7.3. Scientific names and other foreign words and phrases

A. Indicate how the following scientific names should be handled.
1. the parasitic wasp, m. atrata
2. the dandelion, taraxacum officionale, family compositae, class dicotyledonae
3. the honeybee, apis mellifera var. ligustica
4. the human malarial parasite, plasmodium falciparum Bignami
5. the starfish (asterias) belongs to class asteroidea, phylum echino-dermata, in the section deuterostomia.

B. Indicate correct type use (italics or Roman) and format in the following sentences. Follow the most conservative route.
1. When acceptable, use the formulas already given in the book, Official Methods in Microbiology.
2. For information on the in vivo action of green plant pigments, i.e. chlorophyll, see Arnon's article in Scientific American and Calvin and Bassham's book, The Photosynthesis of Carbon Compounds.
3. Our experiments cannot identify the underlying biophysical alter-ations, viz., effects within the membrane itself.
4. Reduced oxygen tension provides the best environment for in vitro parasite development, as shown by Udeinya *et al* (2005).

As foreign words become assimilated, their plural forms give way to English plurals. However, because science tends to be fairly conservative, the acceptability of the English plural forms often differs with the type of publication and its audience. Thus, one journal may pluralize *calyx* as *calyces*, while another uses *calyxes*.

In biomedical writing, certain commonly used Latin phrases cause additional trouble because they most properly follow the noun they modify. These include *in vivo* (in the living body), *in vitro* (in an artificial environment), *de novo* (anew), *in vacuo* (in the absence of air or in reduced pressure) and *in silico* (biological simulation studies done with a computer). To place them before the noun, as though they were regular adjectives, is incorrect. Rather than "*in vivo* tests," say "tests *in vivo*." However, usage is shifting, and these eventually may be accepted as regular adjectives placed before nouns and without italics.

Prefer English equivalents over Latin and Greek abbreviations

An educated literary style once included the use of a number of Latin and Greek terms, particularly in footnotes. These are seldom seen in literary works today, and almost never in biological or medical publications. Avoid abbreviations such as *loc. cit.* (in the place cited), *op. cit.* (in the work cited), and *ibid.* (in the same work). For *viz.*, substitute "namely"; for *circa* use "about." The use of *etc.* (and so forth), while still acceptable, is rapidly falling out of favor; it commonly is not italicized (underlined).

The abbreviations below are still permissible, but are preferably confined to parenthetical references. However, their English equivalent is acceptable or even preferred. Punctuate as for their English equivalent. All these abbreviations are increasingly being used without italics and without periods.

> *i.e.* (*id est*, that is)
> *cf.* (*confer*, compare)
> *e.g.* (*exempli gratia*, for example)
> *et al.* (*et alii*, and others; note that the *al.* requires a period, but *et* does
>   not)

FINE-TUNE NUMBER USE

When you have mastered numbers, you will in fact no longer be reading numbers, any more than you read words when reading books You will be reading meanings.

> – *W. E. B. DuBois*

Numbers are the heart and soul of most scientific research. If they are not reported clearly, a paper's value can be compromised or lost entirely. But while few dispute their importance, many are willing to debate fine points of how they best should be expressed. Should the number ten be written out or expressed as a numeral? Should large numbers be given scientific notation? What should be done with a series that includes numbers of very different magnitude?

One way to handle the situation is by edict. For example, many scientific journals now use Arabic numerals in preference to words for almost every situation in which a number is used. Check the *Instructions to Authors* for your intended journal, and follow their lead.

In the absence of a clear edict, however, the following guidelines may help. Whatever style of expressing numbers you adopt, remember to be consistent.

Numerals versus written numbers

Deciding whether to use numerals or words to express numbers can seem problematic because various systems exist. The most conservative style of scientific writing uses figures (numerals) to express numbers 10 and above, and uses words to express numbers below 10 except when they are used as page numbers, as figure and table numbers, or with units of measurement. Several exceptions and instances of special usage expand on this rule. This conservative style is summarized in Table 7.5.

Table 7.6 summarizes the opposite situation – cases where conservative use specifies that numbers should be expressed as words. In general, the numbers

Table 7.5. *Use numerals – conservative rules*

General guideline	Examples
All numbers 10 and above	trial 14; 35 animals; 16 genera of legumes
Numbers that immediately precede a unit of measurement	a wing 10 cm long; 35 mg of drug; 21 days
Numbers with decimals; fractions that include whole numbers	7.38 mm; 4 1/2 hours
Numbers that represent statistical or mathematical functions or results; percentages; ratios	multiply by 5; fewer than 6%; 3.75 times as many; the 2nd quartile
Numbers that represent exact times or dates; ages; size of samples, subsamples or populations; specific numbers of subjects in an experiment; scores and points on a scale; exact sums of money; numerals as numerals	About 3 weeks ago, at 1:00 a.m. on January 25, 2000, the 25-year-old patients with IQ scores above 125 all awoke simultaneously in the nursing home at 125 Oak Street. They were paid $25 apiece to go back to sleep.
Numbers below 10 that are grouped for comparison with numbers 10 and above in the same paragraph	4 of 16 analyses; the 1st and 15th of the 25 responses; lines 2 and 21
Numbers that denote a specific place in a numbered series; parts of books and tables; each number in a list of four or more numbers.	Trial 6; Grade 9 (but the *ninth* grade); the groups consisted of 5, 9, 1, and 4 animals, respectively.

Table 7.6. *Use words – conservative rules for situations in which numbers should be written as words*

General guideline	Examples
Numbers below 10 that do not represent precise measurements; numbers used in an indefinite, approximate, or general manner	five conditions; trials were repeated four times; a one-tailed *t* test; a three-way interaction; about thirty years old
Numbers below 10 that are grouped for comparison with numbers below 10	the second of four stimuli; five of eight living animals; in six cases, the disease lasted five times as long as in the other four.
Any number that begins a sentence, title, or heading (but reword to avoid this whenever possible)	Five patients improved, and 15 did not. Sixty-nine percent of the sample was contaminated.
Common fractions (those without whole numbers)	one quarter; reduced by half; a three-quarters majority
The numbers zero and one when words would be easier to comprehend than figures, or the words do not appear in context with numbers 10 and above	a one-line computer code; zero-based budgeting; one animal gave birth (*but* only 1 in 18 gave birth).

below 10 would be written, once again subject to a number of modifications. Ordinal numbers, which express degree or sequence, may follow the same rules *(third, 15th)*. Alternatively they may be expressed as numerals whatever their size unless they are single words *(fourth, nineteenth, 44th)*.

When several numbers appear in the same sentence or paragraph, express them all in the same way, regardless of other rules and guidelines. Generally, Arabic numerals would be used whenever you have three or more numbers in a series, even if each of the numbers were below 10.

> The 7 dogs, 8 cats, 9 mice, and 6 gerbils were exposed to applications of flea powder.
> The analysis revealed 22 complete answers, 4 incomplete responses, and 7 illegible ones.

Know when to combine words and numbers

Use a combination of figures and words to express rounded large numbers, starting with millions *(a grant budget of $1.5 million; almost 4 billion species)*.

Numerals and words are also combined when they appear as back-to-back modifiers *(two 13-ml aliquots)*. Generally it is best to keep the numeric form with units of measurement. Hyphenation minimizes potential confusion *(twenty 6-year-old patients* vs. *twenty-six year-old patients)*. If more than two numbers appear back-to-back in a string *(six 3–5 day intervals)*, rewrite the phrase *(six intervals of 3–5 days each)*.

You may spell out whichever number can more easily be expressed in words. Sometimes these combinations are awkward to read; in these cases, spelling out both numbers is preferred.

> *Awkward:* The 1st three animals; the first 3 animals
> *Better:* the first three animals

Do not start sentences with numerals

When a number and unit begin a sentence, you must write them as words, even if they would otherwise be written as figures. Revise such sentences whenever possible.

> *Incorrect:* 550 ml of hydrochloric acid should be added.
> *Correct but difficult to read:* Five hundred and fifty milliliters of hydrochloric acid should be added.
> *Revised:* Add 550 ml of hydrochloric acid.

Prefer Arabic numerals to Roman numerals

Roman numerals should be used only in certain stylized situations, such as the numbering of preliminary pages of a book or the tables in some journals, blood-clotting factors, or cranial nerves. At the same time, if Roman numerals are part of an established terminology do not change them to Arabic numerals. (For example, continue to speak of a *Type II error*.)

Arabic numerals are easier to read and interpret than Roman numerals are. Use them to number experimental research groups, organisms, virus types, and volume numbers in bibliographic material (even though Roman numerals may have been used in the original).

> group 3, echovirus 30
> case 3 in experiment 5
> blood-clotting factor VIII
> *Creative Acupuncture* 9: 6–35
> See the author's note in the preface (p. xiv).

For units such as weights, percentages, and degrees of temperature, use Arabic numerals. For example, write *3.2 m* or *72 °F*, regardless of the way other numerical expressions may be treated. Unless a journal specifies otherwise, do not follow written numbers with a figure in parentheses representing the same number ("send three [3] copies to the editor"). However, it is both acceptable and desirable to include parenthetical material that amplifies understanding of other numerical data.

> He was given 2 mg of tetracycline on each of three occasions.
> A 10% mortality rate is common.
> Necrosis occurred in almost 20% (50/247) of the cases.

The SI metric system for measurements and weights

There actually are several metric systems, including the centimeter-gram-second system and the meter-kilogram-second system. However, these systems are gradually being replaced by a modernized metric system called SI, for Système International d'Unités. It provides unambiguous symbols that are standard in all languages (Young and Huth, 1998). The system is constructed upon seven base plus two supplementary units of measurement (Table 7.7).

Most scientific journals use the SI system and also permit some widely used units outside the SI system, such as liter, hour, bar, and angstrom. Most scientific style manuals include a chart to convert measurements from traditional units to their SI equivalents.

All other units for physiochemical quantities are derived from these SI base units, though they may have special names and their own symbols. For example, the widely used liter is non-SI; its equivalent is one cubic decimeter. (Note that in the United States the symbol "L" is generally preferred, because lower case "l" can be confused with 1.) Prefixes join base units to express multiples. Because kilogram, the base unit for mass, already has a prefix, it is an exception. In this case attach the prefix to the unit stem "gram" rather than adding it to kilogram.

Table 7.7. *Fundamental SI units of measurement*

Quantity	Name	Symbol
Base units		
length	meter (metre)	m
mass	kilogram	kg
time	second	s
amount of substance	mole	mol
thermodynamic temperature	kelvin	K
electric current	ampere	A
luminous intensity	candela	cd
Supplementary units		
plane angle	radian	rad
solid angle	steradian	sr

For quantities much larger or smaller than a given base unit, standard prefixes are used (Table 7.8). The usual practice is to choose the prefix for multiples of 10^2 or 10^{-3} so the number accompanying the unit is less than 1000. Only one prefix may be used for most symbols, and a prefix is never used alone. Both the prefix and the unit it modifies are either abbreviated or spelled out.

> *Incorrect:* Add 6 mµg of substrate.
> *Correct:* Add 6 ng of substrate. [or six nanograms]

When using SI, employ exponents for such expressions as *2 m^2* (rather than *2 sq. m*). Units are created and definitions are modified as measurement technology progresses.

Table 7.8. *Standard SI prefixes common in biomedical writing*

Factor (power of ten)	SI prefix	Symbol
18	exa	E
15	peta	P
12	tera	T
9	giga	G
6	mega	M
3	kilo	k
−3	milli	m
−6	micro	µ
−9	nano	n
−12	pico	p
−15	femto	f
−18	atto	a

Very large and very small numbers

Very large or very small numbers can be expressed in different ways. One is to use SI prefixes. Another is to use scientific notation. Check the *Instructions to Authors* and be consistent throughout the document.

> *SI prefixes:* 8,000,000 N/m^2 (force of newtons per square meter) becomes 8 MN/m^2 (not 8 N/mm^2 because the acceptable prefix should be attached to the numerator)
> *Scientific notation:* $8 \times 10^6 \ N/m^2$

Often, a number can be rounded off without losing meaning. For example, 6,234,275 could be expressed as 6.2 million for most practical purposes. If a quantity must be converted to SI units, multiply the quantity by the exact conversion factor, then round it off appropriately. The format for reporting very large round numbers depends somewhat on the journal. In the absence of other specific instructions, substitute a word for part of the number (such as 1.5 million for 1,500,000). Because of usage differences between Europe and the United States, it is better to avoid the words *billion, trillion*, and *quadrillion*.

When reporting large but exact numbers, U.S. journals use commas between groups of three digits *(695,446)* in most figures of 1,000 or more. (Exceptions include page numbers, binary digits, serial numbers, degrees of temperature, degrees of freedom, and numbers to the right of a decimal point.) For an international audience, do not break up numbers above 999 into groups of three digits with commas. In some countries, a comma indicates a decimal point. Instead, international journals often leave spaces *(695 446)*.

The number of places to which a large decimal value is carried reflects the precision with which the quantity was measured. Omit statistically non-significant decimal places in tabular data. One useful rule of thumb is to report summary statistics to two digits more than are in the raw data. For example, if scores on a test are whole numbers, report descriptive statistics to two decimal places.

Similar entries in a table row or column should be measured to the same level of accuracy, and the number of significant digits must be commensurate with the precision of your experimental method. The best level of precision for numerical data will vary, but rounded-off values often display patterns and exceptions more clearly than precise values.

Percentages

Three similar-sounding words confuse this subject. The term *percent* (sometimes written as two words, *per cent*) means "in, to, or for every hundred"; the symbol % can take its place. Always place a number before the symbol. *Percentage* means "a number or amount stated in a percent." *Percentile* is a statistical term for the value in a distribution of frequencies divided into 100 equal groups.

Except at the beginning of a sentence, use the symbol % and Arabic numbers for percentages. Repeat the symbol for each number in a series or range, including zeroes.

Table 7.9. *An example of misleading use of percentages*

Group	n	Mating success (%)
Experienced	55	50%
Naive, drug-treated	5	60%
Experienced, drug-treated	5	80%
Naive controls	25	41%

> These values were compared with the percentages for 1982.
> Ten percent of our students scored at the 99th percentile.
> The incidence of mononucleosis ranged from 0% to 24%.
> The bacteria were found in 15%, 28%, and 0% of the animals in groups
>   1, 2, and 3, respectively.

For purposes of comparison, percentages are often much more useful than an array of raw data. However, handling percentages properly can be tricky. One absolute requirement: whenever percentages (or other proportional figures) are employed, the finite number *(n)* from which the percentages are derived must be given somewhere. Often these numbers are presented in a separate column in the table.

Some authorities also recommend that the text include the actual number of subjects for each percentage if the cited series includes fewer than 100 subjects. They also recommend that you use decimals in percentages in series only when the percentages are based on more than 1,000 subjects.

> Pulmonary disease was present in 50% (16) of the dogs,
> OR . . . in 16 (50%) of the dogs, OR . . . in 50% (16/32) of the dogs.

Whenever there might be a possibility of misunderstanding, state the basis for the percentages. For example, in reporting certain analyses, it may be essential to specify whether moisture-free ("dry") weight, fresh ("wet") weight, or volume was used.

Journals differ in what denominator magnitude (value of *n*) they will accept as adequate basis for a percentage. Percentages given for compared fractions with small denominators are likely to imply statistically significant differences when none in fact exist. In the example in Table 7.9, the percentages of drug-treated naive animals and drug-treated experienced animals look very different (60% vs. 80%), but in fact because of the small sample sizes, the real difference was only due to the differing behavior of a single animal.

Some clinical journals allow percentages only for fractions with denominators greater than 50. Thus, percentages would be given for the reader's convenience for 31/75 (41%) but not for 12/25. When some fractions would appear with percentages and others without them, it might be stylistically better to omit the percentages entirely. If differences in compared fractions are assessed statistically, the assessment must be based on the absolute numbers, not the percentages.

Report statistics sensibly and accurately

Statistical inference is an orderly means for drawing conclusions about a large number of events on the basis of observations collected on a sample of them. As such, it forms an important part of scientific inquiry.

All measures of variable biological parameters should be reported with statistical measures of this variability. In general, the sample mean and standard deviation or standard error of the mean (always appropriately labeled!) should be stated. Medians and ranges may also be given, particularly if the reported data show a strong departure from normality.

As a biological or medical scientist writing for others in your field, be sure that both the text and table emphasize biology or medicine, not statistics. Statistical methods do not need elaborate presentation, nor do the mathematics of the test results need to be detailed. A simple statement of the chosen test and probability level is usually sufficient. Reference a basic text detailing the procedure if you feel readers might need it.

> *Poor:* To determine whether the two species differed in their egg cannibalism rate (Table 1), we used the Fisher Exact Probability Test, in which $P = (A + B)!(C + D)!(A + C)!(B + D)!/N!A!B!C!D!$, to obtain a $P = 0.56$ which was not significant.
>
> *Better:* The differences in the egg cannibalism rates of the two species (Table 1) were not statistically significant (Fisher Exact Probability Test, $P > 0.05$).

Whenever quantitative differences in data are reported that are found not to be due to chance alone, they should be accompanied by statistical statements that are the result of appropriate statistical tests described in the Methods section. In a table, these often are placed in a footnote. (Some journals use letters for footnotes, others symbols, often with a prescribed sequence.) In the text, statistical results are usually presented in a concise style consistent with standard statistics books (ANOVA: $F_{1,11} = 7.98$, $P < 0.02$; Spearman rank correlation: $r_s = 0.81$, $N = 12$, $P < 0.01$).

Guard against statements that seem to imply value judgments about the results of statistical analyses with phrases like "nearly reached significance." Do not describe differences that are not statistically significant as *insignificant*! Likewise, avoid using the term *significant* to describe results when no statistical tests were run and you merely mean "important."

When statistical analysis was a tedious, largely hand-calculated affair, many a scientist shunned it entirely. Now, with the popularity of statistical analysis software, scientists face a strong temptation to overuse statistics, reporting strings of similar analyses or "massaging" data to an unreasonable degree. Almost nothing is more transparent than reliance upon prepackaged analyses without a corresponding understanding of their meaning.

"I don't know, it's a little formulaic."

© Mark Anderson. Reprinted with permission.

Use specialized symbols and notations sparingly and with care

In many scientific professions, communication depends heavily upon specialized notations such as symbols, equations, and formulas. These also are a type of illustration. They often appear on a line by themselves, like an in-text table. If complex, they may be submitted as a camera-ready photograph or digital file, like other artwork (see Chapter 3).

Scientific symbols and notations often express thoughts not easily or efficiently expressed as words. However, they have many drawbacks. They slow typing and word processing speed. They increase printing costs. And most importantly, they provide a stumbling block for audiences unfamiliar with them. Use such notation judiciously, explaining specialized symbols as necessary and carefully following the recommendations in a comprehensive style manual for your field.

Express mathematical formulations clearly. Short and simple equations, such as $x = 3y - 1$, should be set directly into the text, as done here. If a document has a great many equations that are referred to repeatedly in the text, they can be displayed (set on a separate line) and identified with consecutive numbers placed in parentheses at the right margin. For clarity, equations set off from the text need

---

Exercise 7.4. Number use and interpretation

Treat these sentences conservatively, spelling out numbers or changing them to Arabic numerals as appropriate.

1. A full 3/4 (75 percent) of the experimental animals died with 15 hours, but 17 horses (10%) were still alive forty-five days later.

2. The chemicals for the experiment weighed less than 1/5 of a milligram.

3. Approximately 20,500 cells were calculated to be affected.

4. The control group recovered more quickly but a chi-square test of P equals .11 showed the difference was insignificant. We felt this was significant, however, because it showed the drug's effect.

5. The test plot contained ten species of grasses, two species of legumes, six species of trees, and 15 species of cruciferous plants.

---

to be surrounded by space. Triple-space between displayed equations and normal text. Double-space between one equation and another, and between the lines of multi-line equations. When a series of short equations appear in sequence, align them on their equal signs.

$$x(y) = (3y - 1)(z) \tag{1}$$

$$p(x, y) = \sin(x + y) \tag{2}$$

Entering over-under fractions can be a nightmare. Whenever possible, use a slant line or negative exponent to signify division. Change the format to a single line, like this: $(O - E)^2 / E^2$. If a really complex formula cannot be avoided, consider treating it like a figure. Furnish it in the form of a line drawing. Fractional exponents ($X^{0.5}$) may also be used instead of square root and cube root signs (Swanson *et al.*, 1999).

PRACTICING MIXED CORRECTIONS

When writing or editing a typescript, one is confronted with a potpourri of grammatical and rhetorical writing flaws rather than neatly categorized sets such as those presented in a writing book or style manual. The "test" that follows is given as an opportunity for practice of this slightly more realistic sort.

We hope that one of the messages you have received from this book is that more than one way of revising is always possible and almost always acceptable. As always, judge your choices not only by correctness, but also by their clarity, brevity, readability, and communicative power.

Exercise 7.5. Practicing mixed corrections

Find the errors, comment on them, and write a corrected version of the sentences. Your interpretation of certain sentences may differ from ours, but responses should aim in the same direction – toward increased precision and clarity.

1. The authors conclude that there is evidence that the limiting diameter lies between sixteen and twenty angstroms in these cells taken from mammals.

2. The inhibitory activity of the various combinations was studied and isobolograms plotted.

3. The site of action of EDTA is at the cell surface by increasing cell wall permeability.

4. Measurements were made of the pronounced lesions that were in the heart.

5. Numerous strains of T. cruzi are reported to cause chronic *chagas disease*.

6. In the present study, treatment is terminated when fish appear irritated.

7. The wasp S. maculata is a progressive provisioner and transports the flies held ventrally by the middle legs.

8. Figure 24 is a cichlid fish from a Florida pond where metacercariae (at arrow) were found in the gill cavity.

9. You should mix 1500 grams of dye with 7,000 ml of water.

10. Fruits in the diet of Artibeus included an orange, pear, apple and peach.

11. Ichthyophthirius is one of the few parasites of fish with cilia.

12. The authors encountered amorphous material of varying density.

13. The animals were equally divided into 5 groups of 22 each.

14. Cotton swabs were obtained from tracheas.

15. Many of their published results indicated that perhaps MG organisms may be poorly transmitted at times.

16. The results were obtained from HPLC a useful technique for the analysis of aflatoxins in feeds with excellent resolution.

17. There is a possible cause which must be faced up to. It is in regard to whether aflatoxin enters into the blood stream.

18. An excessive amount of solar radiation received at a rapid rate has been shown by a large body of data to have the capability of inflicting epidermal damage.

19. When the horse was circled to the left and right, lameness was evidenced which was not cyclic but continual.

20. None of these dogs, that were housed in runs and were not challenged by exercise, developed any clinical signs of heartworm disease.

8

The rest of the story

Never be afraid to try something new. Remember, amateurs built the ark; professionals built the Titanic.

Since 1946, an American newscaster named Paul Harvey has been broadcasting a radio segment called *The Rest of the Story*. It always begins as a quaint, apparently historical tale about someone that seems very average until the very end, when Harvey dramatically exposes a missing element that reveals the deeper significance hidden within. Then he concludes: "And now you know . . . the rrrrest of the story!"

You are now at that dramatic moment, ready to share your scientific tale with the world. Only relative details stand between you and scientific publication. We have no way of knowing what will come next in your life, but we are confident that you are on the brink of something great. Go forward with confidence. Soon you will be celebrating, and soon afterward, planning your next project.

PREPARING TO PUBLISH

If you think that something small cannot make a difference, try going to sleep with a mosquito in the room.

You've just finished going through your document for what seems like the hundredth time. Take a break, and get some sleep, then come back to the document one last time. Nine basic questions provide a good framework for a final review of nearly any scientific paper. If any of them cause you problems, refer back to the material in earlier chapters.

1. *Is the title accurate, succinct, and effective?*

Titles are more effective when they begin with a keyword. Check *Instructions to Authors* for any limits on title length. Subtitles, if allowed and used, should be able to stand alone, but not duplicate the main title. Assure that the title is grammatically correct, and pay particular attention to the placement of modifiers. Double meanings that arise from a misplaced or dangling modifier can quickly land you a spot in the Blooper Hall of Fame!

*2.   Does the abstract represent all the content within the allowed
      length?*

An abstract of a research report should include the study design, experimental subjects, methods, results, and interpretations. An abstract of a case report should briefly characterize the patient as well as the unusual features of the case. A review article abstract usually tells what the review is about, rather than representing its content in highly condensed form.

*3.   Does the introductory material set the stage adequately
      but concisely?*

Remember the 3-part format: orient the reader, disclose the gap to be filled, and present the question you propose to answer. At the end of the Introduction section, have you clearly spelled out the focus of your research?

4.   Is the rest of the text in the right sequence?

Most full-length research papers in scientific journals have a fairly conventional format, but the position of the Abstract, Acknowledgments, and footnoted material often varies. Case reports, review articles, editorials, and book reviews appear in many different formats, and are more likely to show deviations in sequence.

5.   Is all of the text really needed?

Sometimes papers are overwritten. Can some of the document be discarded? Does any of the text repeat information presented elsewhere in the document? Remember that your document will be judged by content, not its length.

6.   Is any needed content missing?

Sometimes – especially if a writer is interrupted while working – important material gets left out. Keep this question in mind, and such gaps will probably jump to your attention.

7.   Do data in the text agree with data in the tables?

If you wrote the text with the tables sitting beside you, as we suggested, you should have no problems with this. Check anyway. Surprising things sometimes happen.

*8.   Should any of the tables or illustrations be omitted,
      restructured, or combined?*

The more time you have invested in tables and illustrations already, the more psychologically difficult it can be to change them now. However, if some tables or figures have turned out to be of only tangential importance to the basic research questions, delete them.

9.   Are the correct references included?

Look for essential references that may be missing, and for unnecessary references that may be included. The farther along a typescript goes in the sequence of drafts, the more likely it is that changes have led to errors.

Use only enough references to support key statements. Do not include extras just to show that you are familiar with the related literature. Direct the reader to relevant references for previously described methods, giving only enough detail to orient readers and alert them to any modifications you made.

Theses and dissertations are sometimes an exception to this rule. Advisory committees may require extensive review and referencing to showcase a graduate student's mastery of the literature in a research field. Before the research papers that arise from this work are submitted for publication, however, remove all but the most directly relevant material.

Double-check references and attributions

The last question in the previous section focused on assuring that your document included the relevant references. The next question should be, are these references cited correctly?

Several studies of the accuracy of citations and presentations of others' assertions in the biomedical literature have revealed surprisingly high rates of error. An analysis of 300 randomly selected references in six frequently cited veterinary journals found major errors in 30% of them (Hinchcliff *et al.*, 1993). Misquotation rates of 12% in medical journals (de Lacey *et al.*, 1985) and 27% in surgical journals (Evans *et al.*, 1990) have been reported.

Spelling problems were the most common error, a particularly important concern because misspellings have the potential to impede computerized retrieval systems or to obscure author identity. Another common error was a failure to cite the original source of information, a disturbing finding because it suggests that authors frequently do not read the original reference. Misquotations of findings in studies by others also were common, carrying the risk that through repeated secondary citation, a major inaccuracy may become established as accepted fact.

Make it an absolute policy never to try to save time by copying references from someone else's list. Such shortcuts may seem harmless, but it is amazing how easily inaccuracies can creep into reference citations.

Verify submission format

Long before now you have, of course, chosen a journal. Now it is time to be certain that you have tailored your submission to its requirements. Check the January issue for the journal's current year of publication. There you will often find *Instructions for Authors* spelled out. Journal *ITAs* vary widely in their comprehensiveness, however. You may also need to refer to the "Uniform Requirements for Manuscripts Submitted to Biomedical Journals" excerpted in Appendix 2.

Examine a recent issue for editorial style. Pay attention to the nitty-gritty of matters such as reference citation style, headings and subheadings, use of footnotes, and figure design. Remember that however attractive the pages may look, they are wrong if they are not in the proper format for the publication to which they are being submitted.

Most probably, you will be submitting your document as electronic copy, though some journals still require paper and others want both. Standard practice dictates that typewritten copy should appear in Pica or Elite type, and the spirit of this requirement has carried forward into electronic manuscript preparation. Although computer-generated fonts differ from one another in size, typewritten Pica and Elite type are roughly equivalent to 12-point and 10-point computer-generated type, respectively. Unless specified otherwise, double space everything that is typed, including tables, figure legends, and footnotes. Use wide margins (a full inch at sides, and at least an inch at top and bottom).

When and if you are asked to submit a document in paper (hard copy) form, do not even consider reducing the font size to squeeze artificially within speci-fied page limitations. Also, unless a journal specifically approves it, do not send tables that have been reduced in size on a photocopier. Such seeming attempts at deviousness will only alienate the editors whose approval is critical to your document's acceptance, and it will probably result in its prompt return.

Unless the *ITA*s specify otherwise, use a proportional serif font style such as New York or Times for the basic text in a conventionally published journal. (Sometimes, a sans serif font such as Courier or Helvetica is used to differenti-ate tabular material, computer addresses, or other such inclusions.) Electronic journals may use only sans serif fonts.

Refer back to Chapter 1 and check that you have all the required entries on the first page. The Abstract or Summary usually appears by itself on the second page. Note whether keywords for indexing services appear here in recent issues of the journal. Mimic the style used.

Begin the Introduction on the third page. Either run the text matter continu-ously or start each subsequent major section on a separate page. Many journals require the latter approach.

Footnotes to text material, if used, are grouped on a separate page, as are figure legends. Each table, with its title, should be on a separate page. Rather than interspersing these non-textual materials throughout the text, assemble all of them in numerical order at the back of the typescript. Some journals require notations within the text margins to indicate approximate locations for tables and figures.

Number all pages

When documents were all typewritten by hand, omitting page numbers was a tempting shortcut, because it allowed material to be inserted or changed later without retyping the entire document. Use of word processing removes this excuse. Given the proper formatting directive, it will automatically repaginate subsequent versions. However, if paper copy is required, starting major sections on separate pages still can help to minimize reprinting.

Always number all pages, including (generally in this order) the title page, abstract, the text itself, and such materials as acknowledgments, references, tables, figure legends, and footnote lists. Once a typescript begins to pass through the hands of editors and reviewers, page numbers provide the only clues as to whether it has remained complete. Furthermore, these editors and reviewers must be able to refer to pages by number in their written comments. Some journals also require that lines be numbered along the left margin for easy reference during editing. Most word processing software can do this automatically on command.

Give the paper its final in-house double review

When the typescript finally seems done, read it once more. Have coauthors or a colleague read it as well. It will undoubtedly still harbor a surprising number of "gremlins." Finding them now is a bit embarrassing, but less so than facing them on the journal reviewer's edited copy or the published page!

Submit the document

Increasingly, journal editors are encouraging electronic submissions because this saves time, money, and hassle for everyone involved in the process. Editors can edit the typescript on the computer screen, and, if necessary, reformat it to their specific printing requirements. An added advantage is that material can be sent directly to data banks to be stored and accessed by on-line systems.

Most journals welcome electronic copy from the beginning. Some start with paper copy, and delay a request for electronic submission until modifications based on the review process have been incorporated. Consult the journal's published *Instructions to Authors* for guidelines on electronic submission.

Include a cover letter with the document

Write and edit this letter carefully – it forms an editor's first impression of you and your work. Be certain to spell the editor's name correctly. Assure that this information is current and correct. Sending a submission to the wrong person can delay it considerably!

In the letter, name the journal and say something nice (but not effusive) about why it is the appropriate place to publish this particular paper. State the title of your document. Identify yourself as corresponding author, and include your full current postal and email addresses and your phone number. Mention any additional information that may facilitate editorial processing, such as the type of article (short communication, research article, case study, etc.). It is quite appropriate to offer suggestions for potential non-local reviewers.

Check the ITAs for other requirements

Often, a journal may require special statements, permissions, and such for legal reasons. Below are some common additions that may need to be expressly mentioned in the cover letter:

> State that all authors have contributed significantly to the paper, understand and endorse it, and have read and approved the version being submitted for publication. (Some journals require a

special statement to this effect, signed by all the coauthors; their *ITAs* may specify its wording.)

Include a signed permission statement from anyone you've mentioned in the acknowledgments and anyone cited under "personal communication" for use of their name and/or data.

Certify that no part has been submitted, accepted for publication, or published elsewhere.

State that the article is original work of the authors except for material in the public domain or excerpts from others' works for which written permission of the copyright owners has been obtained.

Indicate that the authors have no relationship, financial or otherwise, with any manufacturers or distributors of products evaluated in the paper; if this is not true, disclose any such relationship in a footnote to the paper.

If the paper depends critically on another unpublished paper or one that is "in press" in another journal, mention this fact. As a courtesy, include electronic or paper copies of the related paper for the reviewers.

Remember Murphy's Laws

Anything that can go wrong will, and at the worst possible moment. If nothing can go wrong, it will anyway.

– Folk wisdom attributed to U.S. Air Force
Capt. E. A. Murphy and others

Expect the best, but prepare for the worst – this has always been, and continues to be, excellent advice. Assume that packages will become lost in the mail, that photographs will become separated from text, and that figures will be misplaced. Be especially careful to fully label the illustrations, usually done with a sticker label on the reverse side. Indicate the top edge of the illustration. Illustrations are processed differently than text at the publishers, and if unlabeled, proper association of figures and text in the final assembly of the journal can be a headache or worse.

Journals still asking for paper documents usually require at least two copies of the typescript, including any supporting materials such as photographs. (Again, check the *Instructions to Authors*.) Save one additional copy for yourself – never mail the sole existing copy of anything! If submission is electronic, maintain a backup copy of the final file in a separate location – not just on your hard drive! One easy way to accomplish this is to email a copy to yourself.

When sending a paper typescript by mail, enclose the cover letter and typescript copies in a strong oversized envelope or reinforced mailing bag. If necessary, add a piece of light cardboard to stiffen the package further. Put illustrations and photographs in a separate smaller envelope inside the mailer to protect them further. When everything is together, seal the mailer and put a strip of tape over the clasp that holds it closed. Mark the envelope "First Class Mail" (or "Air Mail" for overseas) very prominently on both the front and back. Otherwise, the postal service may treat it to a much slower third-class mail delivery. Never guess at the proper postage! Take it to a mailroom and have it weighed. For extra speed

B.C.   **BY JOHNNY HART**

© By permission of John L. Hart and Creators Syndicate, Inc.

and security you may wish to use Priority Mail or a private courier service and request a return receipt.

Now find something else to do. Soon, the journal office may notify you that they have received your submission, but it will be weeks before you hear more than that.

BACK AND FORTH: EDITORIAL REVIEW

Receipt by the editor marks the beginning of a whole series of steps that conclude with publication in printed or electronic media or both. Only two of these steps require direct action from the author: dealing with reviewers' comments and correcting proofs. However, understanding what happens once the editor receives your typescript can help to alleviate those natural feelings of worry and wondering that can gnaw at you while you await a response.

What happens at the editor's office: Round one

When it arrives at the editorial office, your typescript is logged in, dated, and assigned a typescript number which allows the editor to track its progress through the subsequent steps. The typescript is also given a cursory review at this stage to assure that all the illustrations are included and that it meets the journal's criteria for submission for publication. The editor then identifies two or three external referees qualified to review your typescript, and sends copies of your typescript to each.

Referees usually are requested to return their reviews within three weeks. In an ideal world, all referees would return their reviews promptly, because "peer reviewers" usually are researchers who submit their own work to the same journal and generally they are impatient if they do not receive their own reviews in a timely manner. However, because reviewers volunteer their time, some are less conscientious than others about meeting return deadlines.

Once the editor has all of the external reviews in hand, he or she decides if the paper should be accepted or rejected. The paper then is returned to the corresponding author with copies of the referees' comments and the editor's decision and recommendations.

If the submission is rejected, the author has the option of appealing the decision to the editor or editorial board. Alternatively, the author can choose to reformat the article, incorporate whatever of the reviewers' and editor's recommendations seem warranted, and submit the typescript to another journal, thereby beginning the publication process anew.

Acceptance is nearly always contingent on some revision. Be prepared for this fact. Treat the entire process with respect. As noted by Dizon and Rosenberg (1990), "The peer review process is not a perfect system – just a necessary one."

Deal respectfully with reviewers' comments

The system of peer review, wherein anonymous reviewers funnel comments about your typescript back to you through the editor, is rarely a wholly pleasant one no matter how common it is. Even if you have carefully followed all of the suggestions in this book, be prepared for the possibility of negative reviewer comments.

The worst thing that you can do, should critical reviews appear, is to treat them as an affront to your professional image. Instead, calmly and carefully evaluate all the comments received, point by point. Make the suggested changes that seem to have value. Review those that seem wrong. If a reviewer misunderstood you, try to determine why. The misunderstanding may reveal a weakness in your argument or analysis, or a spot where the writing is weak.

Return the revised typescript to the editor, accompanied by electronic copy if requested. In your letter of reply to the editor, respond to each reviewer comment in turn. Indicate acceptance of those suggestions that seem to have merit. If you chose not to accept a reviewer's comment, indicate why not. Diplomatically and briefly explain your reasoning concerning suggested changes that you feel are unjustified. Avoid anger and any tendency to sarcasm in your responses. Editors sometimes pass your comments back to the reviewer, to whom you may not be anonymous. The world is really a very small place.

What happens at the editor's office: Round two

If an author's revisions have been extensive or have substantially changed the paper, the editor may elect to repeat the review process, essentially returning to round one. Once the revised paper is fully acceptable, the editor marks the copy for the typesetter to conform to the particular details of journal design and format. Then the editor forwards it to the publisher.

The publisher typesets the paper and returns it and a galley proof to the author, sometimes by way of the journal's editor, who may also check the proof. Various other paperwork may also appear at this time. Generally the publisher includes an order form for the author to order reprints of the article. If page charges are journal policy, the author receives a bill or invoice for the number of printed pages with the galley proof. Many journals require authors to execute a copyright release form, and such forms are often also enclosed with the galley. In addition to your signature as corresponding author, they may need to be signed by all coauthors.

Correct galley proof conscientiously

"Galley proof" originally was the name for a typeset copy of a document used to permit correction of errors before the type was made up in pages; its name comes from the galley, a tray for holding composed type. With computerized typesetting, the term is also used as a synonym for "page proof" that shows how the made-up pages will appear.

Checking galley proof is an important step in the publication process. Take it seriously, and give the galley the attention and care it deserves. With the increase in electronic submissions, fewer errors are being introduced by the typesetting process, but galleys without errors are exceedingly rare.

Read the proof carefully

Examine individual sentences slowly, word by word and line by line. To detect spelling errors, try reading lines backward to view each word separately. Compare the typeset material with the original typescript to ensure that no material has been omitted or repeated. Examine numbers carefully, especially in tables.

Errors at this stage can be difficult to catch when working alone. If possible, enlist a friend's aid, so that one person can slowly read the original typescript aloud while the other checks the galley.

Mark corrections attentively

Documents slated for paper copy pass through many hands between the author's submission and their final appearance as printed pages. Common sense suggests that a standard method of marking corrections will reduce the chances of misunderstandings. Proofreaders' marks form an internationally recognized convention, although British and American systems differ slightly. With the galley, publishers often include a list of preferred marks, with examples of their use.

Mark corrections in the margin and put proofreaders' marks in the body of the text where the errors occur. Never write the correction itself above the lines of type within the printed matter.

Checking over a galley, the printer looks for marginal notations, and makes only the alterations noted there. He or she will not, and cannot be expected to, make sweeping corrections on the basis of a single command such as "change this word to italics throughout the document." Mark each change on the proof where it occurs. When more than one correction must be written in the margin next to a single line of type, arrange them in sequence from left to right, and separate them by slashes (slant lines).

The time for revision or adding new information has passed. Changes in the typescript at this point should only be to correct errors. Resist any impulse to further polish style. In fact, such changes are usually expressly forbidden, and any changes made that are not the fault of the typesetter may be charged to the author as "penalty copy" at considerable expense. (Rarely, a journal will allow a brief appendix to be added that notes new information that supports work in the paper.)

A proofreader's nightmare

Can you read this? Olny srmat poelpe can.

I cdnuolt blveiee that I cluod aulacity uesdnatnrd waht I was rdanieg.

Bceuase of the phaonmneal pweor of the hmuan mnid, aoccdrnig to a rscheearch at Cmabrigde Uinervtisy, it deosn't mttaer in waht oredr the ltteers in a wrod are.

The olnyy iprmoatnt tihng is taht the frist and lsat ltteer be in the rghit pclae. The rset can be a taotl mses and

you can sitll raed it wouthit a porbelm. Tihs is bcuseae the huamn mnid deos not raed ervey lteter by istlef, but the wrod as a wlohe.

Amzanig, huh? Yaeh, and I awlyas tghuhot sipeling was ipmorantt!

— *Unknown*

Return proofs promptly

Galley proofs are extremely time-sensitive from the publisher's standpoint. Read
and correct the proof and return it immediately to the editor. Delays at this point
are costly to everyone.

Celebrate – You have published!

As the final step in the publication process, the editor organizes and makes up
an issue from proofed papers, and sends the entire issue to the publisher. The
publisher then prints and mails the issue to journal subscribers. Reprints are
usually mailed to authors within a week or two of publication.

Now you can at last rejoice! With pride, add this title credit to your growing
résumé and begin your next publication.

TIPS FOR INTERNATIONAL PUBLICATION

To think justly we must understand what others mean; to know the value of our
thoughts, we must try their effect on other minds.

– Wiliam Hazlitt

Fox Trot

Scientific writing today has taken on a distinctly international nature, but when the writer and readers do not share the same first language, clear communication takes an extra degree of effort. Translation is often touted as the answer. However, there is a shortage of qualified translators, and the expense can be prohibitive. Translation also delays the publication of scientific research. Furthermore, some languages have not developed the vocabulary required for science, so that in effect, translation requires the artificial development of terminology. Various software and online services also promise translation, but as of this writing, none have been refined to the point that they can be recommended for scientific documents.

In this section, we offer some pointers for both the native English speaker writing for a reader with a different first language, and the writer whose first language is not English. For succinct helpful guidelines on the grammatical aspects of these tasks, the appendices in Markel (1994) offer a good place to begin.

Address second-language English readers effectively

Sometime in your writing career, you almost certainly will be called upon to write a document addressed to readers for whom English is a secondary language. Their task will be greatly eased if you pay careful attention to yours.

What MacNeil (1995) calls "the glorious messiness of English" has resulted in an estimated vocabulary of over one million words. (Other major languages have far fewer; French, for example, has only about 75,000.) This massive vocabulary poses formidable obstacles to those attempting to master what has become, to a very real extent, the first truly global language.

Just after World War II, the idea of creating a simplified version of English gained great popularity as a possible tool for better international understanding and hopefully, world peace. Over the years, various experts have proposed special assemblages of restricted vocabularies and simplified grammar. For example, Basic English was designed around an 850-word lexicon; its creator (Ogden, 1930) claimed it would take someone seven years to learn English but only seven weeks for Basic English!

A form called Special English has a core vocabulary of 1,500 words. Like Basic English, it uses the active voice and short, simple sentences that contain only one idea. This system has been used in *Voice of America* broadcasts since 1959; tune in if you'd like to hear how it sounds.

Another variant is Simplified English, a limited and standardized subset of Standard English intended for science or technical communication. Its most extensive use, in a version called Simplified Technical English, is for instruction and maintenance manuals (Gingras, 1987; Sanderlin, 1988), particularly in the aerospace industry. It has been shown not only to reduce ambiguity and improve comprehension, but also to facilitate automated translation and thus make translation cheaper and easier.

Simplified English is both a vocabulary and a technique. It starts with a basic lexicon of less than 300 nontechnical words, grouped by function (with definitions) in a thesaurus. To this, one adds one's own limited list of terms required by the specific document, and includes their definitions in a glossary with example sentences. Words must have only one meaning and they can only be used in certain ways. Use of jargon, vernacular phrases, and abbreviations is discouraged.

Because Simplified English is designed with science in mind, using its reduced vocabulary plus target terms works surprisingly well for most purposes. Often, clarity is actually improved by the change.

> *Instead of:* Unless one *implements* the modifications, there is a *potential* for damage.
> *Write: Make* the modifications, or damage can *occur*.

Although they were developed primarily for non-native English speakers, the constraints imposed by such systems also improve the readability of text for native speakers. For example, Simplified Technical English requires writers to:

- Use the active voice
- Use articles wherever possible
- Use simple verb tenses
- Use language and terminology consistently
- Avoid lengthy compound words
- Use relatively short sentences

Additional guidelines are designed to keep sentence structure as simple as possible. Sentences are to be kept below 20 words in length, and no more than one sentence in ten on a page should exceed 16 words in length. The less skill and training in English the intended audience has, the shorter the sentences should be.

When you are called upon to write a document addressed to non-native English speakers, remember the general principles set forth in these systems. For further guidance, including the Simplified English lexicon and numerous examples of basic usage, see *Science and Technical Writing* (Rubens, 2002) or various online sites.

Choose an effective approach when writing English as a second language

Among multilingual writers whose first language is not English but who choose that language of publication, three writing methods are common:

1. Draft the paper in English from the start, doing the best you can. This is the most desirable way, because it usually results in the most readable text in the least time.
2. Write the first draft in your own language, then translate it into English yourself. This takes longer, and is more apt to lead to grammatical difficulties and stylistic awkwardness.
3. Write the paper entirely in your own language, then employ a professional translator who is familiar with the terminology of your branch of science. This can be expensive. Learn whether you can include the translation fee if you apply for a research grant.

Whichever method you choose, your primary task remains the same as for any other scientific writer – that is, to assure that your material is well organized, complete, and clear. Pay attention to the level and type of details that appear in papers published in your chosen journal, and try to emulate them. Referees and editors will probably not mind correcting minor grammatical mistakes, but they will reject a paper if they cannot even decipher the text's basic meaning.

Seek help from a colleague fluent in scientific English

As you begin writing in English, find a willing native English speaker to serve as your first editor. Such people can be your most important resource – treat them well! Do not overwhelm them with a lengthy manuscript or ask for help with every small grammatical matter in the text. Instead, show them early sections of your paper and use their initial comments about your grammar, style, and organization to improve your writing skills as you progress.

Read in order to write

Learning to write well takes effort and practice, and writing well in a second language takes even more. Although consulting books such as this one can help your effort, ultimately no book can actually teach you how to write, any more than a rule book could teach you how to play soccer or a music theory book teach you to play a symphony. Just as with sport or music skills, writing skills can be developed only by actual practice over time.

In many ways, scientific English in your chosen field of study could be considered to be a "dialect" of the English language (Montgomery, 2003), and learning to write this dialect proceeds much like learning to speak a foreign language. Although one can attempt to memorize words and rules, the fastest learning occurs by imitation and observation. Success comes from studying examples of proper use and trying to emulate them.

A major way that scientists learn their dialect is through constant reading of literature until they develop a sense of what "sounds right" and what doesn't. For many people, this can be a haphazard process, but it doesn't need to be. A more effective approach is to seek out especially well-written recent articles in your field, reread them at frequent intervals, and imitate their writing style as part of your overall language training. If this idea appeals to you, consult Montgomery (2003) for detailed guidance.

At the same time, recognize that cultures differ in their attitudes toward material taken directly from other people's writing. As Day and Gastel (2006) bluntly put it, "In English-language scientific papers for international journals, authors are required to use their own wording for the vast majority of what they say and to clearly designate any wording taken from elsewhere."

Usage and grammar pitfalls for nonnative writers

Most of the usage and grammar questions faced by nonnative English writers are the same ones that native writers face. If this were not true, there would be no place for books like this one!

A few areas seem to cause special problems for nonnative writers, however. In this section, we'll briefly offer some suggestions for dealing with some of them. A highly regarded older book is *Grammar Troublespots: An Editing Guide for ESL Students* (Raimes, 1988); widely available in the online used book market, it is an excellent investment.

Distinguish between count nouns and noncount nouns

Common nouns in English can be count nouns or noncount nouns. The distinction is important because it determines whether to use the singular or plural form of the word, and which articles *(a, an, the)* and limiting adjectives (*fewer* or *less, much* or *many*, and so on) to use (see below).

As the term suggests, count nouns refer to distinct individuals or things that can be directly counted. They usually have singular and plural forms: *gene, genes*. Noncount nouns occur as masses or collections of ideas that can be quantified only in a broad, vague way or with a preceding phrase. They usually have only a singular form: *mankind, honesty*. To confuse the situation, some nouns have more than one meaning; one meaning may be count, and the other noncount. *Water* is a count noun when we speak of a liter of water, but a noncount noun when we say that water is a limited resource.

When you learn a common noun in English, learn whether it is count, noncount, or both. Two dictionaries that include this information are the *Oxford Advanced Learner's Dictionary* (Hornby and Wehmeier, 2005) and the *Longman Dictionary of American English* (Longman, 2004).

Watch use of definite and indefinite articles

The definite article *the* and the indefinite articles *a* and *an* are challenging to multilingual speakers. Many languages have nothing that directly compares to them.

Use *the* with nouns whose identity is known or is about to be made known to readers from general knowledge or some clue in the text.

> *The* amoeba's endoplasm spreads peripherally from *the* ends of *the* pseudopodium.

Use *a* or *an* only with singular count nouns. Use *a* before a consonant sound and *an* before a vowel sound. Pay attention to sounds rather than to spelling.

> *An* amoeba does not have cilia, but *a* protozoan often does.

This rule explains some of the differences between British and American English. The softer British pronunciation of an initial *h* in a word leads to *an historical*, but American pronunciation often accentuates the *h* and favors *a historical*.

To speak of an indefinite quantity rather than just one indefinite thing, use *some, less*, or *much* with a noncount noun. With a count noun, specify the number or use such words as *few, fewer, many*, or *several*. *More* is nice; it can be used with both noun types.

> *Many* unicellular animals can live without *some* sunlight.
> *Less* dietary vitamin C may mean *more*, not *fewer* colds.
> In *several* cases, the animals were unable to reuse *much* nitrogen.

Noncount and plural count nouns can be used without an article to make generalizations.

> Truth is beauty.
> Phenotypes may not reflect genotypes.

Many languages such as Greek, Spanish, and German use the definite article to make generalizations. However, in English a sentence like *The fish are spawning* generally refers only to particular identifiable fish, not to all fish in general.

Get help with prepositions and prepositional phrases

Words such as *to* and *from* are prepositions; they show the relations between other words. Not all languages use prepositions, and English differs from other languages in the way prepositions are used. Even native English speakers sometimes have trouble deciding which preposition to use. You may want to keep a list of prepositional phrases commonly used in your field. Textbooks and websites also can help.

Rather than becoming frustrated, keep the big picture in mind. There is no easy solution to the challenge of using prepositions idiomatically in any language. Each of the most common prepositions has a wide range of different applications, and this range never coincides exactly from one language to another. For example, while Spanish uses one preposition (*en*) in all these sentences, English speakers say:

> The bacterial cultures are *in* the incubator.
> The petri dishes are *on* the laboratory bench.
> Professor Jones arrives *in* the United States *on* January 15th.

English speakers often use prepositions as little more than space-fillers; see the section on "hiccups" in Chapter 5. These should be omitted.

> She wrote *up* the laboratory report for all of us.
> *Better:* She wrote the laboratory report for all of us.

Note that occasionally in English a preposition seems to have no object, but it is not a true hiccup because removing it changes the sense of the verb. Compare these sentences:

> The fruit *drops off* the stem vs. The fruit *drops* the stem.

In such cases, the words that look like prepositions function instead as two-word verbs (phrasal verbs). Some of these phrasal verbs can be separated in a sentence, but others cannot. If in doubt, consult a comprehensive dictionary such as the *Longman Dictionary of American English* (Longman, 2004).

ETHICAL ISSUES

Every scientist is responsible for protecting the integrity of science.
> – *M. Davis* (2005)

Ethics refers to the choices we make that affect others for good or ill. Obviously, this is a multifaceted topic, and no book can describe how to act ethically in every situation.

Various ethical breaches can occur in science, as in any field. However, in science, two ethical errors are considered unforgivable – distorting your own data and plagiarizing the work of others. Both are matters of honesty vs. dishonesty, but in real life application they are not always as black and white as this distinction would make it seem.

It is difficult to assess whether scientific dishonesty is on the rise, or simply being reported more widely in our shrinking world. Every month, it seems, one can find reports of scientists forging, faking, or plagiarizing their way to success. The historical, political, and social context of these issues is beyond the scope of this book, but it makes interesting reading. Good places to start include LaFollette (1992), Buranen and Roy (1999), and the many references included in both.

Respect your data – and your readers

Scientific progress depends upon trust – trust in the personal honesty of other scientists and trust in the honesty of their data. Be careful how you approach your own research. Intentional dishonesty is easy to identify – and to avoid. Simply settle for nothing less than careful research, use of scientific reasoning, an open mind, clear and accurate communication, and a willingness to be honest at all costs (Davis, 2005).

Unintentional distortions can be more problematical. Was that odd result in one dataset simply an anomaly? Can you ethically delete the outlier that keeps your numbers from showing statistical significance to support the result you are almost certain should occur? Should you choose to use graph intervals that downplay differences you can't readily explain?

Ask for guidance from others in your field, but realize that you may be the only one who can answer such questions. Know the conventions for data presentation in your field, and check the accuracy of all details. Try your best to walk a middle line between a meticulousness that leads to overt paralysis and a casual slide down the slippery slope of dishonesty.

Write only what you know to be true

This reminder should be self-evident. It means no falsified data, no fictional notes, no creative quotations. No exceptions.

Practice humility

Be careful not to overstretch the limits when interpreting your data. There are many truths in this world, and no single set of factors can explain everything. Furthermore, whether we choose to consciously acknowledge the fact or not, every one of us is the product of our social and personal beliefs. As Davis (2005) notes, "Individual and cultural prejudices have troubled scientific research and reporting for centuries, and we are not without prejudices today."

Be respectful of others' opinions, even when you do not agree with them. Always remember that any single set of factors can be interpreted in a variety of ways. As a practical example, do not use the word "fact" to refer to what is actually a matter of judgment or opinion.

> *Arrogant and possibly false:* It is a fact that human exploitation has been the major cause of habitat degradation since the birth of the Roman Empire.
>
> *Better:* Based on our research, we believe that human exploitation has been a major cause of habitat degradation since the birth of the Roman Empire.

Avoid ambiguities and double meanings

Unlike creative writing in the liberal arts, scientific communication does not allow readers to interpret words as they choose. Read your sentences carefully, and be sure you are not misdirecting readers through ambiguities or double meanings. Even though technical or legal experts could interpret them as accurate, the use of various abstract words, jargon, and euphemisms is unethical when they are used to mislead readers or to hide a serious or dangerous situation. Governmental groups and politicians are infamous for such cover-ups. Scientific writers should occupy ethically higher ground.

Check again for plagiarism

> What a good thing Adam had. When he said a good thing, he knew nobody had said it before.
>
> *– Mark Twain*

You've probably been warned about plagiarism ever since you began writing. In its simplest definition, plagiarism is the act of taking words or ideas that someone else has written and trying to present them as one's own. Examples encompass everything from buying term papers on the Internet to patching together a thesis introduction from unattributed sentences lifted from various publications.

Drawn from the Latin word for "kidnapping," plagiarism is viewed as a very serious offense all across academia. Almost every writing book denounces it heatedly, variously describing it as illegal, unethical, immoral, or intellectually lazy (Buranen and Roy, 1999). However, perhaps nowhere is the issue of plagiarism (and the related issue of falsified data) taken as seriously as it is in science. People seemingly are willing to accept deception in politics and entertainment, and most buy into fantasy without blinking. However, almost everyone agrees that science must be held to a higher standard, because authenticity and accuracy are the foundation upon which it must stand.

Credit others fully and accurately

Rather than moralize or editorialize, let us remind you once again that you have an obligation to credit others fully and accurately for their work. "Work" includes all the raw material of scholarship, be it words, ideas, drawings, or data. "Others" includes students who have helped with research, friends or informants who have provided information, and colleagues whose work you have built upon.

For a journal article, such acknowledgment is generally enough. If you are publishing a book that includes anyone else's tables, figures, or words at significant length, you will have the additional responsibility for getting written permission from each of these people and, if requested, pay a fee.

Using someone's work without giving credit may go beyond plagiarism into copyright infringement. As a responsible author, you also should understand the fundamentals of copyright law outlined later in this chapter.

Know when to document paraphrased ideas

The most common way to avoid outright plagiarism is to put the essence of another writer's ideas into one's own words without distorting their meaning. The process is called paraphrasing. Quotation marks are not necessary because the paraphrase does not quote the source word for word. However, paraphrased materials still should be credited, because the ideas are taken from someone else.

A major exception to this documentation occurs when the information that is being paraphrased is common knowledge in a field. Common knowledge means that the information is widely known and readily available, as for example in handbooks, manuals, atlases, or other references.

At the other end of the spectrum, for extensively borrowed material that is going to be published, reproduced, or distributed, citation is essential but may not be enough. You may also need to obtain written permission from the copyright holder.

Avoid self-plagiarism

Seduced by the seeming value of lengthy publication lists, some scientists recycle their research. Changing the emphasis slightly, they submit two or three articles where one would really do. Although this practice is legal, it is ethically questionable, and wastes the time and energy of editors, referees, and readers alike. (See this book's earlier section on "salami-slicing science.")

Rarely is such republication justified, but examples might be when the first paper was in another language or in a journal with very limited circulation. If you feel that your situation gives reason for republication, tell the editor the circumstances of its prior appearance. Enclose a copy of the original article so that differences can be verified and the editor can make an informed decision.

In the workplace, employees often borrow and reuse material from in-house manuals, reports, and other company documents. Using such information, called boilerplate, is neither plagiarism nor a violation of copyright.

Protect yourself from potential libel and slander charges

> The experiment went well because Dr. Jones was not involved.
>   *– fictitious email posting*

Scientists tend to ignore the legal problem of potential libel, believing it is something they don't have to worry about. However, in today's litigious society, this can be a naïve assumption.

Libel refers to anything circulated in writing or pictures that injures someone's good reputation, particularly anything about a living person that is both untrue and harmful. (The corresponding term for injury by speech is "slander.")

Libel law is complex and changing, but in general harmful is defined as any statement that can damage a person's status, business or profession, or social life. Groups can be libeled as well as individuals.

> When Dr. Smithson openly charged his rival with bribing the journal editor, the professor sued Smithson for slander.
>
> Dr. Montgomery was quite surprised to find herself sued for libel after her hastily written editorial labeled the American Naturopathic Medical Association as "a bunch of quacks."

Even reporting about ongoing investigations or decisions in fraud cases may now draw complaints. As a result, major journals like *Science* reportedly ask their attorneys to review all unflattering news reports for potential libel, because truth and accuracy are not enough to prevent a journal from being sued or bearing the cost of defending against a lawsuit (LaFollette, 1992).

If you are called upon to write about controversial events or subjects, you likewise might be wise to have a lawyer review your document.

Ask ethical questions about your document

As a final check before you rush to print, review your answers to some essential ethical questions:

1. Is my document honest and truthful?
2. If I were the intended audience, would its message be acceptable and respectful?
3. Am I willing to take responsibility, publicly and privately, for what the document says?
4. Does the document violate anyone's rights?
5. Have I been careful with confidentiality?
6. Have I treated any possible conflict of interest with great caution?
7. Have I been ethically consistent in my writing?

Proceed to publish only when your truthful answers are completely acceptable.

LEGAL MATTERS

Scientists must use each other's ideas and inventions if progress is to be made. However, using something that belongs to someone else brings us into the realm of legal, as well as ethical, issues. The rule is simple – if a work is not yours, find out whose it is and get permission before you use it. The application of the rule is somewhat more complex. Below are some handy things to know. For more detail, Strong (1999) is a useful reference, but when you have really important questions about such things as trade names, copyrights, and patents, consult a lawyer.

Trade names

A manufactured item such as a pharmaceutical product sometimes has as many as three different types of names. One is its systemic chemical name, which is often complex. Another is a shorter, nonproprietary "generic" name. A third is a trade name, also called a proprietary name. This is the name a manufacturer or vendor gives to its product; usually such names are registered as trademarks.

If one manufacturer's product behaves significantly differently from other similar products, readers may need to know which one you used in order to duplicate your experimental results. In such a case, the trade name should be given somewhere (often in parentheses or in a reference or footnote rather than directly in the text).

Otherwise, scientific writing generally avoids trade names. In particular, brand or trademark names should never be used in titles or summaries. One reason is that their use makes it appear as though one is advertising products. Another is that, while generic and systemic names generally stay the same, trade names often differ greatly from one part of the world to another. Furthermore, official trade names can be awkward to use, because many consist of a long string of words,

Table 8.1. *Trade names that companies are working to keep from coming into general use*

Trade name	Generic name
Vaseline®	petroleum jelly or petrolatum
SCOTCH Magic Tape	transparent tape
SPAM® luncheon meat	canned luncheon meat
XEROX® copier	photocopier
VELCRO® brand fasteners	hook and loop fasteners
BOTOX® Purified Neurotoxin Complex	botulinum toxin
SPACKLE®	surfacing compound

some of which may appear in all capital letters. (For example, the full name for those widely known sticky tapes is BAND AID® Brand Adhesive Bandages.)

Distinguish carefully between trade names and common names

Knowing whether a generally used name is proprietary is important. Considerable money has been spent, and many lawsuits have been entered into, to enforce the recognition of trade names! The problem is that when a trademarked product comes into general use, the public often loses touch with the word's commercial origins (Table 8.1). Proper names or their derivatives begin to function as common nouns, and for a period of time both styles exist side by side. Eventually, to the dismay of the company holding the trademark on the product, the product name or a variant of it may become an English word in its own right. (Aspirin, nylon, zipper, and fiberglass are examples of such lost battles.)

Don't slip into the pitfall of using trade names as though they were synonyms for generic products or processes. Usually, a quick perusal of the packaging will reveal a product's status.

Substitute generic or chemical names whenever possible

The use of generic or chemical names for products is usually preferred in the text and obligatory in titles and summaries. Generic drug names can be verified in the most recent edition of the *USP Dictionary of USAN and International Drug Names*. This useful annual guide is considered the standard source for U.S. adopted names (USAN). It includes formal chemical names of drugs, trade names, previously used generic names, and code numbers for investigational drugs, as well as an appendix that details the rules for coining new names. Many other countries have similar means for establishing nonproprietary names (see Council of Science Editors, 2006).

Chemical compounds mentioned in clinical papers can be identified either by a formal chemical name or by a shorter "trivial" (from a chemist's viewpoint) name. *The Merck Index* (O'Neill *et al.*, 2006) is an authoritative source for verification of these names; check that you have the most recent edition.

Cite trade names correctly

Sometimes there are reasons why it is critical to include a trade name in the text of a paper. When this is the case, use the common name first, then the proprietary name.

Like variety names (Yellow Radiance rose), and some market terms (Choice, Prime), trade names should always be capitalized. (With two-word names such as "Sorvall centrifuge" only the first or "significant" word is capitalized.) At least the first time the product is mentioned by full trade name, one should include a suffix superscript of the symbol ® for a mark that has been officially registered with the U.S. Patent and Trademark Office or [TM] for marks that have not been registered but which the manufacturer wishes to identify as its own. (However, many journals omit the symbol.) The symbol need not be repeated in subsequent uses of the trade name. For example, write "the carrier ampholyte, Ampholine®" first, then just "Ampholine" or "ampholyte."

Include the manufacturer's name and address. Often this information is treated as a footnote. (Sometimes the trade name is included in a footnote and omitted entirely from the text.)

> Diets were supplemented with a multi-vitamin tablet (Preventron®).[1] Although other tablets were tried, Preventron tablets were most easily assimilated.
>
> [1]Natural Sales Co., Pittsburgh, PA.

Copyright

Copyright is the right of exclusive ownership by an author of the benefits resulting from the creation of his or her work. It covers the matter and form of a literary or artistic work, i.e., how it is expressed. It does not cover the ideas or data themselves, but just the way in which they have been presented.

Copyright gives authors (or others to whom they transfer copyright ownership) control over how the work is reproduced and disseminated. Once copyrighted, a work cannot be indiscriminately reproduced unless the copyright owner gives permission, usually in exchange for royalties or other compensation.

The issue of copyright affects both your use of others' work and your own published writing. With the advent of the Internet, many copyrighted works formerly available solely in print are now distributed around the world in cyberspace. Copyright law applies to cyberspace works just as it does to their print counterparts. Publications that explain U.S. copyright law in detail are available from the Copyright Office, Library of Congress, Washington, DC 20559 or online <www.copyright.gov>.

How to determine whether published material is copyrighted

A work first published after March 1, 1989, receives copyright protection whether or not it bears a notice of copyright, but almost all published materials include this notice. It usually appears on the back of the title page. In fact, this is often called the "copyright page." If a book was published after January 1, 1978, the term of the copyright is for the author's life plus 50 years. If it was published before 1978, the first copyright term covers 28 years, but it is renewable for an additional 47 years.

All publications created by US government agencies are in the public domain. That is, they are not copyrighted, and may be used freely.

What you own and what you don't own

You own the copyright on any tangible expression that you create. Along with other forms, tangible expressions include written words, illustrations, printed works, electronic software, and recordings. This copyright is yours for the length of your life plus 50 years, unless it was done for an employer or commissioned as work for hire. If you have coauthors, each of you is a co-owner of the copyright, with equal rights.

Copyright does not cover the ideas, procedures, processes, concepts, or discoveries contained in such works. Protection of those things can sometimes be obtained through patents. (See later in this chapter.)

How copyright affects your own publication

When you publish your paper in a journal, copyright is generally transferred to the publisher, who will handle such paperwork as filing the copyright application and responding to future requests to use the material. Before the Copyright Act of 1976, this transfer usually happened somewhat automatically. Now, it must be specifically written out, so most publishers ask authors to sign a copyright transfer form.

If work to which you hold copyright is to be published in electronic format, be sure to fully investigate your rights under current copyright law. Electronic publishing is a rapidly changing area. At this writing, dozens of issues await resolution.

Permissions

In the process of preparing a written paper or an oral presentation, you may find places where you want to use someone else's material. It may be a published photograph, some clip art, or a diagram downloaded off the Web. Can you legally use the material? Later you'll be preparing a classroom term paper. Can you include the material then? What about when you expand the term paper into a journal publication?

In fact, much of this material is probably copyrighted. In many cases you can use it; in other cases, you can't. A legal concept called "fair use" is involved.

Understand "fair use"

Copyright law provides a "fair use" provision that allows others such as teachers, librarians, and reviewers to reproduce a limited portion of copyrighted materials for educational and certain other purposes without compensation to the copyright owners. The law refers to such purposes as "criticism, comment, news reporting, teaching (including multiple copies for classroom use), scholarship or research." The fair use provision does not allow you to copy complete articles and republish them without permission, even if it is not done for profit.

A small amount of material from a copyrighted source may be used in your written work without permission or payment as long as the use satisfies the fair use criteria.

Public domain

This is the most straightforward of the fair use conditions. After the original copyright holders have died and their heirs have exercised their rights for 75 years, anyone can reproduce, record, perform, or otherwise use the material without the permission of the heirs or estate.

Public domain can also be declared right from the start. Items such as clip art collections or certain software programs clearly announce that they are in the public domain.

Items you have permission to use

A second, equally straightforward situation occurs when copyright holders give their permission for others to use their work. In addition to saying yes or no when asked, they can request money or other conditions as they grant the right to use their material.

Other applications of the fair use doctrine

Over the years, the courts have defined certain conditions as fair use of copyrighted material without permission. This doctrine is applied on a case-by-case basis, with decisions generally being based on four aspects: the purpose of the use, publication status, amount used, and potential for competition.

Every case is unique, but in general classroom use has almost always been considered fair. Educational uses have been viewed more favorably than if the use is for profit. If the material has been published (for example, as a book, an article, or electronically) it generally will be viewed more favorably than if it has not been published (like a personal letter or laboratory notes). Use of only part of the work has been viewed more favorably than use of the entire work. Finally, it will be viewed more favorably if your use will not damage the potential market of the original.

It should be noted that photocopying services are sometimes still overly cautious in applying this doctrine because of lawsuits brought against them by publishers during the 1990s. During that time, many copy shops were copying material for classroom use, but also binding, packing, and selling the materials for profit. Now, once burned and twice shy, they may refuse to make copies or scan images for you. However, they usually will let you scan images and make copies yourself. Because you are simply using them for an educational presentation and not making a profit on these materials, there is no violation. (However, if you were a professional speaker, you would need to revisit the question.)

How much can be quoted without permission?

The *Chicago Manual of Style* provides an often-quoted succinct guideline that a quotation of more than 500 words of prose from previously published material still in copyright requires permission from the publisher. Some editors recommend permission for as few as 300 words of prose (Germano, 2001). These 300–500 words apply to the entirety of the article or book in which they will appear. If you are using a series of brief excerpts throughout the text, it is your responsibility to tally them.

Incidentally, the rules are somewhat different for poetry and song lyrics, being limited to four percent of the original work. Play it safe and ask for permissions on these. Publishers of song lyrics, in particular, are notably stern about unauthorized use of their property.

Always remember to give credit

Remember the issue of avoiding plagiarism. Although it may not be an infringement of their copyright, you still are using someone else's material. It is both appropriate and ethical to give the original creator credit for his or her work. Before you copy it, add a citation indicating the author and copyright holder.

The format for such citations may be specified by your publisher or by the copyright holder. Otherwise, however, you can generally follow the examples below.

If you obtained written permission to use an illustration, you might write:

©2007 Robert W. Matthews. Used with permission.

For material that did not require permission because it was taken from the public domain, you could write:

From the public domain via <www.freemaps.org> 28 Feb. 2007
From Freeman, F. N. and Johnson, E. M. (1929, p. 279). "Are you starved for sunlight?" Child-story Readers. Chicago: Lyons and Carnahan.

Patents

Patents do not apply to the expression of ideas, but protect the ideas as they are put into practice as machines, manufacture, processes, or composition. Copyright protection begins as soon as the expression is created but patents must be registered to serve as protection. Copyrights protect for a long time; U.S. patents, only for 17 years.

What can be patented, and how?

In general, patents cover the creations most people call "inventions." However, biotechnology has added a new dimension with the decision that it is possible to patent life forms if they have been synthesized by human efforts and do not exist in nature without human intervention.

In general, to be patentable, an invention must be proven to be novel, not obvious, and useful. These criteria all must be supported in written documentation, requiring you to carefully search and read the literature on your subject. You must also keep careful records, preferably dated and signed by witnesses, to be able to prove that you invented it first.

An important related question concerns when to publish information about the invention. If it is described to the public before you have registered the patent, it will be considered public information and will probably not be patented.

(Incidentally, note that the U.S. patent literature is said to be the largest and most comprehensive collection of technical information in the world. Certainly, disclosures on how inventions are produced and how they function can be a storehouse of information for other scientists. When doing a literature search, don't forget to explore your research subject in this area if it seems at all appropriate.)

General information on U.S. patents can be obtained from the government website <www.uspto.gov>. The laws regarding patents can be complex, and are somewhat different in different countries. If you are thinking of patenting an invention, get the best help you can find and afford.

Appendix 1

Suggested responses to exercises

CHAPTER 1

Exercise 1.1. Search strategy and Boolean logic (page 10)

1. A, H, J
2. B, E, G
3. D, F
4. A, B, D, E, F, G, H, J
5. F
6. C, I

Exercise 1.2. Message, format, and audience (page 19)

1. Probably not. Simple novelty or extension of a previous record usually is not enough to warrant publication. A case study must change, improve, or enlarge how people think.
2. The paper your colleague has proposed would have a purpose – to report the case findings – but as a research paper it would not have a message. However, a critical review of case records, coupled with a careful and critical assessment of the literature, might result in a valuable document. A case-series analysis or review article would help busy clinicians get information without laboriously sifting through the primary literature. It would tell investigators where things stand on particular aspects of the disease. And, if well written, it could suggest directions new research should take.
3. Yes, with proper choice of format. Written as a "me-too" series of case histories, the paper will probably be rejected. However, a case-series analysis that would include these data could be a useful contribution.
4. Only one primary research publication is justifiable, because all of the results bear upon your single message. However, this could be supplemented with general articles written for the popular press to reach other target audiences.
5. Psychological researchers, clinicians, psychologists, teachers, school admin-istrators, parents.

Exercise 1.3. Organizing ideas (page 27). No response needed.

CHAPTER 2

Exercise 2.1. Spelling and grammar programs (page 38)

A.

1. Twice as many women as men experience migraines.
2. Wanted: Nonsmoking, nondrinking worker to care for cow.
3. I realized that because she was a baboon that grew up wild in the jungle, Wiki had special nutritional needs.
4. The patient with a severe emotional problem was referred to a psychiatrist.
5. Veterinarian Joe Mobbs hoists to its feet a cow injured while giving birth.
6. He wanted a wart removed that had appeared on his left hand about two years ago.
7. Birth control users who smoke are in danger of having retarded children.
8. The woman wants us to operate on the dog's tail again. If it doesn't heal this time, the dog must be humanely killed.

B.

1. fowl, means, quadrupeds
2. prolific, native
3. congenital
4. prostate
5. dying, algae
6. Danes, Husky
7. coma
8. pistil, its
9. patient, scar
10. words, tip

Exercise 2.2. Title choices (page 47)

1. *Comments:* Overuse of prepositions and trivial phrases takes title over the 10–12 word limit. Two-part title is not accepted by some journals.
   Revision: Verruca [*or* Plantar's Wart] Recurrence after Curative Excision
2. *Comments:* Some (but not all) editors ban titles that make claims about the findings in the paper.
   Revision: Correlation of Columbine Flower Characteristics and Pollinators
3. *Comments:* Unintended humor arises from careless word choice.
   Revision: Veterinarian Offers Medical Assistance After Panda Mating Fails
4. *Comments:* A century ago, long titles like this one were common. Today they are no longer accepted.
   Revision: Bionomics, Behavior, and Taxonomy of Some East Asiatic Crabronine Wasps
5. *Comments:* Another overly wordy two-part title, with unintended humor. Titles should not be thinly disguised abstracts.
   Revision: National Health Study on Lung Cancer in Women

Exercise 2.3. Tense use (page 51)

1. Work by Matthews (2007) shows that *Vespula* nests readily in the laboratory. [Sentence is also correct as it stands, though slightly less smooth.]
2. In our study, bird size increased with width of wooded habitat, as Figure 2 indicates.
3. Beal (1960) also observed [or observes] that size increases with meadow width.
4. In our study we found that there were significantly fewer antibody-producing cells in copper-deficient mice than in copper-supplemented mice (see Figure 3).
5. Correct as it stands; these results cannot be generalized.
6. Conover and Kynard (1981) reported that sex determination in the Atlantic silverside fish is under the control of both genotype and temperature.
7. Correct as it stands.
8. Correct as it stands.
9. ABSTRACT: The cell-to-cell channels in the insect salivary gland were probed with fluorescent molecules. From the molecular dimensions, a permeation-limiting channel diameter of 16–20 angstroms was obtained.
10. SUMMARY: Germinal and somatic functions in *Tetrahymena* were found to be performed separately by the micro- and macronuclei, respectively. Cells with haploid micronuclei were mated with diploids to yield mono-somic progeny.

CHAPTER 3

Exercise 3.1. Table and figure choices (page 76)

1. Present the data in a table; some readers might be interested in carrying out their own calculations of relationships among the data.
2. Present these data in a table (if exact values are of interest) or by ranges on a map (to show geographical patterns).
3. Present your data in tables or graphs; the relationships are as important as the actual values. Omit the rat photo; it adds no new information.
4. Reading from left to right, the table columns might correspond to the temporal order in which the data were collected, like this:
   Age; Sex; Complaint; Physical Findings; Laboratory Data; Autopsy Findings
5. Use the electronmicrograph; it presents new evidence of the bacterial structure. Omit the roentgenogram; no new evidence is provided by a typical example of previously published information.
6. You could present it in a table, a graph, or in the text, but readers will see the point more quickly in a genealogical chart, which is a type of graph.
7. A bar graph would emphasize the difference in mortality, but the same point could be made with equal efficiency in the text. In a lecture or talk, a bar graph might be perfect for added visual emphasis, but readers can scan the text of a paper again if they have missed a point.

CHAPTER 4

Exercise 4.1. Slide presentation format (page 92)

A.   Several answers possible.
B.   Several answers possible.
C.   1 – f, 2 – d, 3 – c, 4 – i, 5 – b, 6 – l, 7 – m, 8 – n, 9 – k, 10 – a.

Exercise 4.2. Answering questions (page 96). More than one answer is possible. Judge by suitability.

CHAPTER 5

Exercise 5.1. Person and point of view (page 109)

1.   As a laboratory technician, you will find that the new procedure is an improvement; you will not need to sterilize the skin. *OR* Laboratory technicians will find the new procedure an improvement because they do not need to sterilize the skin.
2.   Change "the authors herein" to "we."
3.   Change "the authors wish to gratefully acknowledge and thank" to "we thank."
4.   The disease is contagious and contamination should be avoided (van der Veen, 1850); cleanliness is essential. *OR* Van der Veen (1850) found that the disease is contagious and contamination should be avoided. I agree that cleanliness is essential.
5.   I believe that I have discovered a new species of *Australopithecus.*

Exercise 5.2. Readability (page 112)

1.   The Haversian system consists of a central canal containing blood vessels and a nerve, surrounded by concentric rings of bony matrix. Between them, scattered tiny spaces called lacunae are filled with bone cells and connected by canaliculi to one another and the central canal. Through these canals the cells are nourished and kept alive.
2.   The kidney, a very important organ, has the ability to secrete substances selectively which enables it to maintain proper composition of the blood and other body fluids. Some metabolic end products are injurious if allowed to accumulate.
3.   Sex-linked genes explain red-green color blindness in humans. If a woman heterozygous for color blindness marries a normal-visioned man, half of her sons will be color blind. Her normal sons will show no trace of anomaly and will never transmit it to their children. All of her daughters will have normal vision. However, half of these will be heterozygous for the defect and can have color-blind sons. The homozygous daughters will never pass the trait on to either sons or daughters.

Exercise 5.3. Shortened forms (page 122)

1. Do not use abbreviations (TCGF, SPAFAS) in titles. Do not abbreviate U.S. except as an adjective.
2. Do not use undefined abbreviations in abstracts. Do not abbreviate units of measurement (hrs.) when they are used without numerals.
3. This alphabet soup sentence is annoyingly cryptic.
4. Do not abbreviate units of measurement used without numerals.
5. Abbreviation of state names is inconsistent and that of South Carolina follows neither approved system.

Exercise 5.4. Clarity and brevity (page 123)

A.

1. mature iron from muscle; iron that is from mature muscle.
2. chronic symptoms of depression; symptoms of chronic depression.
3. excretion of renal lithium; renal excretion of lithium.
4. In their abdomens, the three patients all had tumors that were confirmed to be metastatic and malignant. (Avoid saying "cases" had tumors.)
5. We examined various combinations of immunospecific drugs to see whether any inhibited leukocytes in the peripheral blood of humans. (Avoid saying a study "examines" something.)

B.

1. These observations suggest a female sex pheromone. (Still marginally incorrect, for an "observation" can't suggest anything, but the meaning would be clear to readers.)
2. Following the outlined procedure might be wise.
3. The study shows an apparent link between cigarette smoking and lung cancer. (Longer but more technically correct: Based on this study, cigarette smoking and lung cancer may be linked.)
4. A cause-and-effect relationship appears likely.
5. The results indicate that the mixture was somewhat saturated with oil. *OR* On the basis of these results, the mixture was somewhat saturated with oil.

C.

1. The new organism is green, round, 5×10 mm, and active *OR* motile.
2. Twenty to thirty electrophoretic steps usually will be needed.
3. If we meet now about the data, consensus should be easy to attain.
4. The case load included 15 juveniles and 10 adults. (By definition, juveniles are young and adults are mature; here, "case load" is not jargon, but specialized vocabulary of the field.)
5. Figure 1. Lateral white cells in abdominal ganglion of live cockroach. Ventral view, anterior at top. (Scale bar, 0.1 mm.)

6. The absence of color was unique.
7. To determine the organism's mobility, state-of-the-art equipment was used.
8. To understand the effects of heat on the organism, we plan to refrigerate it.

CHAPTER 6

Exercise 6.1. Jargon (pages 130)

A.

1. enough
2. can
3. inhibited
4. in theory, theoretically
5. regularly

B.

1. The "etiology of this disease" means the "study of the cause of this disease." The author intended to say "the cause of this disease."
2. Literally, "histopathology stages" would be stages in the study of the pathology of tissues. The author probably intended to say "histopathological."
3. A "necrology" is a list of persons who have died within a certain time. The author probably meant "necropsy." Avoid saying that the necropsy could "confirm" something; necropsy is the tool that the scientist uses to confirm it.

C.

1. After the operation, the cow ran into a defective electric fence and had to be killed.
2. Position the slide carefully to see the unique shape clearly.
3. I think the drug can relieve and curtail disease symptoms.

Exercise 6.2. Handling language sensitively (page 134)

1. A researcher must be sure to double-check all references.
2. There were 200 Asian participants.
3. Depressed individuals and those with epilepsy reacted to the drug in different ways.
4. The chairperson confronted the person for plagiarizing.
5. The ten women in the study included one with cerebral palsy.
6. Breast cancer is one of the oldest diseases known.
7. We need 14 women who are willing to staff the project.
8. As a scientific writer, you should state your point clearly at the beginning.

Exercise 6.3. Devil pairs (page 137)

1. like; as
2. whereas; while
3. various; varying
4. effect; effect
5. effect; effects (awkward usage); affect
6. principle; principal; principle
7. complement; compliment; complement

Exercise 6.4. Which and that (page 138)

1. New fossil evidence indicates that *Cantius*, a primitive primate, had a grasp-ing big toe, which may have figured in the evolution of all modern primates.
2. The use of low weight dextrin should be avoided in these patients. These drugs appear to pass through the damaged endothelium of pulmonary vessels.
3. Occasionally a client will notice a parasite on a fish. The situation is more worrisome to the owner than to the fish.
4. We conclude that during the next year, 10.5 thousand (*OR* 10,500) tons of lead will be emitted into the air in addition to the 90 thousand (*OR* 90,000) tons that are being emitted now.
5. We could not find the proposal that was missing.

Exercise 6.5. Fuzzy words and disguised verbs (pages 141)

A.

1. By early adulthood, more males than females expressed severe symptoms of copper deficiency.
2. Under standard conditions, diazepam inhibited the initial rate of protein phosphorylation (Fig. 1).
3. Soap acts at the cell surface.
4. Stanozolol prolonged appetite.
5. We isolated *A. hydrophila*.

B.

1. Physicists hope to solve the question of whether science can harness alter-native energy sources.
2. Data were transformed to perform relevant statistical analyses.

Exercise 6.6. Active and passive voice (page 143)

1. One might expect this treatment to be effective. *OR* We expect this treatment to be effective.
2. The pathologist had no feed to analyze.
3. Jones and her colleagues inoculated 25 chickens.

4. I traveled to Georgia to collect Lepidoptera.
5. Mark passages A and B for revision.
6. This dictionary does not include modern technical words that had no equivalent in ancient spoken Greek and Latin.
7. At the request of the university president, administrative personnel at the Biology Building are studying three incineration systems.

Exercise 6.7. Subject–verb agreement (page 144)

1. The remaining fluid was drawn off, and the kidneys were washed.
2. Due to the small number of test animals used, the data were not statistically significant OR (if no statistical tests were involved) Due to the small number of test animals used, the data were not meaningful.
3. Extensive karyorrhexis, karyolysis, and hepatocyte degeneration were evident within the centrilobular regions. ("Cellular" is redundant, for hepatocytes couldn't degenerate any other way.)
4. The data indicate that Jones was the first to discover the phenomenon.
5. Not one of the animals was harmed in the course of this study.
6. After a sample was assessed by radiocarbon dating, sections were subjected to potassium–argon analysis.
7. Neither the rats nor the chimpanzee was kept in the laboratory. OR Neither the chimpanzee nor the rats were kept in the laboratory.

Exercise 6.8. Dangling participles and other misplaced modifiers (page 147)

1. Toward the anterior chamber, a lamination was evident.
2. Using dimethyl sulfoxide, we observed no bacteria.
3. After experimentation, bacteria multiplied.
4. A correlation between the variables was evident with this method.
5. With an inverted ocular, intestinal sections can be examined for metazoan parasites.
6. Two of the researchers' stopwatches that had been left leaning against cabinets were badly damaged.
7. For sale: Laboratory table with thick legs and large drawers; suitable for researcher.
8. Last night, the campus police reported that two microscopes were stolen.
9. To encourage condom use, the French government has prepared commercials blunt enough to shock even liberal Americans.

Exercise 6.9. Collective nouns, comparisons, and lists (page 152)

A.

1. An appropriate dose is 10–50 parts per million of chloramphenicol.
2. The university president convened a committee of scientists.
3. We infused 12 liters of serum into the elephant.

B.

1. The authors' mild pulmonary hypertensive stage was similar to this stage in our study.
2. Group A was more unusual than Group B.
3. The cat recovered better than any of the other cats did.
4. The emergency medical kit contained a bandage, an applicator, a towel, a brush, and a rubber sponge.
5. The fox was heavier than any of the other animals in the study group.
6. Of the two alternatives, this one is the more interesting.

CHAPTER 7

Exercise 7.1. Punctuation (page 161)

1. Indicate optimum instrument settings for temperature, humidity, rainfall, and performance.
2. When examined closely, the skeleton bears many bumpy spines that project from the surface of the animal.
3. Class Echinoidea, which includes sea urchins, sand dollars, and heart urchins, is not closely related to class Ascomyceteae.
4. The adults are radially symmetrical, but the larvae are bilateral. It is generally held that this phylum evolved from bilateral ancestors and that radial symmetry arose as an adaptation to a sessile way of life.
5. The clinician asked, "How did the patient die?" The answer was not obvious.
6. The essay, "The Future of Veterinary Medicine," appeared in the early 1960s.

Exercise 7.2. Capitalization (page 164)

1. The Afghan hound ate plaster of Paris.
2. The study sample included 15 Greyhounds, 14 Malamutes, and 10 Spanish Terriers.
3. Adenine and guanine are nucleotides called purines.
4. A person can live normally without the adrenal medullae, but not without the cortices.
5. These bacteria inhabit all biomes in the Northern Hemisphere.
6. *What's So Funny about Science?* by Sidney Harris
7. Assessment of the Role of Alcohol in the Human Stress Response
8. A synopsis of the taxonomy of North American and West Indian birds

Exercise 7.3. Scientific names and other foreign words and phrases (page 169)

A.

1. the parasitic wasp, *M. atrata*
2. the dandelion, *Taraxacum officionale*, family Compositae, class Dicotyledonae

3. the honeybee, *Apis mellifera* var. *ligustica*
4. the human malarial parasite, *Plasmodium falciparum* Bignami
5. The starfish *(Asterias)* belongs to the class Asteroidea, phylum Echinodermata, in the section Deuterostomia.

B.

1. When acceptable, use the formulas already given in the book, *Official Methods in Microbiology*.
2. For information on the action of green plant pigments, *i.e.*, chlorophyll, *in vivo* see Arnon's article in *Scientific American* and Bassham's book, *The Photosynthesis of Carbon Compounds*.
3. Our experiments cannot identify the underlying biophysical alterations, namely, effects within the membrane itself.
4. Reduced oxygen tension provides the best environment for parasite development *in vitro*, as shown by Udeinya *et al.* (2005).

Exercise 7.4. Number use and interpretation (page 179)

1. Three-quarters (75%) of the experimental animals died within 15 hours, but 17 horses (10%) were still alive 45 days later.
2. The chemicals for the experiment weighed less than 0.2 mg.
3. We calculated that 20,500 cells were affected.
4. The control group recovered more quickly, but the difference was not statistically significant (chi – square test, $P = .11$).
5. The test plot contained 10 species of grasses, 2 species of legumes, 6 species of trees, and 15 species of cruciferous plants.

Exercise 7.5. Practicing mixed corrections (page 180)

1. *Comments:* Wordy; change numbers to Arabic; use first person.
    Revision: We conclude that these mammalian cells have a limiting diameter of 16–20 Å.
2. *Comments:* Subject–verb disagreement; use of passive could be changed.
    Revision: We studied the inhibitory activity of the various combinations and plotted isobolograms.
3. *Comments:* Wordy, awkward; "at . . . by" construction sounds like location; "increasing" may be interpreted two ways.
    Revision: At the cell surface, EDTA increases cell wall permeability. (Remember not to start a sentence with an abbreviation.)
4. *Comments:* Wordy.
    Revision: The pronounced heart lesions were measured.
5. *Comments:* Two meanings possible for "numerous" – many strains, or strains which have many individuals; incorrect use of italics and capitalization. An exception to the usual rule regarding diseases, Chagas is

capitalized because it is derived from a proper noun, the name of its describer.

Revision: Many strains of *T. cruzi* cause Chagas disease.

6. *Comments:* A report of one's current research requires past tense; "irritated" gives sentence an amusing double meaning. (Author probably meant it in the sense of "inflamed," not "annoyed.")

   Revision: Treatment stopped when fish showed signs of physical irritation.

7. *Comments:* Dangling phrase – whose middle legs, those of the wasp or those of the fly? Which does "ventrally" refer to? Scientific name needs italics. Progressive provisioner is an acceptable technical term.

   Revision: A progressive provisioner, *S. maculata* carries flies beneath its body with its middle legs.

8. *Comments:* How can a figure be a fish? Does a pond have metacercariae or a gill cavity?

   Revision: Metacercariae (arrow, Figure 24) were evident in the gill cavity of a cichlid fish found in a Florida pond.

9. *Comments:* Unnecessary words; measurements could be simplified.

   Revision: Mix 1.5 kg dye with 7 L water.

10. *Comments:* Generic names should be underlined or italicized. A list in which some items begin with a vowel and some do not requires an article with each; a series requires a comma before "and." If true, pluralization would make the sentence read more smoothly.

    Revision: Fruits in the *Artibeus* diet included an orange, a pear, an apple, and a peach. *OR* Fruits in the *Artibeus* diet included oranges, pears, apples, and peaches.

11. *Comments:* Misplaced modifier, sounds like fish have cilia. Generic names should be underlined or italicized.

    Revision: Ichthyophthirius is one of the few ciliated parasites infesting fish.

12. *Comments:* "Varying" means changing; authors probably meant "various." Use of "the authors" is unclear; if it means authors of this sentence substitute "we."

    Revision: We found amorphous material of various densities.

13. *Comments:* "Equally" and "each" are redundant; "divided" has two meanings.

    Revision: The animals were placed in 5 groups of 22.

14. *Comments:* Sounds like a magician, pulling swabs out of tracheas.

    Revision: With cotton swabs, we obtained tracheal samples.

15. *Comments:* Too much hedging; use present tense for published findings that can be generalized. The qualifiers "many" and "sometimes" (or "at times") both are needed to avoid changing the meaning.

    Revision: Many of their published results indicate that MG organisms sometimes are transmitted poorly.

16. *Comments:* Misplaced phrase – feeds with resolution? Punctuation needed; active tense improves sentence.

    Revision: We used HPLC, a technique with excellent resolution, to analyze aflatoxins in feeds.

17. *Comments:* Hiccups; redundancy; wordiness.
     Revision: A possible cause is aflatoxin entering the bloodstream.
18. *Comments:* Wordy and pretentious.
     Revision: Too much sunlight can burn skin.
19. *Comments:* For a restrictive clause, "that" is preferable; passive, colorless verb; "continual" is used improperly; some redundancy.
     Revision: When it circled, the horse was continuously lame.
20. *Comments:* Restrictive clause should not be set off by commas; rewording would make sentence read more smoothly.
     Revision: The unexercised dogs housed in runs developed no clinical signs of heartworm disease.

Appendix 2

Excerpts from "Uniform requirements for manuscripts submitted to biomedical journals: Writing and editing for biomedical publication"*

International Committee of Medical Journal Editors

About the uniform requirements

A small group of editors of general medical journals met informally in Vancouver, British Columbia, in 1978 to establish guidelines for the format of manuscripts submitted to their journals. The group became known as the Vancouver Group. Its requirements for manuscripts, including formats for bibliographic references developed by the National Library of Medicine, were first published in 1979. The Vancouver Group expanded and evolved into the International Committee of Medical Journal Editors (ICMJE), which meets annually. The ICMJE gradually has broadened its concerns to include ethical principles related to publication in biomedical journals.

The ICMJE has produced multiple editions of the Uniform Requirements for Manuscripts Submitted to Biomedical Journals. Over the years, issues have arisen that go beyond manuscript preparation, resulting in the development of a number of Separate Statements on editorial policy. The entire Uniform Requirements document was revised in 1997; sections were updated in May 1999 and May 2000. In May 2001, the ICMJE revised the sections related to potential conflict of interest. In 2003, the committee revised and reorganized the entire document and incorporated the Separate Statements into the text. The committee prepared this revision in 2005.

---

* Excerpt reproduced with permission from International Committee of Medical Journal Editors, http://www.icmje.org/index.html. The ICMJE has not endorsed nor approved the contents of this reprint. This document is updated at least yearly; the latest version is located at <www.ICMIE.org>, which is the appropriate citation for this document. It may be downloaded and reproduced for educational, not-for-profit purposes without regard for copyright.

221

IV. MANUSCRIPT PREPARATION AND SUBMISSION

IV. A. Preparing a manuscript for submission to a biomedical journal

Editors and reviewers spend many hours reading manuscripts, and therefore appreciate receiving manuscripts that are easy to read and edit. Much of the information in journals' instructions to authors is designed to accomplish that goal in ways that meet each journal's particular editorial needs. The guidance that follows provides a general background and rationale for preparing manuscripts for any journal.

IV. A.1.a. General principles

The text of observational and experimental articles is usually (but not necessarily) divided into sections with the headings Introduction, Methods, Results, and Discussion. This so-called "IMRAD" structure is not simply an arbitrary publication format, but rather a direct reflection of the process of scientific discovery. Long articles may need subheadings within some sections (especially the Results and Discussion sections) to clarify their content. Other types of articles, such as case reports, reviews, and editorials, are likely to need other formats.

Publication in electronic formats has created opportunities for adding details or whole sections in the electronic version only, layering information, cross-linking or extracting portions of articles, and the like. Authors need to work closely with editors in developing or using such new publication formats and should submit material for potential supplementary electronic formats for peer review.

Double spacing of all portions of the manuscript – including the title page, abstract, text, acknowledgments, references, individual tables, and legends – and generous margins make it possible for editors and reviewers to edit the text line by line, and add comments and queries, directly on the paper copy. If manuscripts are submitted electronically, the files should be double spaced, because the manuscript may need to be printed out for reviewing and editing.

During the editorial process, reviewers and editors frequently need to refer to specific portions of the manuscript, which is difficult unless the pages are numbered. Authors should therefore number all of the pages of the manuscript consecutively, beginning with the title page.

IV. A.1.b. Reporting guidelines for specific study designs

Research reports frequently omit important information. The general requirements listed in the next section relate to reporting essential elements for all study designs. Authors are encouraged in addition to consult reporting guidelines relevant to their specific research design. For reports of randomized controlled trials authors should refer to the CONSORT statement. This guideline provides a set of recommendations comprising a list of items to report and a patient flow

Reporting guidelines [for specific research design]

Initiative	Type of study	Source
CONSORT	randomized controlled trials	http://www.consort-statement.org
STARD	studies of diagnostic accuracy	http://www.consort-statement.org/stardstatement.htm
QUOROM	systematic reviews and meta-analyses	http://www.consort-statement.org/Initiatives/MOOSE/moose.pdf
STROBE	observational studies in epidemiology	http://www.strobe-statement.org
MOOSE	meta-analyses of observational studies in epidemiology	http://www.consort-statement.org/Initiatives/MOOSE/moose.pdf

diagram. Reporting guidelines have also been developed for a number of other study designs that some journals may ask authors to follow (see Table: Reporting Guidelines). Authors should consult the information for authors of the journal they have chosen.

IV. A.2. Title page

The title page should carry the following information:

1. The title of the article. Concise titles are easier to read than long, convoluted ones. Titles that are too short may, however, lack important information, such as study design (which is particularly important in identifying randomized controlled trials). Authors should include all information in the title that will make electronic retrieval of the article both sensitive and specific.

2. Authors' names and institutional affiliations. Some journals publish each author's highest academic degree(s), while others do not.

3. The name of the department(s) and institution(s) to which the work should be attributed.

4. Disclaimers, if any.

5. Corresponding authors. The name, mailing address, telephone and fax numbers, and e-mail address of the author responsible for correspondence about the manuscript (the "corresponding author;" this author may or may not be the "guarantor" for the integrity of the study as a whole, if someone is identified in that role. The corresponding author should indicate clearly whether his or her e-mail address is to be published.

6. The name and address of the author to whom requests for reprints should be addressed or a statement that reprints will not be available from the authors.

7. Source(s) of support in the form of grants, equipment, drugs, or all of these.

8. A running head. Some journals request a short running head or foot line, usually of no more than 40 characters (count letters and spaces) at the foot of the title page. Running heads are published in most journals, but are also sometimes used within the editorial office for filing and locating manuscripts.

9. Word counts. A word count for the text only (excluding abstract, acknowledgments, figure legends, and references) allows editors and reviewers to assess whether the information contained in the paper warrants the amount of space devoted to it, and whether the submitted manuscript fits within the journal's word limits. A separate word count for the Abstract is also useful for the same reason.

10. The number of figures and tables. It is difficult for editorial staff and reviewers to tell if the figures and tables that should have accompanied a manuscript were actually included unless the numbers of figures and tables that belong to the manuscript are noted on the title page.

IV. A.3. Conflict of interest notification page

To prevent the information on potential conflict of interest for authors from being overlooked or misplaced, it is necessary for that information to be part of the manuscript. It should therefore also be included on a separate page or pages immediately following the title page. However, individual journals may differ in where they ask authors to provide this information and some journals do not send information on conflicts of interest to reviewers.

IV. A.4. Abstract and key words

An abstract (requirements for length and structured format vary by journal) should follow the title page. The abstract should provide the context or background for the study and should state the study's purposes, basic procedures (selection of study subjects or laboratory animals, observational and analytical methods), main findings (giving specific effect sizes and their statistical significance, if possible), and principal conclusions. It should emphasize new and important aspects of the study or observations.

Because abstracts are the only substantive portion of the article indexed in many electronic databases, and the only portion many readers read, authors need to be careful that abstracts reflect the content of the article accurately. Unfortunately, many abstracts disagree with the text of the article. The format required for structured abstracts differs from journal to journal, and some journals use more than one structure; authors should make it a point to prepare their abstracts in the format specified by the journal they have chosen.

Some journals request that, following the abstract, authors provide, and identify as such, 3 to 10 key words or short phrases that capture the main topics of the article. These will assist indexers in cross-indexing the article and may be published with the abstract. Terms from the Medical Subject Headings (MeSH) list of Index Medicus should be used; if suitable MeSH terms are not yet available for recently introduced terms, present terms may be used.

IV. A.5. Introduction

Provide a context or background for the study (i.e., the nature of the problem and its significance). State the specific purpose or research objective of, or hypothesis tested by, the study or observation; the research objective is often more sharply focused when stated as a question. Both the main and secondary objectives should be made clear, and any pre-specified subgroup analyses should be described. Give only strictly pertinent references and do not include data or conclusions from the work being reported.

IV. A.6. Methods

The Methods section should include only information that was available at the time the plan or protocol for the study was written; all information obtained during the conduct of the study belongs in the Results section.

IV. A.6.a. Selection and description of participants

Describe your selection of the observational or experimental participants (patients or laboratory animals, including controls) clearly, including eligibility and exclusion criteria and a description of the source population. Because the relevance of such variables as age and sex to the object of research is not always clear, authors should explain their use when they are included in a study report; for example, authors should explain why only subjects of certain ages were included or why women were excluded. The guiding principle should be clarity about how and why a study was done in a particular way. When authors use variables such as race or ethnicity, they should define how they measured the variables and justify their relevance.

IV. A.6.b. Technical information

Identify the methods, apparatus (give the manufacturer's name and address in parentheses), and procedures in sufficient detail to allow other workers to reproduce the results. Give references to established methods, including statistical methods (see below); provide references and brief descriptions for methods that have been published but are not well known; describe new or substantially modified methods, give reasons for using them, and evaluate their limitations. Identify precisely all drugs and chemicals used, including generic name(s), dose(s), and route(s) of administration.

Authors submitting review manuscripts should include a section describing the methods used for locating, selecting, extracting, and synthesizing data. These methods should also be summarized in the abstract.

IV. A.6.c. Statistics

Describe statistical methods with enough detail to enable a knowledgeable reader with access to the original data to verify the reported results. When possible, quantify findings and present them with appropriate indicators of measurement error or uncertainty (such as confidence intervals). Avoid relying solely on statistical hypothesis testing, such as the use of P values, which fails to convey important information about effect size. References for the design of the study and statistical methods should be to standard works when possible (with pages stated). Define statistical terms, abbreviations, and most symbols. Specify the computer software used.

IV. A.7. Results

Present your results in logical sequence in the text, tables, and illustrations, giving the main or most important findings first. Do not repeat in the text all the data in the tables or illustrations; emphasize or summarize only important observations. Extra or supplementary materials and technical detail can be placed in an appendix where it will be accessible but will not interrupt the flow of the text; alternatively, it can be published only in the electronic version of the journal.

When data are summarized in the Results section, give numeric results not only as derivatives (for example, percentages) but also as the absolute numbers from which the derivatives were calculated, and specify the statistical methods used to analyze them. Restrict tables and figures to those needed to explain the argument of the paper and to assess its support. Use graphs as an alternative to tables with many entries; do not duplicate data in graphs and tables. Avoid non-technical uses of technical terms in statistics, such as "random" (which implies a randomizing device), "normal," "significant," "correlations," and "sample."

Where scientifically appropriate, analyses of the data by variables such as age and sex should be included.

IV. A.8. Discussion

Emphasize the new and important aspects of the study and the conclusions that follow from them. Do not repeat in detail data or other material given in the Introduction or the Results section. For experimental studies it is useful to begin the discussion by summarizing briefly the main findings, then explore possible mechanisms or explanations for these findings, compare and contrast the results with other relevant studies, state the limitations of the study, and explore the implications of the findings for future research and for clinical practice.

Link the conclusions with the goals of the study but avoid unqualified statements and conclusions not adequately supported by the data. In particular, authors should avoid making statements on economic benefits and costs unless their manuscript includes the appropriate economic data and analyses. Avoid claiming priority and alluding to work that has not been completed. State new hypotheses when warranted, but clearly label them as such.

IV. A.9. References

IV. A.9.a. General considerations related to references

Although references to review articles can be an efficient way of guiding readers to a body of literature, review articles do not always reflect original work accurately. Readers should therefore be provided with direct references to original research sources whenever possible. On the other hand, extensive lists of references to original work on a topic can use excessive space on the printed page. Small numbers of references to key original papers will often serve as well as more exhaustive lists, particularly since references can now be added to the electronic version of published papers, and since electronic literature searching allows readers to retrieve published literature efficiently.

Avoid using abstracts as references. References to papers accepted but not yet published should be designated as "in press" or "forthcoming"; authors should obtain written permission to cite such papers as well as verification that they have been accepted for publication. Information from manuscripts submitted but not accepted should be cited in the text as "unpublished observations" with written permission from the source.

Avoid citing a "personal communication" unless it provides essential information not available from a public source, in which case the name of the person and date of communication should be cited in parentheses in the text. For scientific articles, authors should obtain written permission and confirmation of accuracy from the source of a personal communication.

Some journals check the accuracy of all reference citations, but not all journals do so, and citation errors sometimes appear in the published version of articles. To minimize such errors, authors should therefore verify references against the original documents. Authors are responsible for checking that none of the references cite retracted articles except in the context of referring to the retraction. For articles published in journals indexed in MEDLINE, the ICMJE considers PubMed the authoritative source for information about retractions. Authors can identify retracted articles in MEDLINE by using the following search term, where pt in square brackets stands for publication type: Retracted publication [pt] in pubmed.

IV. A.9.b. Reference style and format

The Uniform Requirements style is based largely on an ANSI standard style adapted by the National Library of Medicine (NLM) for its databases. For samples of reference citation formats, authors should consult National Library of Medicine website, <http://www.nlm.nih.gov/bsd/uniform_requirements.html>

References should be numbered consecutively in the order in which they are first mentioned in the text. Identify references in text, tables, and legends by Arabic numerals in parentheses. References cited only in tables or figure legends should be numbered in accordance with the sequence established by the first identification in the text of the particular table or figure. The titles of journals should be abbreviated according to the style used in Index Medicus. Consult the list of Journals Indexed for MEDLINE, published annually as a separate publication by the National Library of Medicine. The list can also be obtained through the library's website, <http://www.nlm.nih.gov/tsd/serials/lji.html>. Journals vary on whether they ask authors to cite electronic references within parentheses in the text or in numbered references following the text. Authors should consult with the journal that they plan to submit their work to.

Journals vary on whether they ask authors to cite electronic references within parentheses in the text or in numbered references following the text. Authors should consult with the journal that they plan to submit their work to.

IV. A.10. Tables

Tables capture information concisely, and display it efficiently; they also provide information at any desired level of detail and precision. Including data in tables rather than text frequently makes it possible to reduce the length of the text.

Type or print each table with double spacing on a separate sheet of paper. Number tables consecutively in the order of their first citation in the text and supply a brief title for each. Do not use internal horizontal or vertical lines. Give each column a short or abbreviated heading. Authors should place explanatory matter in footnotes, not in the heading. Explain in footnotes all non-standard abbreviations. For footnotes use the following symbols, in sequence:

*, †, ‡, §, ||, ¶, **, ††, ‡‡

Identify statistical measures of variations, such as standard deviation and standard error of the mean.

Be sure that each table is cited in the text.

If you use data from another published or unpublished source, obtain permission and acknowledge them fully.

Additional tables containing backup data too extensive to publish in print may be appropriate for publication in the electronic version of the journal, deposited with an archival service, or made available to readers directly by the authors. In that event an appropriate statement will be added to the text. Submit such tables for consideration with the paper so that they will be available to the peer reviewers.

IV. A.11. Illustrations (figures)

Figures should be either professionally drawn and photographed, or submitted as photographic quality digital prints. In addition to requiring a version of the figures suitable for printing, some journals now ask authors for electronic files of figures in a format (e.g., JPEG or GIF) that will produce high quality images in the web version of the journal; authors should review the images of such files on a computer screen before submitting them, to be sure they meet their own quality standard.

For X-ray films, scans, and other diagnostic images, as well as pictures of pathology specimens or photomicrographs, send sharp, glossy, black-and-white or color photographic prints, usually 127×173 mm (5×7 inches). Although some journals redraw figures, many do not. Letters, numbers, and symbols on figures should therefore be clear and even throughout, and of sufficient size that when reduced for publication each item will still be legible. Figures should be made as self-explanatory as possible, since many will be used directly in slide presentations. Titles and detailed explanations belong in the legends, however, not on the illustrations themselves.

Photomicrographs should have internal scale markers. Symbols, arrows, or letters used in photomicrographs should contrast with the background.

If photographs of people are used, either the subjects must not be identifiable or their pictures must be accompanied by written permission to use the photograph. Whenever possible permission for publication should be obtained.

Figures should be numbered consecutively according to the order in which they have been first cited in the text. If a figure has been published, acknowledge the original source and submit written permission from the copyright holder to reproduce the material. Permission is required irrespective of authorship or publisher except for documents in the public domain.

For illustrations in color, ascertain whether the journal requires color negatives, positive transparencies, or color prints. Accompanying drawings marked to indicate the region to be reproduced might be useful to the editor. Some journals publish illustrations in color only if the author pays for the extra cost.

Authors should consult the journal about requirements for figures submitted in electronic formats.

IV. A.12. Legends for illustrations (figures)

Type or print out legends for illustrations using double spacing, starting on a separate page, with Arabic numerals corresponding to the illustrations. When symbols, arrows, numbers, or letters are used to identify parts of the illustrations, identify and explain each one clearly in the legend. Explain the internal scale and identify the method of staining in photomicrographs.

IV. A.13. Units of measurement

Measurements of length, height, weight, and volume should be reported in metric units (meter, kilogram, or liter) or their decimal multiples.

Temperatures should be in degrees Celsius. Blood pressures should be in millimeters of mercury, unless other units are specifically required by the journal.

Journals vary in the units they use for reporting hematological, clinical chemistry, and other measurements. Authors must consult the information for authors for the particular journal and should report laboratory information in both the local and International System of Units (SI). Editors may request that the authors before publication add alternative or non-SI units, since SI units are not universally used. Drug concentrations may be reported in either SI or mass units, but the alternative should be provided in parentheses where appropriate.

IV. A.14. Abbreviations and symbols

Use only standard abbreviations; the use of non-standard abbreviations can be extremely confusing to readers. Avoid abbreviations in the title. The full term for which an abbreviation stands should precede its first use in the text unless it is a standard unit of measurement.

IV. B. Sending the manuscript to the journal

An increasing number of journals now accept electronic submission of manuscripts, whether on disk, as attachments to electronic mail, or by downloading directly onto the journal website. Electronic submission saves time as well as postage costs, and allows the manuscript to be handled in electronic form throughout the editorial process (for example, when it is sent out for review). When submitting a manuscript electronically, authors should consult with the instructions for authors of the journal they have chosen for their manuscript.

If a paper version of the manuscript is submitted, send the required number of copies of the manuscript and figures; they are all needed for peer review and editing, and editorial office staff cannot be expected to make the required copies.

Manuscripts must be accompanied by a cover letter, which should include the following information.

- A full statement to the editor about all submissions and previous reports that might be regarded as redundant publication of the same or very similar work. Any such work should be referred to specifically, and referenced in the new paper. Copies of such material should be included with the submitted paper, to help the editor decide how to handle the matter.
- A statement of financial or other relationships that might lead to a conflict of interest, if that information is not included in the manuscript itself or in an authors' form.
- A statement that the manuscript has been read and approved by all the authors, that the requirements for authorship as stated earlier in this document have been met, and that each author believes that the manuscript represents honest work, if that information is not provided in another form (see below); and
- The name, address, and telephone number of the corresponding author, who is responsible for communicating with the other authors about revisions and final approval of the proofs, if that information is not included on the manuscript itself.

The letter should give any additional information that may be helpful to the editor, such as the type or format of article in the particular journal that the manuscript represents. If the manuscript has been submitted previously to another journal, it is helpful to include the previous editor's and reviewers' comments with the submitted manuscript, along with the authors' responses to those comments. Editors encourage authors to submit these previous communications and doing so may expedite the review process.

Many journals now provide a pre-submission checklist that assures that all the components of the submission have been included. Some journals now also require that authors complete checklists for reports of certain study types (e.g., the CONSORT checklist for reports of randomized controlled trials). Authors should look to see if the journal uses such checklists, and send them with the manuscript if they are requested.

Copies of any permission to reproduce published material, to use illustrations or report information about identifiable people, or to name people for their contributions must accompany the manuscript.

Selected resources

Alley, M. (1996). *The Craft of Scientific Writing.* 3rd edn. New York: Springer.

Alley, M. (2003). *The Craft of Scientific Presentations.* New York: Springer.

Alley, M. and Neeley, K. A. (2005a). Discovering the power of PowerPoint: Rethinking the design of presentation slides from a skillful user's perspective. *Proceedings of the 2005 American Society for Engineering Education Annual Conference and Exposition,* ICME2005–2461.

Alley, M. and Neeley, K. A. (2005b). Rethinking the design of presentation slides: A case for sentence headlines and visual evidence. *Technical Communication,* **52**, 417–426.

Alred, G. J., Brusaw, C. T., and Oliu, W. E. (2003). *Handbook of Technical Writing.* 7th edn. New York: St. Martin's Press.

Anholt, R. R. H. (2006). *Dazzle 'Em with Style: The Art of Oral Scientific Presentation.* 2nd edn. Burlington, MA: Elsevier Academic Press.

Aslett, D. (1996). *How to Have a 48-Hour Day.* Cincinnati, OH: F & W Publications, Inc.

Atkinson, C. (2005). *Beyond Bullet Points.* Buffalo, NY: Microsoft Press.

Baron, D. N. (1994). *Units, Symbols, and Abbreviations: A Guide for Biological and Medical Editors.* 5th edn. London: Royal Society of Medicine.

Bell, S. J. (2004). End PowerPoint dependency now! *American Libraries* **35**(6), 56–59.

Benson, B. W. and Boege, S. (2002). *Handbook of Good Laboratory Practices.* Bristol, PA: Hemisphere Publishing.

Bjelland, H. (1990). *Writing Better Technical Articles.* Blue Ridge Summit, PA: TAB Books.

Boice, R. (1990). *Professors as Writers: A Self-help Guide to Productive Writing.* Stillwater, OK: New Forums Press.

Boice, R. (2000). *Advice for New Faculty Members: Nihil Nimus.* Needham Heights, MA: Allyn & Bacon.

Bolker, J. (1998). *Writing Your Dissertation in Fifteen Minutes a Day.* New York: Henry Holt.

Briscoe, M. H. (1996). *Preparing Scientific Illustrations: A Guide to Better Posters, Presentations, and Publications.* 2nd edn. New York: Springer-Verlag.

Buranen, L. and Roy, A. M. (eds.) (1999). *Perspectives on Plagiarism and Intellectual Property in a Postmodern World.* Albany: State University of New York Press.

Calisher, C. H. and Fauquet, C. M. (1992). *Stedman's ICTV Virus Words.* Baltimore, MD: Lippincott, Williams & Wilkins.

Campbell, J. B. and Campbell, J. M. (1995). *Mosby's Survival Guide to Medical Abbreviations, Acronyms, Prefixes and Suffixes, Symbols and the Greek Alphabet.* St. Louis, MO: Mosby Inc.

Cooper, H. (1998). *Synthesizing Research.* 3rd edn. Thousand Oaks, CA: Sage.

Council of Science Editors. (2006). *Scientific Style and Format: The CSE Style Manual for Authors, Editors, and Publishers.* 7th edn. New York: Cambridge University Press.

Darwin, F. (ed.) (1897). *The Life and Letters of Charles Darwin, Including an Autobiographical Chapter.* New York: D. Appleton and Company.

Davis, M. (2005). *Scientific Papers and Presentations.* 2nd edn. Burlington, MA: Academic Press (Elsevier).

Day, R. A. and Gastel, B. (2006). *How to Write and Publish a Scientific Paper.* 6th edn. Westport, CT: Greenwood Press.

de Lacey, G., Record, C., and Wade, J. (1985). How accurate are quotations and references in medical journals? *British Medical Journal*, **291**, 884–886.

Dizon, A. E. and Rosenberg, J. E. (1990). We don't care, Professor Einstein, the Instructions to the Authors specifically said double-spaced. In *Writing for Fishery Journals*, ed. J. Hunter. Bethesda, MD: American Fisheries Society. pp. 65–74.

Dorland's Illustrated Medical Dictionary. (2003). 30th edn. Philadelphia, PA: W. B. Saunders Co.

Dupré, L. (1998). *BUGS in Writing: A Guide to Debugging your Prose*, revised edn. Reading, MA: Addison Wesley Longman, Inc.

Evans, J. T., Nadjari, H. I., and Burchell, S. A. (1990). Quotational and reference accuracy in surgical journals: A continuing peer review problem. *Journal of the American Medical Association*, **263**, 1353–1354.

Flower, L. (2000). *Problem Solving Strategies for Writing.* 5th edn. San Diego, CA: Harcourt Brace Jovanovich.

Germano, W. (2001). *Getting It Published.* Chicago: University of Chicago Press.

Gingras, B. (1987). Simplified English in maintenance manuals. *Technical Communications*, **34** (1), 24–28.

Gould, C. (1998). *Searching Smart on the World Wide Web. Tools and Techniques for Getting Quality Results.* Berkeley, CA: Library Solutions Press.

Gurak, L. J. (2000). *Oral Presentations for Technical Communication.* Needham Heights, MA: Allyn & Bacon.

Hailman, J. P. and Strier, K. B. (1997). *Planning, Proposing, and Presenting Science Effectively.* Cambridge, UK: Cambridge University Press.

Handbook of Current Medical Abbreviations. (1998). 5th edn. Philadelphia, PA: The Charles Press.

Hinchcliff, K. W., Bruce, M. J., Powers, J. D., and Kipp, M. L. (1993). Accuracy of references and quotations in veterinary journals. *Journal of the American Veterinary Medical Association*, **202**(3), 397–400.

Holt, J. G., Kreig, N. R., Sneath, P. H. A., Staley, J. T., and Williams, S. T. (eds.) (1994). *Bergey's Manual of Determinative Bacteriology.* 9th edn. Baltimore, MD: Lippincott, Williams & Wilkins.

Hornby, A. S. and Wehmeier, S. (eds.) (2005). *Oxford Advanced Learner's Dictionary.* 7th edn. New York: Oxford University Press.

International Code of Botanical Nomenclature (St. Louis Code), adopted by the Sixteenth International Botanical Congress, St. Louis, 1999, 2000. Konigstein: Koeltz Scientific Books.

International Code of Zoological Nomenclature. (1999). 4th edn. London: International Trust for Zoological Nomenclature.

International Committee of Medical Journal Editors. (2006). *Uniform Requirements for Manuscripts Submitted to Biomedical Journals.* www.ICMJE.org.

International Committee on Taxonomy of Viruses. (2000). *Virus Taxonomy: Classification and Nomenclature of Viruses. Seventh Report of the International Committee on*

Taxonomy of Viruses. ed. M. H. V. van Regenmortel, C. M. Fauquet, D. H. L. Bishop *et al.* New York: Academic Press.

International Union of Microbiological Societies. (1992). *International Code of Nomenclature of Bacteria.* 1990 Revision, ed. P. H. A. Sneath, E. F. Lessel, V. B. D. Skerman, H. P. R. Seeliger, and W. A. Clark. Washington, DC: American Society for Microbiology.

Iverson, C. I. (ed.). (1997). *American Medical Association Manual of Style: A Guide for Authors and Editors.* 9th edn. Baltimore, MD: Lippincott, Williams & Wilkins.

Jablonski, S. (ed.) (2004). *Dictionary of Medical Acronyms and Abbreviations.* 5th edn. Philadelphia, PA: W. B. Saunders Co.

Jeffrey, C. (ed.) (1992). *Biological Nomenclature.* 3rd edn. New York: Cambridge University Press.

Keller, J. (2004). Is PowerPoint the devil? *Chicago Tribune,* 23 January.

LaFollette, M. C. (1992). *Stealing into Print: Fraud, Plagiarism, and Misconduct in Scientific Publishing.* Berkeley: University of California Press.

Lawrence, S. (1981). Watching the watchers. *Science News,* **119**, 331–333.

Lederer, R. (1987). *Anguished English.* New York: Dell Publishing.

Leigh, G. J. (1998). *Principles of Chemical Nomenclature: A Guide to IUPAC Recommendations.* Malden, MA: Blackwell Science.

Longman Dictionary of American English. (2004). 3rd edn. St. Laurent, Quebec, Canada: Pearson Longman ESL.

Macdonald-Ross, M. (1977a). Graphics in text. In *Review of Research in Education* No. 5, ed. L. S. Shulman. Itasca, IL: F. E. Peacock.

Macdonald-Ross, M. (1977b). How numbers are shown. *AV Communication Review,* **25**, 359–409.

Mack, K. and Skjei, E. (1979). *Overcoming Writing Blocks.* Los Angeles: J. P. Tarcher. Distributed by St. Martin's Press, New York.

MacNeil, R. (1995). The glorious messiness of English. *Reader's Digest,* Oct. 1995, pp. 151–154.

Maggio, R. (1991). *The Bias-free Word Finder: A Dictionary of Nondiscriminatory Language.* Boston, MA: Beacon Press.

Maggio, R. (1997). *Talking About People: A Guide to Fair and Accurate Language.* Westport, CT: Greenwood, Oryx Press.

Markel, M. (1994). *Writing in the Technical Fields: A Step-by-Step Guide for Engineers, Scientists, and Technicians.* New York: IEEE Press.

Mayer, R. E. (2001). *Multimedia Learning.* New York: Cambridge University Press.

Medical Terms and Abbreviations. (2002). 2nd edn. Philadelphia, PA: Lippincott, Williams & Wilkins.

Montgomery, S. L. (2003). *The Chicago Guide to Communicating Science.* Chicago: University of Chicago Press.

Nelson, V. (1993). *On Writer's Block.* Boston, MA: Houghton Mifflin Co.

Ogden, C. K. (1930). *Basic English: A General Introduction with Rules and Grammar.* London: Kegan Paul, Trench, Trubner.

O'Neill, M. J., *et al.* (2006). *The Merck Index: An Encyclopedia of Chemicals, Drugs, and Biologicals.* 14th edn. New York: John Wiley & Sons.

Peek, R. P. and Newby, G. B. (eds.) (1996). *Scholarly Publishing. The Electronic Frontier.* Cambridge, MA: The MIT Press.

Peterson, I. (1993). Going for glitz. *Science News,* **144**, 232–233.

Publication Manual of the American Psychological Association. (2001). 5th edn. Washington, DC: American Psychological Association.

Raimes, A. (1988). *Grammar Troublespots: An Editing Guide for ESL Students*. New York: St. Martin's Press.

Robbins, N. B. (2005). *Creating More Effective Graphs*. New York: Wiley-Interscience.

Rogoff, J. B. and Reiner, S. (1961). Electrodiagnostic apparatus. In *Electrodiagnosis and Electromyography*, ed. S. Licht. 2nd edn. Baltimore, MD: Waverly Press.

Rubens, P. (2002). *Science and Technical Writing: A Manual of Style*. 2nd edn. Oxford: Routledge.

Safire, W. (1990). *Fumblerules: A Lighthearted Guide to Grammar and Good Usage*. New York: Doubleday.

Sanderlin, S. (1988). Programming instruction manuals for non-English readers. *Technical Communication*, **35**(2), 96–100.

Schaie, K. W. (1993). Ageist language in psychological research. *American Psychologist*, **48**, 49–51.

Schwartz, M. and the Task Force on Bias-free Language of the Association of American University Presses. (1995). *Guidelines for Bias-free Writing*. Bloomington, IN: Indiana University Press.

Shortland, M. and Gregory, J. (1991). *Communicating Science: A Handbook*. New York: John Wiley & Sons.

Simons, T. (2004). Does PowerPoint make you Stupid? *Presentations*, March 24–31.

Skerman, V. B. D. (ed.) (1989). *Approved Lists of Bacterial Names*. Washington, DC: American Society for Microbiology.

Stedman's Medical Dictionary. (1995). 26th edn. Baltimore, MD: Williams and Wilkins.

Stix, G. (1994). The speed of write. Trends in scientific communication. *Scientific American*, **271**, 106–111.

Strong, W. S. (1999). *The Copyright Book: A Practical Guide*. 5th edn. Cambridge, MA: MIT Press.

Swanson, E., O'Sean, A. A., and Schleyer, A. T. (1999). *Mathematics into Type* (Updated edn.) Providence, RI: American Mathematical Society.

Swinford, E. (2006). *Fixing PowerPoint Annoyances*. Sebastopol, CA: O'Reilly Media.

Truss, L. (2003). *Eats, Shoots and Leaves: The Zero Tolerance Approach to Punctuation*. NY: Gotham (2006 paperback reprint).

Tufte, E. R. (2001). *The Visual Display of Quantitative Information*. 2nd edn. Cheshire, CT: Graphics Press.

Tufte, E. R. (2003). *The Cognitive Style of PowerPoint*. Cheshire, CT: Graphics Press.

USP Dictionary of *USAN and International Drug Names* [annual]. Rockville, MD: U.S. Pharmacopeia.

Walker, T. J. (1998). The future of scientific journals: free access or pay per view? *American Entomologist*, **44**, 135–138.

Weiss, E. H. (1990). *100 Writing Remedies: Practical Exercises for Technical Writing*. Phoenix, AZ: Oryx Press.

Wheatley, D. W. and Unwin, A. W. (1972). *The Algorithm Writer's Guide*. London: Longman.

Woodford, F. P. (1968). *Scientific Writing for Graduate Students: A Manual on the Teaching of Scientific Writing*. Bethesda, MD: Council of Biology Editors.

Woolsey, J. D. (1989). Combating poster fatigue: how to use visual grammar and analysis to effect better visual communications. *Trends in Neurosciences*, **12**, 325–332.

Yang, J. T. (1995). *An Outline of Scientific Writing for Researchers with English as a Foreign Language*. Singapore: World Scientific.

Young, D. S. and Huth, E. J. (1998). *SI Units for Clinical Measurement*. Philadelphia, PA: American College of Physicians.

Index

236